THE LOVE AND SERVICE OF GOD, INFINITE LOVE

containing

A Message From Our Divine Lord For The Clergy Of The World

D1446656

" I will not now call you servants. I have called you friends." (JOHN XV.)

The
LOVE AND SERVICE OF GOD, INFINITE LOVE

containing

A Message From Our Divine Lord For The Clergy Of The World

Translated from the original French
by

Fr. Patrick O'Connell, B.D.

Delegate of the Central Council of the Priests'
Universal Union of the Friends of the Sacred Heart

TAN BOOKS AND PUBLISHERS, INC.
Rockford, Illinois, 61105

Nihil Obstat: Jacobus Browne
                  Censor Deputatus

Imprimatur: ✛ Jacobus
               Episcopus Fernensis
               die Ia Junii 1950

Originally published in 1950 by the Irish Members of the Priests' Universal Union of the Friends of the Sacred Heart and printed in the Republic of Ireland by John English & Co., Ltd., Wexford.

ISBN: 0-89555-310-4

Library of Congress Catalog Card Number: 86-51580

Printed and bound in the United States of America.

TAN BOOKS AND PUBLISHERS, INC.
P.O. Box 424
Rockford, Illinois 61105

1987

DECLARATION

In giving these pages to our venerated confreres in the Priesthood and to the public, we have no intention of pronouncing on the mystic communications which they contain; we conform ourselves to the established discipline and declare that we submit filially and entirely to the judgment of our Holy Mother, the Church.

Dedicated by the Translator and his Brother to

the memory of their dear Parents

DAL VATICANO.

SEGRETARIA DE STATO,
DI SUA SANTITA,

4th January, 1950.

HIS EXCELLENCY, THE MOST REV. PAUL ROSTANGO,
BISHOP OF IVREA.

YOUR EXCELLENCY,

The August Pontiff (Pius XII) has graciously accepted the copy of
the book entitled *The Love and Service of God-Infinite Love* presented
to Him by the Central Council of the Work of Infinite Love (the Priests'
Universal Union and its Branches) of which you are the President. In
this act of homage He has seen a clear proof of filial piety towards Himself and of active zeal for the spreading of ideas and sentiments which
are, and which will be still more, a cause of spiritual revival and a leaven
for the spiritual life.

His Holiness rejoices at the new light which this volume throws on
the Work of Infinite Love and at the enthusiasm which it will arouse,
as this work responds to the urgent needs of the present time. The
thoughts expressed in this volume go to the very foundation of the
spiritual life ; they will aid the thoughtful in purifying their hearts, in
becoming recollected and in ascending towards the heights of sanctity.

The Holy Father, pleased with the act of homage and, wishing that
this volume may hasten the reign of Evangelical justice and be a source
of holy joy, blesses Your Excellency, the Institute of Bethany of the
Sacred Heart and the Associations attached to it.

I thank Your Excellency for the copy which you have so kindly presented to myself and kissing your sacred ring with profound respect,
profess myself to be

Your Excellency's

Most Devoted Servant,

J. B. MONTINI

FOREWORD

As explained in the volume just published, Mother Louise Margaret, under obedience to her Director, noted down all the communications which she received from Our Divine Lord and, during her visit to Rome, submitted them, as well as all her other writings, to the Congregation of the Council. Part of these she had already put in order and published under the title *The Sacred Heart and the Priesthood*, a further portion also arranged by her, was published after her death under the title *The Book of Infinite Love*. The remainder of her writings, with the exception of the conference which, as Rev. Mother, she delivered to the Sisters were published in the order in which she wrote them, in three volumes under the title *In the Service of Jesus-Priest*. The portion of these three volumes which have reference to her life and work form the subject-matter of the volume just published (*The Life and Work of Mother Louise Margaret*). The remainder of her writings contained in these three volumes, as well as her conferences to the Sisters, published now for the first time, have been arranged in order of subject-matter, translated into Italian and published this year. The Sisters of Bethany of the Sacred Heart kindly sent us the Italian manuscript as soon as it was prepared in order to make it possible for us to publish an English version during the Holy Year. As we had already made a translation of the three volumes of *In the Service of Jesus-Priest* from the original French, it was only a question of rearranging it according to the order of Italian manuscript and adding the conferences to the Sisters.

In the foreword to *The Sacred Heart and the Priesthood* we mentioned that, for the full understanding of this book, the three volumes of *In the Service of Jesus-Priest* should be read. All the information contained in these three volumes, and some additional, is now available in the two new volumes.

When the Italian edition of this present volume was published at the beginning of this year, His Holiness Pope Pius XII hastened to send His approbation and Apostolic Blessing in a letter written by Cardinal Montini which we have given above.

It can only remain for us to thank Almighty God for enabling us to bring this work to a successful conclusion, and the many friends who kindly read the manuscripts before going to press.

PATRICK O'CONNELL

3rd March, 1950

TABLE OF CONTENTS

Contents

Contents

Contents

xiv

Contents

Contents

" I am come to cast fire on the earth. And what will I,
but that it will be enkindled."

The book which we joyfully present to the public is a humble attempt to satisfy this desire of Our Lord by making known to the world
the immensity of the love of God, in order that by this knowledge,
men may be urged on to make a generous return of love for love.

It is appearing at a most opportune time : at a time when, in the
words of the present Holy Father, " the world is presenting to our
eyes the sad spectacle of her dissensions and her contradictions and
of the gravest sins of impiety and hatred against God." These things
demand a greater return for love and more generous reparation from
those who have remained faithful.

But there is another reason why the appearance of this volume is
opportune. The collection of extracts from the writings of Mother
Louise Margaret, of which it is composed, is indeed intended for the
general body of the faithful, but it contains a message which is directed
specially to the clergy. There could be nothing more seasonable than this
message of love to the clergy of the present day, for at this very time, the
Vicar of Christ Himself, the bishops and priests of the world are made the
targets of the venemous attacks and the persecution of the powers of evil.

To-day, the world is thirsty for love, though perhaps not fully conscious
of the fact—but for a love which will fully satisfy the immense desires
of its people, who have been created for the Infinite. The world has
need of God-Love. It wishes to see in Him a Father Who inclines merci-
fully towards its miseries, and Who is ready to pardon its transgressions.
And God Himself appears willing to respond with benign complacency
to its expectations by multiplying His loving invitations. The object
of the book which we present is to convey one of these loving invitations.

This book may be said to be a commentary on the " Deus Caritas est "
of St. John (1 John IV, 16). To say that it contains no new revelation
is the same as to say that it is orthodox ; all the ideas in the book are to
be found in one form or another in the Sacred Scripture, but these ideas
are brought together and presented in a new light and help us to understand better the message of love contained in the Gospels. The book
brings us back to the fundamental truth of Christianity and focusses
our attention on what constitutes its very essence.

We confidently recommend this book to the pious attention of both clergy and laity, because the highest authority in the Catholic Church after a careful examination of all the writings it contains, has recognized their great value and has declared them to be free from error.

No doubt, our faith rests on the truth of the Gospel and our interior life is nourished by it, but because the supernatural communications contained in these writings help us to understand better the truths of the Gospel and to apply them to our lives, we appreciate these writings and joyfully recommend their reading.

Mother Louise Margaret, from whose writings these selections have been taken, is already widely known and appreciated, not only in Italy but in other countries as well. She transmits a divine message, but in no way assumes the role of teacher. On the contrary, in her humility she regarded herself as an ignorant sinner and expresses her great repugnance to be even the bearer of a message to those whom she reverenced as her Fathers and Teachers in the faith.

Even as a child she was always on the side of the Church in family discussions; as Superioress, she always bowed before the decisions of the Church, and when there was question of suppression of the monastery founded by her, she never murmured.

The humble servant of God, Mother Louise Margaret, would be ready to repeat the same words with regard to that which has survived her and which she has left as a precious heritage : her writings, her Congregation, the Sacerdotal Work.

It pleased Divine Goodness to select our diocese of Ivrea as the cradle of this spiritual heritage, but " The Sacerdotal Work" has long since passed the boundaries of the diocese and, we may say, has reached the farthest parts of the earth.

If, as the Gospels says, the tree is known by its fruits, we have reason to have confidence in the vitality of the "Work" and its branches from the consoling fruits it has produced in the most diverse spheres of Catholic life.

The Love and Service of God-Infinite Love appears at the beginning of the Holy Year. May this humble contribution to the Kingdom of Infinite Love over all the earth, by means of a holy and sanctifying Priesthood, help to hasten the new era of sanctification and peace and that " great returning" wished for by the present Holy Father Pius XII.

PAULO ROSTAGNO,

✠ *Bishop of Ivrea.*

Ivrea, 24th June, 1949 (Feast of the Sacred Heart of Jesus).

INTRODUCTION

" Divine Love is the theme we must preach to our fellow-man,[1]
'Tis the heavenly elixir for the evils of mankind ;
'Tis the hearth of live fire which God's love will enkindle
In a world that's grown cold and all selfish with crime.

Then hail ! Twentieth Century, in Divine Love your hope is,
Your enemies without number, it will teach you to conquer
Return to your God and learn to love Him.
Jesus Christ goes before you, showing you His Heart."

Thus wrote Mother Louise Margaret Claret de la Touche at the dawn
of the twentieth century.   We who have arrived at its mid-day feel more
than ever how opportune these words are.   We feel the need for love
in the world ; for we see men frozen by egoism, tortured by hatred,
disappointed with life, but nevertheless striving after a good of which
they are ignorant, but to which they aspire unconsciously.

Man has suffered from his own hatred for others and from that of
others for him ; he has experienced profound disillusionment at seeing
the failure of so many schemes to which he pinned his faith.   Man is
hungry for God and he does not know Him.

We must show him God and bring him back to His divine arms.   But
that can be done only on one condition : that we represent God to him
as He is, that is to say, as a Father Who loves to an infinite degree.

" Deus est Caritas."   " God is love." (1 John IV, 14)   It is for this
God-Love that man is hungry, it is of Him that the world has need.

And God Himself, like the Good Shepherd of the Parable in the Gospel,
has condescended to come in search of lost humanity by calling His
children once more to the knowledge of His love.

Yes, God, Who in the inspired pages of the Prophets of old, had, a
thousand times, published His great love for men ; God, Who sent His
Son into the world with the great mission to reveal His love and to enkindle its fire in all hearts : " I am come to cast fire on the earth, and what

---

[1] See Vol I for the Life and work of Mother Louise Margaret.

will I, but that it be enkindled " (Luke XII, 49) ; God, Who by the voice of His saints had, in the course of the centuries, recalled this great truth to men, and had made to St. Margaret Mary such touching and effective revelations ; God, in fine, Whom the resistance and coldness of men has never been able to weary, has deigned to repeat His message of love once more to men in order to bring them back to the knowledge of Himself Who is Infinite Love, and by this means to be able once more to clasp them to His breast.

Mother Louise Margaret was the instrument chosen by God for this new manifestation of His love.[1]

God commenced by making her penetrate into the depths of the mystery of Infinite Love and by filling her with His love. Then He communicated to her His plans : to renew the world by means of love and to make use of His priests for this design. He traced out for them the plan of a universal organization destined to unite the priests of the whole world in a great pacific army to fight for the reign of love.

Mother Louise Margaret might therefore be said to have a double mission.

The first was to repeat to the world the ancient and ever new message of the love which God has for His creatures, to lead souls to a more profound knowledge of Infinite Love, Which is God Himself, and by the example of her life, which was a generous response to love, to show what sanctity and faith in love can produce—a mission to bring men back to the essence of Christianity, which can be summed up in one word : Love. The second mission was to transmit to priests the designs which God has on them in this great enterprise of renewing the world by means of love : to express the desires of His Divine Heart in this Work of Infinite Love.

But, shut up in the silence of her convent, what could Mother Louise Margaret do to carry out this mission entrusted to her by God ? What co-operation could she give ?

First and above all she gave the complete donation of herself, of her sufferings, of her total immolation. And this gift of herself was so complete and fervent that she became as the root hidden in the ground of the work that was to come into being.

---

[1] See *The Life and Work of Mother Louise Margaret.*

Then, she gave the co-operation of her writings in which, by Divine command, she noted down the messages and lights which she received from God. These writings have been translated into many languages and have found their way to every corner of the world, even to the mission-fields of Africa, India, China, and Japan. They have been highly appreciated everywhere they have gone, and have been an inspiration to priests everywhere, particularly to those on the mission fields.

The present volume is composed of extracts from the Intimate Notes, letters and conferences to the Sisters of Mother Louise Margaret. Most of these extracts have already been published in the French edition of the three volumes of *In the Service of Jesus-Priest* in their chronological order. In *The Sacred Heart and the Priesthood* which was published during the lifetime of Mother Louise Margaret and *The Book of Infinite Love,* which was published after her death, the communications which she received were arranged by herself in order of subject-matter, in the present volume the same has been done for the remainder of her writings. It is the fruit of many years of careful study.

The first part of this book contains the writings which have reference to the doctrine of Infinite Love and the application of that doctrine to our lives.

The second part contains the writings which have reference to the Work demanded by Jesus, the Priests' Universal Union of the Friends of the Sacred Heart and its branches, and gives the doctrine on which the Work is based and the general outlines of its organization.

PART I.

THE DOCTRINE OF INFINITE LOVE

It has been made abundantly clear in " The Life and Work of Mother Louise Margaret " that she made no claim to be the author of the explanation of the doctrine of Infinite Love contained in her writings ; that, on the contrary, she insisted on her ignorance of that sublime subject and even her incapacity to write down what it was given to her to know about it.   She also insisted that the doctrine on Infinite Love was not new when she said : " The doctrine on Infinite Love is certainly no new doctrine ; it appears in the front page of Genesis . . . . it shines forth in the meditations of the Word . . . . it manifests itself in the Holy Gospels, it shines with a special light in the Redemption."

The doctrine that God is Love can be but dimly perceived in the Old Testament ; it was Christ Himself Who explained it by His words, by His life and by His sublime sacrifice.   Christ not only revealed the doctrine of Infinite Love, but was Himself the living Tabernacle of Infinite Love.

The role of Mother Louise Margaret was like that of all God's servants, the role of a messenger.   Revelation was complete with the death of Christ ; its recording was finished with the death of the last of the Apostles ; the work of explaining it to succeeding generations is the duty of Christ's Church.   But Christ reserved to Himself the right to intervene whenever it seemed good to Him, to insist that not only the letter but the spirit of His doctrine be maintained, and to throw light on what He had revealed.   The light on the mysteries of Infinite Love which we find in the writings of Mother Louise Margaret is such new light.

In a letter to Monsignor Filipello she wrote :

" I see Infinite Love in all the mysteries of our Faith, explaining them, defining them, illuminating them with an intense light, which, however, is so mild that the eyes of the soul can gaze upon it without being dazzled."

CHAPTER I.

INFINITE LOVE

1. GOD IS LOVE

God is Love ! His great occupation is to love ; He loves from eternity to eternity ! While Infinite Love excercising Itself on Itself, takes complacence in the marvellous exchange which takes place between the Father to the Son, and between the Son and the Father to the Holy Ghost, in the ineffable communication which the Three Divine Persons make to each other of the same Love which is Their Essence and Their Being, It acts outside Itself also and, as the proper action of Love is to love, It loves every creature, every work that has issued from God's powerful word ; everything that was, everything that is, and everything that will be. God loves. That is what He occupies Himself with in the sovereign possession of His Being and in the serene peace of His immortal glory.

He loves ! That is His life, His action, His pleasure, His divine food and His ineffably sweet repose. He loves, He wishes to love. He must continue to love ; His Love is Himself, and, if He ceased to love, He would suddenly cease to be God.

God is Love ! He gives love without reckoning. He pours it out in splendid abundance on the entire creation. Nothing escapes from this divine deluge, which strives to engulf everything.[1]

2. GOD IS, ABOVE ALL, LOVE

We do not know God ! God is love, and we do not know it. When He strikes us with sorrow, at first we are sometimes astonished, then we recognize His power, we bow before it, but we do not think of His love.

However, if one might say that something had precedence in God in Whom everything is eternal, I would say that before being powerful, before being wise, before being just and good, God was already Love ; and doubtless, one may say so, for before He acted on nothing-

---

[1] Intimate Notes 20-12-1905.

ness, He had not shown the totality of His power; before He created angels and men and formed the universe, He had not displayed His marvellous Wisdom ; before He had formed inferior creatures towards whom He could incline, He had not manifested all the extent of His Goodness ; before evil existed, He had not exercised the plenitude of His Justice. And He was already Love !

Nothing in God was before Love, and Love was before all things.

When my soul contemplates these divine mysteries, it prostrates itself in adoration. O God-Love ! if we could only realize that ! if we would only go up towards Thee always and without hesitation and as by first impulse ! towards Thee, the only source of being, the only life, the only movement ! We have faith, perhaps, but we believe in a God Who is only power and justice.

We do not believe in Thee ; Thou, Thou art Love ! not a feeble, powerless, soft. love, Oh ! no. O God-Love, I know that Thou feelest an insult, I know that Thou art powerful to avenge it. I know that justice is displayed prominently in Thy works, but I also know that mercy dominates it.[1]

3. THE ABYSSES OF LOVE

For some time I have been applying myself intently to the contemplation of Love, and my soul has retained such sweet and strong impressions that I wish to note down some of them.

I saw before me an immense abyss, so vast that no human eye could sound its depths ; it was Love Creator.

Infinite Love had need of diffusing Itself outside of Itself and It had resolved to create man in order to be able to bestow Itself on him, and, as a young mother with her own hands prepares the cradle for the child to which she is about to give birth, as she endeavours to make it not only commodious and comfortable, but also handsome and pleasant looking, so, Almighty God, Who was to be at the same time Father and Mother, lovingly prepared man's cradle, the universe. He took pleasure in enriching it and adorning it with all that could contribute to the utility, the service, and the joy of His beloved creature.

At times Almighty God stopped in His work and contemplated what was already created. He saw that nothing was wanting

---

[1] Intimate Notes : No date.

to it and found that all was good (Gen. 1, 31). Finally, when the great palace of the universe was ready to receive the royal guest for whom it had been prepared, God created man, and it was in him that Infinite Love was well pleased.

The Most Holy Trinity having deliberated, man was formed, and the divine breath, the Spirit of God, Love, gave him life, life of the soul and of the body, a life perfect and pure, a life such as God made for man.

Then I saw another abyss. Man had sinned, he had transgressed God's commands, and this rebellious creature was to be punished. Infinite Sanctity demanded its rights, and Justice was about to annihilate this being that had responded to the liberality of Love-Creator only by disobedience and pride.

But Love-Mediator, placing Itself between man, the sinner, and God Whom he had outraged, formed a profound abyss and Justice could no longer reach man.

For long centuries this Love-Mediator preserved the sinful creature from the blows of Divine Justice : He guided the Patriarchs and revealed Himself to them ; He spoke to the Prophets ; He preserved the true notion of God among the chosen people ; He laboured to prepare the whole human race for the work of the Redemption.

A third abyss of Love is now shown to me, so vast, so profound, so incomprehensible, that an incomprehensible love alone could explain it. It was Love-Redeemer.

The Word became incarnate, He visited the earth, He revealed to man the hidden mysteries of salvation ; He gave all his blood, and in this generous laver, culpable humanity was cleansed. The whole life of Jesus, all His adorable immolations were comprehended in that.

Love-Priest had offered Love-Victim ; the world was redeemed, Divine Justice was disarmed ; definite reconciliation between the Creator and the creature was effected. Jesus died to give us life ; when risen again, He completed the formation of His Church ; then He ascended to His Eternal Father.

A new abyss of love was shown to me ; it was Love Illuminator ! The Holy Spirit, the Spirit of God, the substantial love of the Father and the Son descended on the Church to fertilize it, as He had formerly fertilized the virginal womb of Mary.

The Church had given birth to numerous children and the Holy Spouse continued to enlighten it ; mysteries were revealed more clearly ; souls, warmed by Love, served God as He wished to be served, in spirit and in truth ; the preaching of the Apostles, the blood of the martyrs, the teaching of the Doctors, the decrees of the Councils, these living lights which are the Saints, come each at the appointed time, raised up by Love-Illuminator to complete the marvellous adornment of the Divine Spouse of Christ.

A fifth abyss was shown to me ; the times were accomplished ; new heavens and a new earth had appeared, and Love-Glorifier was going to crown the elect ; nothing was wanting to the divine plenitude ; all creatures had returned to the bosom of the Father, and Love, by glorifying them, glorifies Itself.

An immense abyss, it contained all beings ; like a torrent of divine delights, it inundated the elect, and, like a consuming and avenging fire, it devoured the accursed. Love reigned as sovereign and undisputed Master, It had done its work ; it had gained the victory ; all glory was rendered to It. And I perceived yet another abyss, the dimensions of which no human words can express nor has any human intellect ever measured. It was Love without form, Love without exterior manifestations : it was God Himself.

Prostrate on the edge of this unfathomable abyss, my soul adored in silence, and I seemed to hear a voice saying to me : " Infinite Love envelopes, penetrates, and fills all things. It is the only source of life and of all fertility ; It is the eternal principle of beings and their eternal end. If you wish to possess life and not to be sterile, break the bonds that bind you to yourself and to creatures and plunge into this abyss."[1]

4. THE QUALITIES OF LOVE

During all these days I dwelt on these four words of St. Paul : " breadth and length and height and depth." (Ephes. III, 17, 18)... The Charity of God, which is immense, infinite, could not be measured by the human eye or by the gaze of the soul. Then the Being, Love, in a mysterious manner, condensed this divine Charity, and rendered it visible in the Heart of the Word Incarnate. Created beings have been able to see in this Heart, created, but adorable and divine, the breadth and length and height and depth of Infinite Love.

---

[1] Intimate Notes 28-10-1901.

Breadth; because It embraces the multitude of beings ; there is not a single creature which Infinite Love does not nurse in Its arms ; not a single one which It has not willed, looked on with consideration and loved ; not one which It has not endowed and provided with everything which constitutes its form and existence.

There is first of all the angel, a pure creature, an immaterial spirit, a flame of living fire. Then there is the man, uniting in himself an immortal soul, the lights of the intellect and of reason to the material form of a body and flesh ; a creature worthy of admiration and enveloping a spiritual soul, a created light vivified by the divine life, with a perishable, mortal veil.

Then there is the animal, by the blessing of God increasing and multiplying, and being guided surely by its instinct towards its earthly end. Next, there is the tree of the forest, each spring feeling the sap of life ascend its century-old trunk and escape in the form of green buds ; and the flowers of the fields bending beneath the wind and blooming for the glory of their Creator. Lowest down in the scale are the bodies without life receiving their form and brilliancy from the divine Principle.

Length; it is the duration without limit of this love. Creatures commenced one day to receive the love of God, and that day was the day of their creation ; but in God, love for His creatures had never a beginning. He bore their *idea exemplaris* in Himself from all eternity. He loved them, then, long before He created them. He loved them as soon as He had conceived them in His thought. But has He conceived them some day? Has He not borne their *idea exemplaris* in Himself as long as He is God? And when has He begun to be God?

From all eternity, Infinite Love has, then, enveloped all creatures. Will It cease one day to love them? Never ! The love of God is immutable, it will never change. What He loved once, He loves always, and if sometimes He strikes, if He destroys, it is always love that guides Him. He has loved from all eternity ; He will love for all eternity.

Length; Who will measure the length of Infinite Love? Who will place a beginning for It or assign an end? God has always loved ; He will always love, for all eternity.

Height; Infinite Love has ascended to incomprehensible heights. In the Father, It has ascended even to the generation of the Divine

Word, of the Omnipotent Word, of the Eternal Wisdom, the only Son, equal in all things to the Father.

In the Father and the Son, It has ascended even to the procession of the Holy Ghost, the Principle of all love and of all sanctity, God, like the Father and the Son.

In the Divine Trinity, It has ascended even to the forming of the most perfect unity, so that the Father and the Son and the Holy Ghost are only one Love, one only God in Three Divine Persons.

In this one God, It has ascended even to the idea of the creation, even to the accomplishment of this great work, even to the divine liberality with which creatures have been favoured. This divine Love appears in its sublimity when it conceived the idea of the Incarnation; when, after the Fall of Man, It disarmed Justice, when, in spite of incessant sins, It preserved its merciful patience.

This love was sublime when the Word became Incarnate ; when He became a little child, poor, humiliated, suffering ; when He lived among us in simplicity and goodness, and in the gift of His whole Self ; when He was in a death agony in the Garden at the sight of our iniquities ; when He appeared bound with chains, scourged, mocked, crucified ! Sublime in the Tabernacle, where He remains chained as a prisoner during the ages ; sublime in the Holy Sacrifice of the Mass, in which He immolates Himself, and in the Blessed Eucharist, in which He makes Himself our food.

O the sublimity of the Infinite Love of God ! who will be able to raise himself up to Thee, to comprehend Thee ?

Depth : And who will be able to descend to Thy unfathomable depths ? Infinite Love, this marvellous edifice, composed of Omnipotence, infinite Wisdom, sovereign Goodness, unchangeable Justice, divine Mercy, absolute Good, perfect Beauty, has foundations so deep that nothing has been able to shake them. Time which destroys everything has been unable to do anything against It. The tide of human iniquities has come and broken itself against It, as the wave in its fury breaks itself at the foot of the granite rock. All eternity will not be sufficient for the elect to penetrate the lowest depths of this abyss of Love !

Depth : Let us go to the Heart of Jesus : through the wide opening which the lance has made in It, let us look into this abyss of divine Charity ; let us endeavour to sound its depths. But no, the soul is seized with dizziness before this abyss of love ; one must shut one's eyes, abandon every support and let himself fall, fall, fall without end into these divine depths, without seeking to understand, without wishing to explain.

Love is not explained ! It is desired, it is wished for, it is tasted ; we are inebriated by it, we live on it, we do not know it ! O the depths !¹

5. THE MOVEMENTS OF LOVE

What do you wish to say, my soul, and why wish to speak of what goes beyond anything that you can conceive ? The reason is because I feel myself urged on by a force, powerful and sweet at the same time, to manifest the Infinite Love that is in God and which is God Himself.

It is especially after Holy Communion that I feel this divine plenitude increase within me, and that the lights on these mysteries of divine Charity come to me more clearly and more numerous.

What then shall I now say ?

It is that God is Love, and that this Love, Which is His essence, causes at the same time both the Unity of His nature and the Trinity of His Persons ; that this Infinite Love living and giving life, living in Itself and by Itself and giving life outside Itself, not only tends by Its own nature to communication but that, by the fact of the intensity of Its life and Its immortal fecundity, It is communication itself. Infinite Love, because It is living and fertile is a movement. This movement takes place in God Himself by the communication between the Three Persons.

I cannot find words to speak of this divine movement of Love in Itself. It is like an uninterrupted circulation which goes from the Father to the Son and to the Holy Spirit ; it is a unique, vital movement ; so compressed and so intense that at the first look my soul casts on it, it seems to be an immobility.

This movement of Love takes place also outside God. The most marvellous production of this exterior movement of Love is the Humanity of Jesus. .

I would wish to be able to explain the difference that there is between the movement which Infinite Love makes in Itself and that which It makes outside Itself.

The interior movement, if I am not mistaken, does not tend to any

---

¹ Intimate Notes : 1901.

creation, to any new production ; it is a movement of repose and enjoyment ; a complete movement[1] which can neither increase nor diminish nor change. It is the plenitude of Love which satisfies Itself in a perpetual and always equal movement between The Three Persons.

The exterior movement tends to creation, to an incessant production.

It is—how shall I express it?—a movement of activity, and it satisfies itself by a perpetual production of graces, of gifts, of spiritual life, of creation, of material lives.

These two movements, or rather this single movement, is not less prolific in the one than in the other of its forms.

It is prolific in God by the eternal generation and the eternal procession ; it is prolific outside God by grace and creation.[2]

6. THE INCARNATION

In these serene heights on which He dwells, in this great eternal silence in which He reposes, without interrupting the permanent act which He operates, God dreams dreams of Love.

Could He, Infinite Love, dream of anything else ? What could He do except works of love ? God had then dreamt of loving and of being loved, no longer solely by Himself, but by new beings created by Him, on whom He could pour out the lifegiving floods of His overflowing love and from whom He could receive in His turn the sovereignly sweet homage of a submissive and grateful love.

The angels and the worlds and men had successively issued from His omnipotent Word, and the Spirit of Love had had His complacence in these excellent works.

Man, the last born of creation, was cherished by God as a Benjamin, and for him God dreamt new dreams of love. Oh ! how beautiful the dreams of God are !

---

[1] Mother Louise Margaret takes the word ' movement ' in the sense of activity and not of change. Besides, a little later on, she expresses her thought with admirable preciseness when she says that in God this movement is a movement of repose and enjoyment. It is interesting to see how St. Thomas in his commentary on *De Trinitate* (Question 5. Art. 4) and in his *Summa Theologiae* (Part I, Question 9) explains that one may, by metaphor, speak of movement in God as Plato, St.Augustine Denys, and Holy Scripture itself have done. The Holy Doctor remarks that this metaphor of movement is applied both to imminent operations of the Divine Intellect and will and to the action which produces exterior things. (Ch. V. Héris, O.P. S.T.M.)

[2] Intimate Notes : without date.

Like a skilful sculptor, He had modelled humanity ; with a breath of His mouth He had given it life, and He had seen it so beautiful in the first whiteness of its innocence that He became smitten with an ardent desire to unite Himself to it and to unite it closely to Himself.

Sin had soon come and covered the divine masterpiece with its foul slime ; but the dream of God had remained.

The time having come, the Word descended ; He clothed Himself in passible, mortal flesh. And thus the divine dream became realized. God and man now formed but one in Jesus Christ. They formed but one Divine Person. But God is Love, and Love is insatiable of union. He dreamt of new unions, and it was the Blessed Eucharist, it was the Church, to the body of which He united His Spirit intimately ; and it was the Priesthood in which He deposited His Heart.

Infinite Love had dreamt of union ; omnipotent Love had realized it ; most wise and most just Love had accomplished it in this admirable manner which renders all honour to God ; all-good and all-merciful Love had, in accomplishing it, raised up fallen humanity. It has rehabilitated it and crowned it by the Incarnation [1]

7. THE WORKS OF LOVE

" If I had time and if I were less ignorant, I would like to write what I see of Infinite Love, in order to make it understood by others. It is the desire to be more loved which induces God to manifest thus the Love which is in Him, and which is Himself.

It is the superabundance of His Love which has made Him Creator ; it is His Love which has inspired the Incarnation and made Him Redeemer and Saviour. It is His Love which has formed the Church and the Priesthood, which invented the Blessed Scarament and all the Sacraments. It is His Love which has arranged Purgatory for souls that have not been sufficiently purified by the trials of life. It is His Love which has prepared the sojourn of peace, joy and glory for souls of good will. It is from Love unknown and outraged that Hell has been produced. Love everywhere, Love in everything ! Why? Because God Himself is

---

[1] Intimate Notes : Oct. 1906.

Love and because He can produce nothing, touch nothing which
has not the imprint of this same Love."[1]

8. HELL, A WORK OF LOVE AS WELL AS OF JUSTICE

I have been told that a priest, a Religious who has left the right
path, was teaching a doctrine contrary to that of the Holy Church
and was denying the existence of Hell, alleging that God is too good
to punish eternally. My God, how sad it is to see those who ought
to be the light of the world and the pillars of the Church, cast dark
shadows on souls, and uproot the foundations of the Faith.

But it is precisely because I believe in Thy Love, O my great God,
powerful and good, that I believe in hell. If Thou wert not Love, if,
selfishly shot up in Thy happiness, Thou didst cast on beings inferior
to Thyself only indifferent looks, perhaps Hell might not exist.
But Thou ! Thou hast created everything through Love; Thou
hast formed man to Thy divine image, Thou hast vivified him by
Thy breath, Thou hast filled him with Thy gifts, and Thou hast
demanded from this creature so richly endowed only a little confidence, a little fidelity and love. And when he despises Thee and
revolts against Thee, wouldst Thou remain unmoved as if Thou
wert an incomplete being, devoid of love and feeling. O my God,
I believe in the rigours of Thy Justice, because I believe in the excessive tenderness of Thy Heart.

I love Thee, My God, Infinite Love, Who dost bend down
towards Thy creature, Who dost sustain him and raise him up ; but
I love Thee also, disowned and outraged Love, Who dost redress
Thy wrongs and punish. If hell did not exist I would not love Thee
so much.

When I see a prince allow all crimes go unpunished in his kingdom ; when I see his largesses bestowed with equal profession on
felons and traitors as on loyal subjects, and see the royal greatness
and majesty dragged in the mire, I cannot but despise him and call
him unjust and cowardly ! No, if there were no hell, I could not
love Thee .... If there were no hell, three splendid jewels would
be wanting to the crown of Thy sublime perfections ; there would be
wanting justice, power and dignity !

I adore Thee also, I love Thee passionately, Thou great, majestic,
terrible God ; consuming in eternal flames those who have resisted
the embraces of Thy love.

---

[1] Intimate Notes : 20-1-1918.

And besides, it is not Thou, my God, sovereignly good, who dost condemn and damn ; it is those wicked people themselves who, refusing to throw themselves into the flames of eternal love, precipitate themselves into those of Thy eternal Justice !

Yes, I love Thee such as Thou art. I adore Thee crowned with the infinite collection of all perfections, as just as Thou art good, as great by Thy power and by Thy holiness as by Thy mercy, and always Love, Love which creates, which gives, which pardons, which vivifies ; Love which commands, which corrects, which chastises.[1]

Reply to an Objection

God would not be God, if He were not sovereignly perfect. He would not be perfect, if He were only good and were not at the same time infinitely wise, infinitely great, infinitely just, infinitely holy. Now, it belongs to His greatness, His justice, and His holiness not to give the creature possession of infinite happiness and of eternal glory unless the creature merit them by trial. The trial consists precisely in man, who has free will, having to choose between good and evil ; hence the necessity of evil for the trial. God is not the author of evil, He merely permits it for the trial. But the doctrine of the Church on grace, which tells us that God always gives man sufficient grace to resist evil, shows God to be infinitely good, since He offers the creature an all-powerful help to triumph in the trial which He imposes on him. The doctrine of the Church and its teaching makes the whole question clear. To wish to solve it by philosophy alone without relying on the lights of Faith is to condemn oneself to wander perpetually in the darkness.[2]

---

[1] Intimate Notes : Dec. 1903.
[2] Intimate Notes : Dec. 1903.

CHAPTER II.

MERCY.

God is Love, even when He creates hell ; and how many times does He not offer His Mercy to souls who have outraged His Love before allowing them to precipitate themselves into the flames of eternal Justice ? Mercy is a form of Love adapted to us sinners. That is why it interests us specially and touches us deeply. He who does not meditate on it and endeavour to understand it, will be in a state of doubt concerning the divine liberality. He will remain incapable of establishing with God those relations of boundless confidence which God has the right to expect from His creatures, and his soul will remain engulfed in his miseries and sins.

1. THE CREATIONS OF MERCY

The idea of Infinite Mercy has dominated my soul to-day. I have seen it divinely creative. On the days of creation, when the foundations of the earth did not exist, God, Infinite Love, created everything by His Word. God spoke and everything was made.

Holy Scripture represents to us the adorable Trinity performing its work of love.

The Father speaks the creative word ; the Word arranges all things, and, as infinite Wisdom, He finds His complacence in the midst of creation ; the Holy Spirit, by His divine warmth, disposes the waters of the earth for fertility. The Word, at the first hour, under the form of Divine Wisdom, with infinite grace, created from nothing the multitude of beings ; with the Father and the Holy Ghost, He causes life to shoot forth, and every creature assumes its being and its form under the breath of Love.

In the days of Redemption, God in a certain manner makes a new creation, not material, but purely spiritual ; and it is again by His Word that He wills to operate and produce. It is no longer then under the form of Divine Wisdom, but under that of Divine Mercy, that the Word is Creator.

Having become incarnate in Jesus, Infinite Mercy creates no longer out of nothing. but out of fallen man, beings of justice, ways of holiness, new purities, children of God. Oh ! these creatures of Mercy ! Still more beautiful, more worthy of the Wisdom and

12

Love of God than those which appeared at the commencement of time.

Divine Mercy rejoices in the midst of them, and as Divine Wisdom found its complacence in the midst of its work, so Divine Mercy takes its delights in the midst of the souls which it purifies and saves.[1]

2. LOVE AND MERCY

I meditated on the Prodigal Son. Oh ! what a sweet and consoling meditation ! This parable is an exquisite portrait, traced by the hand of Jesus Himself, of the Infinite Mercy of the Heart of God. How good He is to trace in detail all its lineaments and to show all its divine beauties.

God is Love, He is Infinite Love, this divine essence in itself has no form. It is a vast, limitless sea, a light confined by no obstacle ; but outside Itself, Infinite Love takes different forms in order that we may be able to recognize It. One of the forms of Love, the most attractive for our sinful souls, is Mercy. Mercy is a form of Love adapted to us sinners, but it is truly Love, Infinite Love, always the same, uncreated, eternally living and operating.

Now, Infinite Love has five divine terms, five sacred properties, five operations ; and all the forms of this Love, because they are Love, have also these same terms, these same properties, these same operations.

Infinite Love is Creator, Mediator, Redeemer, Illuminator, Glorifier.

Mercy is creative, in as much as it creates a new purity in the repentant soul. It is mediatory, in as much as it places itself between sin and Divine Justice, and brings repentant Love and pardoning Love together. It is redemptory, in as much as it ransoms the soul from sin, and delivers it by purifying it. It is illuminating, in as much as it, and it alone, at the same time enlightens and shows the misery of the sinner and the goodness of God. It is glorifying, because it is mercy which gives heaven to men, and by their salvation gives glory to God.[2] & [3]

---

[1] Intimate Notes : 25-1-1907.
[2] Intimate Notes : October, 1905.
[3] See The Sacred Heart and the Priesthood, Chap. VIII. Mercy, the Seventh Sacerdotal Virtue of the Heart of Jesus.

CHAPTER III.

JESUS, THE EXTERNAL MANIFESTATION OF INFINITE LOVE.

The human soul finds it difficult to raise itself to the contemplation of Eternal and Infinite Love, which is God. Our God has condescended to assume our human nature and to render His Love perceptible in the Person of Jesus, and especially in His Sacred Heart. Jesus has, in a mysterious way, made His Sacred Heart, the place of abode, the meeting place of His faithful servants.

1. JESUS CHRIST

Jesus Christ! in pronouncing this name I bring to the mind a world of mysteries, of profound, sweet thoughts, an infinity of divine realities.

Jesus Christ! He is the Alpha and the Omega, the principle and the end of all things. By His radiant figure, He dominates the long series of the ages that have passed ; He throws admirable light on the depths of the future.

Jesus Christ! the unknown of yesterday, the persecuted of to-day, the crucified, perhaps, of to-morrow, the divine pivot around which all things revolve. He is the Master of minds, the Saviour of the world ! Jesus Christ ![1]

2. JESUS, GOD AND MAN

When the Word of God willed to unite Himself to man by the Incarnation, He, doubtless, chose for Himself a most beautiful, most pure, and most exquisite humanity ; He did not, however, create it different from others. With the exception of sin, which, since original sin had sullied humanity, the human nature of Christ was in nothing unlike the human nature of others. There were the same faculties in His intellect, similar sentiments in His Heart ; there was the same capability of suffering, the same liability to death in His flesh.

---

[1] Intimate Notes : 1909.

The union with the Word had expanded, amplified, perfected the human nature of Christ; it had not changed it. Christ was, and always is, at the same time the Son of God and the Son of Man, true God and true man; and it is Love which has willed it so. Love always thirsts for union, in order that one Man having been united to God in the Person of Christ, all men, His brethren, like Him in everything, should be sharers in this union. It was necessary that this be so for the raising up of the entire human race, and in order that man, in spite of his persistent weakness and misery, might have the confidence to say to God : " Father."

God, Infinite Love, most pure Intelligence, loves the human nature which His divine hands formed out of spirit and of matter; He has no horror for this material part which His power has drawn from nothing. He does not fear to unite Himself to it, in order to make it ascend even to Himself. The sculptor does not hate the clay from which he draws his masterpieces; he does not despise this kneaded slime which can give him so much glory.[1]

3. JESUS CHRIST BECOME MAN THROUGH LOVE

" One is good, God." (Matt XIX, 17). He alone is the supreme Goodness, supreme Wisdom, supreme Power, supreme Perfection! What then could be better for us than to follow and imitate God Himself? But God Himself in His divine essence cannot be perceived by our senses, and we have an imperious need of something which we can perceive or touch.

And it is for that reason that God in His Infinite Goodness has condescended to assume a visible form, in order that we may have a greater facility and a more powerful attraction to love our Creator.

Our First Parents, in their ambition, had sought to make themselves equal to God by the knowledge of good and evil, and had fallen into sin, losing the good which they knew, and subjecting themselves to the evil which they had not known up to that moment. It was then that God resolved to come amongst men in human form in order that, without presumption or danger, they might be able to aspire to a likeness to God, fly from evil, and give themselves to the practice of good.

In taking our human nature, the Incarnate Word united in Himself

---

[1] Intimate Notes : October, 1906.

these two extremes : Divine Greatness and human lowliness.

When we wish, we can, as it were, ascend to supreme happiness by means of union with Christ and likeness to Him.

This Incarnate God has come on earth to glorify His Father by making known to men His name and His love.   Before His coming, the name of the Lord was holy and terrible, now the name of the Father is holy and sweet.   The old law was a law of fear ; the new law is a law of love.

It was for the love of His Heavenly Father and of men that the Word became man, and He has done so through the operation of the Holy Spirit, Who is the Spirit of Love.

The Incarnation is therefore a work of Love, of gratuitous and Infinite Love.[1]

4.   THE SACRED HEART OF JESUS, THE EXPLANATION OF THE MYSTERIES OF LOVE

Yesterday evening, finding myself at the feet of Jesus in prayer, I said to Him: **" The more people offend Thee, my Saviour, the more I wish to love Thee ; the more people attack Thy Divinity the more I wish to adore Thee ! "**

And this thought was suggested to me : The Apostle St. Thomas truly loved Our Lord, and one day, in an impulse of generosity, he said : " Let us go that we may die with Him " (John XIV,16) but he did not believe in His Divinity ; he did not believe in His Resurrection ; he thought that Jesus was powerless to take up again the life which He had sacrificed for the salvation of the world, and he doubted His divine power.

What was the remedy that Jesus used to cure the incredulity of His apostle ?   He made him put his finger into the wounds of His hands and feet.   And as soon as Thomas had put his hand into this wound of love, as soon as he had explored the Heart of His divine Master, he cried out : " My Lord, and My God." (John XX, 28.)

It seemed to me that Our Lord had suggested this thought to me for the sole purpose of giving me to understand that the knowledge of His Heart, that is to say, of His Infinite Love, would be capable of combating the errors of our day and of triumphing over them.

The mystery of the Incarnation, that of the Redemption, all the

---

[1] Intimate Notes : 28-11-1908.

divine mysteries can be explained only by Love. But can Infinite Love be comprehended, grasped by poor, finite, limited creatures ?

It is only in the Sacred Heart of Jesus that we can understand It. We see in this Heart a love human and divine, and by this human love, but more than human, we arrive at the knowledge of divine Love, of God Himself.

The Heart of Jesus shows forth to us goodness, mercy, sacrifice ; then we believe in Love.[1]

5. THE LIVING TABERNACLE OF LOVE

Nothing outside of Thee can satisfy me, and since Thou hast revealed Thyself to me, I have known that I have been created solely for Thee.

Long had I sought Thee, O my God, where Thou wast not, long had I desired Thee without knowing what I desired. I had sought Thee in human affections and, if sometimes the consolation obtained seemed to be a tiny trickle from Thy divine tender love, it was mostly only an empty mirage.

I had sought Thee in nature which produces its marvels at Thy word, and it replied : " I am a manifestation of the Divine Power but I am not your God."

I had sought Thee through the arts, I had sought Thee in all beauty and harmony, and they replied to me : " We cannot give you your God." I had sought Thee by my intellect in everything that appeared to be noble and true ; I had sought Thee by my heart, in everything that appeared to me to be just and good ; but in all these things, joined to what they received from Thee, I found so much infirmity and weakness, that my soul was not able to satisfy itself in them.

I had sought in the vain pleasures and frivolities of the world, not Thee, O my God, for I knew Thou wert not there, but some sort of means to forget the sadness of my heart ; and not only had I not found such, but I discovered a still more painful and deceptive void.

Nevertheless, I have found Thee, my God.
In the Heart of Thy Son incarnate, in the living Tabernacle of Love,
I have found all forms of beauty, grandeur, tender love, and purity ;

---

[1] *Intimate Notes* : 5-5-1903.

I have found Mercy, this unique meeting place of the fallen creature and the ever-glorious Divinity.

In the Sacred Heart of Jesus I have found paths accessible to my weakness to ascend to Thee ; I have entered into His Heart, and by visiting Its mysterious dwellings I have been insensibly and, as it were by degrees, elevated to the luminous and serene heights where Thy Divinity radiates Its influence.

I adore Thee, O my God, Who hast abased Thyself through Christ even to my humanity, and Who dost unite Thyself so closely to my race in His adorable Heart.

I adore Thee in this Temple sanctified by the actual and continuous presence of Thy divine being ; I annihilate myself in adoration before Thy Sovereign Majesty, but, at the same time, love raises me up to Thee.   I adore Thee and love Thee, and love and adoration are so mingled and blended in my soul, that I cannot say whether I adore Thee more than I love Thee, or whether I love Thee more than I adore Thee.

I adore Thee because I find in Thee all power and all holiness, all justice and all wisdom, because Thou art my Creator and my God. I love Thee, because I find in Thee all beauty and all goodness, all tender love and all mercy, because Thou hast given me the gift of an inestimable treasure.

Christ is my treasure.   He is mine, at each moment I can draw from Him to my heart's desire, and I find Him always abounding in riches : I take from Him the means to pay my debts, to relieve my needs, to procure for me delights, to buy for myself a crown.

Oh ! what an ineffable gift is not this Jesus with His Heart overflowing with tender love ; what a treasure is contained in It ! How It never fails ! the more I draw from It, the more It increases !

O my God, Thou hast so loved Thy creatures that Thou hast given them Thy only Son, and in order that the majesty of Thy Word might not frighten them, Thou hast clothed Him in flesh similar to ours in order that our souls might be unfailingly drawn by Him. Thou hast embellished Him with the most attractive charms, but above all, Thou hast formed for Him an infinitely perfect Heart Which was to be the abode of Thy delights ; Thy divine plenitude dwelleth there, and the humblest of Thy creatures has his place there.   This adorable Heart, great as Thyself, O my God, since It contains Thee, becomes nevertheless my dwelling since It loves me ; in It, I come face to face with Thy divine Majesty, and when Thou seest me in that sacred place of refuge, Thy just anger becomes appeased and Thy justice is disarmed.

I adore Thee, my God, through Jesus and in Jesus ; I adore this Jesus, Thy Son, Whose humanity makes Him my brother, and Whose Divinity makes Him my God ; I love Thee with Jesus and for Jesus ; love Thee by the Heart of Jesus, Which love has made mine, I love Thee in Jesus, in Whom my love reaches Thee, through Whom it can always move Thee and take hold of Thee.[1]

6. THE SACRED HEART

St. John, wishing to convey to us an idea of the Divine Being, wishing to sum up in a single term all the grandeurs, all the beauties, all the attributes of God, said : " God is Charity " (1 John IV, 16). God is Love. And if we wish to depict Jesus Christ, God and Man, in a single word, if we wish to express in a single term all that He is, all that He has done, and the very reason of His being, we can say : Jesus Christ is His Heart, is His Sacred Heart !

Divine Charity, Infinite Love, is God whole and entire ; God, both what He is Himself and what He does outside Himself ; God with His power, His justice, His wisdom ; God Who is, God Who creates, God Who redeems, God Who enlightens, and Who recompenses. It is God, without division, without exclusion, without reserve, splendidly summed up in a splendid phrase : " Deus Caritas est !" (1 John, IV, 16).

The Sacred Heart is Jesus Christ whole and entire, God and Man, the Word Incarnate. It is not only His Heart of flesh beating in His breast, this meek and humble Heart which we adore as the symbol and the organ of His incomparable Love, it is His whole being, divine and human : His divinity, His soul, His body, each of His sacred members, all His thoughts, His acts, His divine words.

The Sacred Heart is God made man, It is Jesus Christ humiliated, delivered up, crucified, expiring ; It is Eucharistic Jesus Christ, ineffable victim of love, Jesus immolated on the altar, Jesus a prisoner in the Tabernacle.

In order to designate one God in Three Persons, a single word of three syllables has sufficed : ' Caritas !' In order to designate Jesus

---

[1] Intimate Notes : 18-3-1900.

Christ with His two natures in one Person, a term composed of two
words united together has been found necessary : " The Sacred
Heart !" The first word designates the Divinity, the second, the
Humanity ; and it is necessary that they be joined together to designate
Jesus Christ.

God is explained completely and entirely by this word : ' Caritas,'
for love explains everything though it is itself inexplicable. Jesus
is completely explained by this name : " The Sacred Heart." His
sublime goodness, His devotedness, His Mercy, all His divine
virtues, His sacrifice, His death, all this is explained by His love.

The Sacred Heart is divine Charity Incarnate, Infinite Love
humanised ; it is the Charity of St. John come to reside in a heart
of flesh.[1]

7. THE SACRED HEART, THE BLESSED EUCHARIST, LOVE

The devotion to the Blessed Eucharist and the devotion to the
Sacred Heart are not only two sister devotions, in reality they are
one and the same devotion. They complete each other and develop
each other ; they blend so perfectly with each other that one cannot
go on without the other, and their union is absolute. Not only can
one of these devotions not be prejudicial to the other, but because
they complete each other and perfect each other, they also reciprocally increase each other.

If we have devotion to the Sacred Heart, we will wish to find It,
to adore It, to love It, to offer It our reparation and our praise, and
where shall we look for It but in the Blessed Eucharist where It
is found eternally living?

If we love this adorable Heart, we will wish to unite ourselves
to It, for love seeks union ; we will wish to warm our hearts by the
ardours of this divine fire, but to reach the Sacred Heart, to take
hold of It, to put It in contact with our own, what shall we do?
Shall we scale heaven and bear away the Heart of Jesus Who reigns
triumphant in glory? Doubtless we will not.

We will go to the Blessed Eucharist, we will go to the Tabernacle,
we will take the White Host, and when we have enclosed it in our
breast, we will feel the Divine Heart truly beating beside our own.

The devotion to the Divine Heart infallibly brings souls to the

---

[1] Intimate Notes : No date.

Blessed Eucharist ; and faith in and devotion to the Blessed Eucharist necessarily lead souls to discover the mysteries of Infinite Love of which the Divine Heart is the organ and the symbol.

If we believe in the Blessed Eucharist, we believe in Love. It is the mystery of Love. But, in itself, love is immaterial and imperceptible, to fix our minds and our senses, we seek an outward form for love. This form, this sensible manifestation, is the Divine Heart.

The Sacred Heart, the Blessed Eucharist, Love, are one and the same thing : In the Tabernacle we find the Host, in the Host, Jesus, in Jesus, His Heart, in His Heart, Infinite Love, divine Charity, God, and the Principle of life, living and giving life.

But still more : The ineffable mystery of the Eucharist can be explained only by Love. By the love of God, yes, but by the love of Jesus, God and man. Now the love of Jesus is the love of His Heart ; to sum up all in one word, it is His Heart ; therefore the Blessed Eucharist is explained only by the Sacred Heart.

The Blessed Eucharist is the sublime completion of the love of Jesus for men ; it is the highest, the last expression, the paroxysm, if I may so express myself, of this incomprehensible love.

Nevertheless, we could have believed in love without the Blessed Eucharist ; the Incarnation would have sufficed to show us the love of God ; a single drop of the bitter chalice of His Passion would have been superabundant to prove to us that love. We would have been able to love the Heart of Jesus, we would have been under an obligation to love It, to believe that It is sovereignly good, even if He had not gone to this divine excess of the Blessed Sacrament. But because He has invented this marvel, how we should love this Sacred Heart of Jesus so divinely tender, so inexpressibly tender and liberal ; so . . . shall I dare to say it ? . . . so madly and so passionately fond of His creatures !

Yes, the Blessed Eucharist augments and inflames our love for this Divine Heart. But because we know that we shall find this Divine Heart only in the Blessed Eucharist, because we are athirst for union with this Heart so tender and so ardent, we go to the Blessed Eucharist, we prostrate ourselves before the Blessed Sacrament, we adore the Host radiating its influence from the monstrance ; we go to the Holy Table with ardent avidity ; we lovingly kiss the consecrated paten on which the divine Host reposes each day. We surround with honour, respect, and magnificence, the Tabernacle in which Jesus, living and loving, makes His dwelling.

Oh ! it is impious to say that the worship of the Sacred Heart can injure devotion to the Blessed Eucharist. What ! will the knowledge of Him Who gives the gift make us despise the gift ?   No, the more we love the Divine Heart, the truer our worship of It is, the more extensive and enlightened it is, the more also will our worship and our love for the divine Eucharist develop and grow strong.[1]

8. THE SACRED HEART OF JESUS DESIRES TO POUR OUT ITS LOVE

The Heart of Jesus still suffers from the abundance of love which, as it were, oppresses It and dilates It ; It is relieved when It can pour it out into the hearts of Its creatures thus making Itself loved by them.

Of ourselves we cannot love God ; the love which we are able to have for Him has been deposited by Him in our hearts in the beginning ; it is by this love that we love Him ; thus we bring relief to the Sacred Heart by loving God, since in order to love Him we have need to receive a little of the overflowing love of His Divine Heart.

And as our hearts are narrow and weak, although they can only contain a little particle of love, they are dilated and oppressed by it, and thus the suffering of the Divine Heart passes into ours.

Oh ! how God loves His creatures all unworthy and sinful and corrupt as they are !   He draws them to Himself and wishes them to be altogether His own.[2]

---

[1] Intimate Notes : 16-10-1903.
[2] Intimate Notes : 19-8-1894.

CHAPTER IV.

INFINITE LOVE AND THE HUMAN SOUL.

God loves! this truth impresses me, but if it is added; God loves me, how much sweeter and consoling it becomes!

Not only does Infinite Love fill the whole universe, but It diffuses Itself in my soul to make it live of It. It fills it even to overflowing and establishes with it ineffable relations of intimacy by communicating to it Its own life.

The soul can then truly say: " My God," and can enjoy this sweet possession.

1. THE INTIMACY OF THE SOUL WITH GOD

Just now after Holy Communion, I remained for a moment suffering and then I found myself suddenly plunged into an abyss of Infinite Love. This divine love enveloped me, came down in streams on me, I felt myself impregnated with it like a sponge plunged into water. The most sweet voice of Jesus said to me : " Fill yourself with this love and diffuse it over the world." Oh ! how good it is to be in this sea of Infinite Love ! Without effort, without meditation, without thought, I saw the divine mysteries with wonderful clearness. A mystery of love has been unfolded to me that delighted me. How shall I describe it ? It was Infinite Love in the Father living and giving life, then this same Love manifested to men by Jesus Christ, by the Word Incarnate, making Itself perceptible to the intellect and to the heart of the creature. Finally, this same divine Love acting in man by the Holy Spirit, enlightening him, moving him.

The knowledge of Infinite Love renders the mystery of the most Blessed Trinity more luminous, more transparent to my soul than very pure crystal exposed to the sun. But what delights me entirely are these intimate relations which the adorable Trinity has and wishes to have with man. I cannot better express what I see of them, what I know of them, what has been shown to me about them in this mirror of divine Love, than by comparing the dependence of the creature on the Blessed Trinity, the close and necessary bonds which unite them, with the bonds which exist between the mother and the little child still shut up in her womb. O my God ! what marvels of love in Thee and how few souls know them !¹

2. EFFUSIONS OF LOVE

This morning after Holy Communion, I remained sunk in an abyss of adoration and love   Profoundly annihilated in myself, I seemed to hear above me the multitude of heavenly spirits singing and extolling divine Mercy ; and it was because Jesus had just united Himself to me, the most miserable, the weakest and the most impure of His creatures.

O Love ! Jesus living in me wishes to console me for my poverty and my misery by showing me that He was able to draw glory for Himself and praise for His mercy from these things.

Jesus, my life, my light, Thou Who dost unite Thyself to my sinful soul, I love Thee ; yes, I love Thee, but I love Thee too little. I would wish to love Thee passionately, with all the powers of my soul, with all the ardour of my heart, with all the energy of my will ; I would wish to go into a transport of love to unite myself indissolubly to Thy Heart.

When I possess Thee, my sweet Mercy, when Thy love exercises its divine influence on my soul, my exterior senses no longer receive any impression from it and I remain as if suspended in the expectation and desire of more complete union.

Thy Love, O great sovereign God, which is Thyself, is my life.   I exist only for Thy Love ; the reason of my existence is Love. Thou hast given me this existence, O my God, to magnify Thy Love, Thou hast raised me up each time that I fell in order to exalt Thy Mercy ; Thou hast lavished Thy gifts upon me only in order to reveal the excess of Thy tender love.

I am not myself ; Thou, my God art all ; I am the little that I am only by Thee and for Thee.

I feel myself constantly urged to write anew ; however, I am always repeating the same thing ; always the same note, the same melody is given forth from my soul, always praise, always the excess of Thy liberality, O Infinite Love !   Yes, I must repeat again, Infinite Love envelops us and embraces us ; it fills the world, it overflows into the boundless immensity, the human soul alone remains

---

¹ Intimate Notes : 20-12-1904.

closed to it, not entirely, for it would be annihilated, but it makes itself too narrow for love to enter.

All creatures receive with life this effusion of Infinite Love ; they turn towards their Creator and they open out to the vital influences which flow from God to them, but the soul of man made free to love God more than any creature,—this soul uses its freedom to close itself and bar itself against love.[1]

3. THE POSSESSION BY LOVE

I see God, immense, elevated, sublime ; and from the ocean of Infinite Love that is in Him, an imperceptible drop flows out. It is my soul. And what are all the powers, all the faculties, all the lights, all the graces which constitute the being of my soul and which are both its form and its life ? Do they not flow out from the Divinity ? my soul which has come out of God, and which lives by God, is to be one day lost in the abyss of God.

I feel that Infinite Love surrounds me and sustains me as the life of my life, the reason of my being ; that It not only has produced me by Its divine fruitfulness but that It, so to speak, creates me anew at each moment by the act of conserving my being.

This knowledge of the complete possession by God of my inmost being produces in me a most sweet sentiment, very delicate and very pure, very strong also, which is not, it seems to me, either adoration, or love, or confidence, or respect, but a sentiment composed of all that is strongest and most delicate of these.

It is something indefinable which I cannot express by any term and which, in my ignorance, I cannot explain : sacred repose, peaceful abandoned love, boundless confidence.

I feel myself so little, and God so great, leaning down lovingly towards His creatures, liberal to excess and containing in Himself depths of mercy, abysses of love which my soul feels, which it relishes, in Which it loses itself.

I do know whether I endeavour to love God with my whole soul, but I feel that my whole soul is penetrated by God ; I feel Him sometimes invade my being from all sides ; He invades my intellect by divine lights. He penetrates into my heart by burning ardours, He enters into my will and draws it to Himself.[2]

---

[1] Intimate Notes : 20-12-1901
[2] Intimate Notes : No date.

4. A MOTIVE FOR LOVE

O my adorable Master, I was not worthy to serve Thee in the Order dear to Thy Heart, above all I did not deserve to find Thee so merciful and kind to me, a poor creature sullied by sin.

However, if I was to find a place of refuge, was it not near Thy Divine Heart overflowing with mercy that I should find it, near this Sacred Wound, the fountain of love, open to those who thirst?

Yes, O Jesus, I was sullied, but Thou wast pure, I was a sinner but Thou wast holy, I was weak, but Thou wast strong, I was a nothing but Thou wast God!

Thou wast Love, Infinite Love, which overflows, which flows down, which fills; a love unique and divine which nothing can explain, but which alone can explain all things.

Thou hast been delivered up for me, O Jesus, to the death on the cross; that seems inexplicable, but the reason was because Thou hast loved me.

Thou hast pardoned my faults, Thou hast drawn me to Thyself, Thou hast lavished Thy favours upon me; all that again seems inexplicable, but the reason again was because Thou hast loved me.

And why hast Thou loved me, my sweet Master? Because Thou art Infinite Love, and Love cannot help loving.

Yes, everything is explained by Love; and then the heart remains there fainting away; the soul remains as it were motionless in mute adoration; and there is no more thinking, no more words, nothing but a silence of love. [1]

5. EVERYTHING IN GOD IS LOVE

God does not love man merely in an abstract, far-off manner. No, God loves him and takes an interest in him every minute.

It is love that directs all that God permits to happen to each one of us, not a blind, unintelligent love, but a love guided by infinite Wisdom, a love which looks to the best interests of each individual soul—which sometimes may be suffering.

But it is Love that directs everything.

God is Love! He has created us only to pour out into us the abundance of His Infinite Love; He can perform only works of love; all His thoughts, all His acts, all His divine designs are Love.

---

[1] Intimate Notes : 1901.

. . . But then everything that happens to me, whether it be the result of His Will or of His permission, everything which comes from Him, whether it be a joy or a sorrow, is all from Love. If persecution drives me into exile, if sickness stretches me helpless on a bed of suffering, if separation from, or the death of loved beings wounds my heart, if acts of ingratitude or calumny rend and defame me, if the disorders of a member of my family break my heart, all that is from Love! Does that mean that this act of injustice, that this evil which crushes me are the work of Love? Oh! certainly not; Love does not work evil or death, for It is resurrection and life. But I might be ignorant of this evil; I might be indifferent to it; I might even, by a fatal deviation, rejoice in it. If then I suffer, it is Love which wishes this suffering for me; it is Love which directs it to me, and makes me taste it. And if it is a joy which is given to me, a pure, legitimate joy, it is a smile from Love to comfort me and gladden me. Oh! my dear sister in Jesus, how this knowledge of Love lights up this life; how it transforms it, how it transfigures events and things. Being thus enveloped in Love, living in It, receiving everything from It, we feel ourselves living in God and, as it were, carried in His bosom.

Together, if you wish, we shall go to Love; we shall penetrate our souls with It; we shall fill our hearts with It; we shall light our lives by It. To find It, we shall enter into the living Tabernacle where It dwells in Its plenitude : the adorable Heart of Jesus. There in that sacred hearth of divine Charity, accessible, however, to our human weakness, we shall see Infinite Love; we shall know what It is in Itself, by seeing what It is in Jesus. Is not the wounded Heart of Jesus the divine door which introduces us into Love? Better than I, doubtless, my sister in Christ, you know the paths which lead to Infinite Love : paths of duty, of complete renunciation of self, of suffering in all its forms.[1]

6. GOD IS ALWAYS GOOD

God is always good, Goodness itself, infinitely good even when He wishes us to be afflicted, when He abandons us, when He imposes privations upon us, when He leaves us without help or support.

When He lavishes His sweetest graces on us, when He permits us

---

[1] Letter to Madam X : 1906.

to taste inward consolations in our souls, which He Himself sometimes presents to us, is He better? No, for His Goodness is always
immutably perfect like His divine Being.

What shall I say that Thou art, O my God, my Creator and my
Father? Thou art eternally Good.[1]

7. THE LOVING VIGILANCE OF GOD

At the end of another year two thoughts present themselves to our
minds, two sentiments make themselves felt in our hearts : a sentiment of sorrowful regret when we think of the many hours lost, of
days badly spent, of faults which have escaped our vigilance, or for
which our own perverse will is responsible.

By an act of very special love, God has chosen us as His very
special portion, He has sustained our courage by many helps re-
peatedly given ; and by a marvellous prodigality of His grace, He
has established us in a state of perfection and has strengthened us
for His holy service. Has He not then, the right to expect from us
greater fidelity and a more generous return of love? The thought
that we have disappointed His Divine Heart and that through our
fault we have deprived Him of some accidental glory which our
constancy in virtue and our generosity in sacrifice would have pro-
cured for Him, is the motive of our present sadness.

But another sentiment succeeds to that of sorrow ; it is a sentiment
of confidence and of humble gratitude. While, during the course
of the year, we were cowardly following Him from a distance, while
we were parsimoniously measuring out for God our acts of self-
renunciation and immolation, He has not allowed his loving vigilance to sleep for a moment, nor has He been parsimonious in pouring out His graces upon our souls. By His Providence, He has
entered into all the details of our lives and, not content with giving
us what is necessary, with a truly maternal tenderness of love, He
has gone so far as to give us that additional gift of peaceful repose and
interior joy in which every soul finds its happiness.

In presence of such goodness on the part of God, we can only
prostrate ourselves before Him with sentiments of love and, weeping
over our past ingratitude and over the lost hours which will never
return, go forward with humble confidence to meet the future.[2]

---

[1] Intimate Notes : 29-3-1900.
[2] Conference to the Sisters : 13-12-1907.

8. TRUE LOVE

On the morning of the third day of our retreat, I was in a state of interior solitude and of painful insensibility and helplessness.

During recreation this feeling of helplessness increased and at the same time I felt a great need of God ; soon our Lord made me experience the most painful and the most delicious effects of love and suffering, and, for nearly two hours, I remained in that state with my eyes or my lips fixed on the crucifix, conversing with Our Lord and receiving lessons from His divine mouth.

Innumerable pages would be required to write all that He said to my heart, and all that I said to His ; however, I will note here some of what was said between us.

When I asked Him why He always mingled suffering with all His favours to me, as at that moment when His divine love, while inebriating me with delights, made me suffer terribly, He said to me : " I love you as My Father has loved Me." (Cf. John XV, 9).

And I saw how the Father had crucified His Son, Jesus, through the ardent love which He had for that Son, the Word, Who, loving men, wished to save them.

Thus Our Lord makes us suffer in our souls, our hearts, and our whole being, out of love for our souls that He wishes to be all-pure.[1]

9. THE MYSTERIES OF LOVE

When finishing these pages written with hardly any reflection and without sequence, and returning in spirit over those thirty-eight years that have elapsed, I wish to dwell on a singularly striking thought. On the part of this little creature, the web of whose life these years have woven, what is there ? Faults without number, acts of cowardice and resistance, and infidelity. On the part of God, what have I seen ? Love, yes love, nothing but love ! God is Love and Love is in God and Love overflows from God. And sometimes without any other reason but Its own abundance, Infinite Love escaping from the Divine Being descends into a soul. It envelops it, It overwhelms it, It fills it to overflowing, although no previous good or merit has been able to attract It into the soul. These are the mysteries of Love.

Like an infinitely tender father, the Divine Master took me in

---

[1] Intimate Notes : 27-8-1895

His arms when I was yet an infant ; for a long time He guided me Himself, protecting me in the midst of the dangers of the world, instructing me interiorly, and disposing things in such a manner, that happenings that were in appearance most prejudicial to His divine designs, in the end helped to further them. When temptations and trials were shaking my soul, my adorable Master sent me His servant.

In His all-wise Providence, God has given me, from the beginning of my life, a necessary brake for my ardent nature, and by this inestimable gift of the Cross which He has given to His own Son, He had attracted me to Himself and revealed to me His Love. I recognize that all the sufferings which it has pleased God to send me have been the sources of graces. All the graces also, all the ineffable marks of the tender love of God for me have been sources of suffering. Ah ! if I had always known how to make good use of the Cross ! If I had known how to welcome it with joy, to carry it with love ! But even while knowing that it was good and that it came from God, how many times have I not groaned beneath its weight and rejected it ! I bless my adorable Master for the incomparable privilege of suffering which He has given me; I bless the events and the things which have concurred to make me suffer ; I bless and I love all those who have been, in the hands of Jesus, the instruments of my sufferings. If it has happened to me in the course of these pages to employ any terms that resemble complaints, I disavow them and wish to efface them.

O Infinite Love, Principle of Life, Source of graces, I recognize Thee in all things. I adore Thee in the ineffable mystery of Thy essence and in the repose of Thy glory ; I adore Thee in Thy sublime Unity which nothing divides, and in the Trinity of Thy Persons ; I adore Thee in Thy divine fertility which is exercised in Thyself and which manifests itself externally ; I adore Thee in Thy perfection without shadow ; I adore Thee in the manifestations of Thy Wisdom, Thy Power, Thy Justice, and Thy Goodness !

I annihilate myself before Thee like a tiny atom, and, while my eyes shed tears for having, by my faults without number, tarnished the mirror in which Thou hast wished to reflect Thyself in me, from my heart there bursts forth a hymn of gratitude and love for all the blessings which Thou hast lavished on me. I give myself back to Thee Who hast created me for Thyself alone, and I offer myself to be consumed by Thy fires and to serve for Thy glory by my own annihilation.[1]

---

[1] Intimate Notes : 19-11-1905.

SECOND PART.

THE RESPONSE TO LOVE.

In the preceding pages, we have endeavoured to penetrate with the eyes of our soul into the abysses of Infinite Love. We have contemplated It in these mysteries, we have adored It in Its living Tabernacle, the Heart of Jesus Christ.

In the following pages we shall see the consequences which this knowledge of God under the aspect of Infinite Love will have for our spiritual life.

We shall read in them of the fruits of this doctrine in the soul of her who has lived it profoundly and whose mission it was to teach a form of spirituality, which, because it contains the essence of Christianity and the purest spirit of the Gospel, is both simple and sanctifying.

This form of spirituality is based on belief in the infinite love of God or rather in the belief that God is Infinite Love. It is but another view of the devotion to the Sacred Heart of Jesus, which is based on belief in the boundless love of the Sacred Heart for each one of us.

From this faith in God-Love there follows as a natural consequence an ardent desire to love Him and to make Him loved. To acquire this faith in the love of God for us, knowledge is required ; knowledge which will enkindle in our heart ardent love, fervour, and zeal. We do not mean empty, sentimental love, but love which thirsts after holiness and perfection, and perfect conformity with the will of God, and which is ready to make a total donation of its whole being to Him in Whose love the soul has absolute trust.

It is a simple form of spirituality, which makes the soul repose on the Heart of God and invites it to allow itself to be guided by Him with the confidence of a child.

It is a joyful form of spirituality, for, by habituating the soul to see at all times and in all things the love which God has for it, it fills it with sentiments of gratitude and makes it sing the praises of God.

It is a highly sanctifying form of spirituality, for it constantly recalls the soul to the practice of the great commandment in which is summed up the whole law and the Prophets : " Thou shalt love the Lord thy God . . . "

It is a form of spirituality adapted to all classes of people, to all the circumstances of life ; to hours of joy as well as hours of sadness, for it teaches us to see evidences of the love of God in all things, to adhere to the will of God at every time and in every place and to transform all our acts into acts of love.

It might be defined as a recall to the teaching of the Divine Master who has shown us God as " Our Father " and has told us that " the very hairs of our head are numbered " ; a return to the spirit of filial love, of serene confidence and loving abandonment to God.

Is not that precisely what the Christian soul most needs and desires ?

CHAPTER I.

THE KNOWLEDGE OF GOD

It is by the path of knowledge that man arrives at love. The more this knowledge shows him the perfection, beauty, goodness and greatness of the person loved, the more intense his love will become. The more therefore we increase our knowledge of the infinite perfections of God, the more ardently we will love Him. We shall see in the following pages what outbursts of love and praise and gratitude this knowledge of God has produced.

1. THE WORKS OF GOD SPEAK TO US OF HIS LOVE

How admirable are Thy works, O My God, how beautiful and peaceful this nature Thou hast created by the power of Thy word ! How bountiful Thy Heart is to deign to surround us with riches and beauties so pleasant to the eye !

Our entire life should be spent in continual acts of thanksgiving, and the incense of our gratitude should, at every moment, go up to Thy throne.

We have received everything from Thy liberality, O Lord. If the combined works of creation form a spectacle worthy of our admiration, the contemplation of its marvellous details shows forth still better Thy power and goodness. Let my cries of love and gratitude go up to Thee, O my God, at every moment ! Praised, loved and adored everywhere and continually be the only and thrice holy God, Creator, Ruler, Conserver and Dispenser of all these beauties, of this harmony of nature which enchants our eyes, delights our min ds fills our hearts and plunges the soul into adoration, gratitude, admiration and love [1]

2. TO SEE GOD IN HIS WORKS

If by the grace of God and our own puny efforts we have already attained to the possession of the love of God, let us seek to preserve it with great care and to make it ever more perfect.

We have many means to do this : detachment from the goods of

---

[1] Intimate Notes : 1892.

the world, interior mortification, habitual recollection, and attention to our actions in the spirit of peace and repose.

But among other means there is one particularly efficacious : it is to form the habit of seeing God in all things and of making all things lead us to God.

By this simple method we can remain in the Divine Presence with ever new pleasure and truly without interruption.

It is so easy to find God in all things ! And where can we not find the great God, by Whom all things have been made ?

From the sole fact He is the Creator of the world, we know that it is impossible to find anything that does not speak to us of Him.

God has made all things out of nothing. From the smallest blade of grass to the highest peak of the mountain, from the simplest phenomenon of nature to the finest works of the human intellect, everything bears the trace of divinity ; every creature bears the imprint of the Divine Hand which has formed it. If any of these pleases us on account of its beauty, it is because of the reflection of the beauty of God which we can see in it ; if its goodness captivates our hearts, it is because Infinite Goodness has filled it with its charms ; if its simplicity attracts us, it is because the divine simplicity is hidden within it. Divine Providence reveals itself in the nest suspended in the branches of the tree ; the wisdom and power of God appear in the tiniest insect.

The holy habit of seeking God in all things will make us ascend naturally from all created things to God.

By this holy habit, we shall arrive at that continuous presence of God which He expects of us.[1]

Why are so many souls who have the faith so poor in love for God? It is because they do not know Him as He is.

God is not a being indifferent to our evils, selfishly shut up in the enjoyment of His glory, careless about our wants and soon tired with our weakness. But, how many people have this false idea about Him! We must endeavour to seek in God a Father Who holds us in His Hand and ever watches over us.

2. TO KNOW GOD AS HE IS

And what shall I say to you that you do not know already? I shall repeat for you words eternally ancient and eternally new, the

---

[1] Conferences to the Sisters : 19-10-1907.

words of salvation, the words of peace and of joy which the Blessed
Apostle spoke, centuries ago, to the faithful of Ephesus, without
being tired repeating them, the grand sweet words which throw
light on everything, which explains everything, words full of meaning
and marvellously sweet to the heart of man : " God is Love." (1 John
IV, 16). Our God, our Creator, and our Father : He Who, with His
divine hand, has moulded the slime of our bodies and Who, with the
breath of His mouth, has communicated an immortal life to our
souls ; the God from Whom we have received everything, Who is our
principle and our last end : this God is Infinite Love ! If in the
possession of His beatitude, God could feel pain, He would have this
infinite suffering of not being known. Yet, even among those who
by holy Baptism have been made children of God, how few there
are who know Him as He is. Far from going to seek in God
the means of knowing Him and loving Him, man, thinking only of
his own nature, makes for himself a God like himself ; he attributes
to Him his own mean and selfish thoughts, his own fickle and inconstant sentiments, his own despicable inclinations. God is so
little known as He truly is, that if we ask the generality of Christians
about Him, each one of them will represent Him in a different light.
Some see in Him only His justice and have for Him only sentiments
of fear ; others see in Him only goodness, without resolution, and put
themselves to very little trouble to serve Him with fidelity ; others
believe Him to be in truth powerful, but are always criticizing His
wisdom ; others admit His wisdom but limit His omnipotence.
Thus, these people making for themselves a God according to their
own stature, always incomplete and defective, cannot love Him with
that ardent and absolute love, with that pure and unshakeable love
to which He has a right. Oh ! how much misunderstood our God
is ! He possesses in Himself all perfections in perfect equilibrium,
He is not less just than good, He is not less powerful than wise ; He
exceeds in nothing and nothing is wanting in Him. Very far from
sharing in our weaknesses, He wishes on the contrary, to make us
sharers in His divine strength ; far from sharing our vulgar sentiments, He wishes by His knowledge and His love to raise up our
minds and purify our hearts. But what man is ignorant of especially,
is that God is Infinite Love. His power, His justice, His goodness
and His wisdom are Divine attributes ; they are ineffable qualities
which our intellect can distinguish in Him ; but what He is above all,
by the very essence of His being, is Love, Love living and giving

life, the principle of being and the source of all good. God is Love. He has created us only to pour into us the abundance of His Infinite Love ; He can perform only works of love ; all His thoughts and all His acts, all His divine designs are Love.[1]

4. THE STUDY OF GOD

We have different means at our disposal to increase in ourselves the love of God ; one of the principal of these is to acquire a real and profound knowledge of God.

The knowledge which we have of mankind does not always produce love in us. In fact, the more attentively we consider creatures, the more we discover the imperfections that are inherent in their inferior condition, and the sight of these imperfections is too often an obstacle to the love of God, especially for those souls who are not deeply imbued with the charity of Christ. But the knowledge of the infinitely perfect Being, free from all imperfection and arrayed in marvellous splendour, cannot fail to excite in us sentiments of love.

To know God is for the upright virtuous man a sure means of loving Him. If he knows Him better, he will love Him better, if he knows Him, not as He is—for that is beyond the power of human intellect—but at least as far as He permits His creatures to know Him in this life, he will doubtless love Him still more perfectly.

If our love for God, Who is worthy of being loved with an infinite love, is, however, so weak, so cold and languid, is it not perhaps in great part because our knowledge of Him is uncertain and superficial, because we have not taken care to apply our spiritual energy to that study which is the source of pure and holy love ?

To know our God : that is what should be the continual aspiration of our minds, as to love Him should be the uninterrupted movement of our hearts.

Having been created by Him, we should direct our whole being to Him ; endowed by His divine liberality with an intellect which makes our human nature superior to every other nature of the earth, we should direct towards Him absolutely all the operations of our mind : He is the Master of all.

It is also an act of justice to direct every thought and every act

---

[1] Intimate Notes : April, 1906.

of our memory to God, to make our intellectual faculties labour for Him Who has given them to us.

It is a great mistake to think that we are not capable of applying ourselves to the study of God, for are not our minds full of attention for useless knowledge, for vain and hurtful reflections?

But how shall we be able to study God?

We are certainly not thinking of putting into your hands tracts on theology or of urging you to undertake speculative studies which would serve rather to fill your minds than to warm your hearts.

But there are other ways of studying God.

What do we do when we wish to know a person with whom we are living? We observe his acts, his gestures, his gait; we listen to his words; we keep our eyes constantly fixed on him and watch everything that he does; we examine his works; in a word, we put ourselves as much as possible in contact with him.

To seek to know God is not to study an abstract science or a historical fact lost in the shadows of the past.

God lives with us and we live with Him. He holds us in His hand and ever watches over us. We walk, so to speak, side by side with the Divine Being, we do not leave Him for an instant. To study God is to observe Him, to think of Him, to listen to His words, to consider His works, not to lose sight of Him for a moment in order to see Him in His slightest gestures.[1]

5. INFINITE LOVE IS HEAT FOR THE HEART AND LIGHT FOR THE INTELLECT

" Now this is eternal life : That they may know Thee, the only true God, and Jesus Christ, Whom Thou hast sent." (John XVII, 3).

This morning, I feel myself urged to write again of Infinite Love and yet what shall I say that I have not said already?

I see in the bosom of God an overflowing plenitude of the love which is His essence, His life, His movement, His fecundity.

This plenitude has a continual need to pour itself out, to flow; it goes by a natural inclination towards creation, towards man in particular. It is a need of Love to fill the emptiness of the creature and to give life to all things. Infinite Love is sometimes felt by the heart of man, but it is not known by his intellect; that is why so many

---

[1] Conferences to the Sisters : 2-8-1907.

shadows lurk in his intellect; especially in what regards the knowledge of God, of His mysteries, and of supernatural truths. Love should not be for man a mere sentiment which he conceives by His sensitive faculties.

In the same measure in which a person conceives Infinite Love by His mind and by His heart, he will also conceive the knowledge of eternal truths and of all the mysteries of God. Infinite Love, like a divine fire, is heat for the heart of man and light for his intellect. If a man goes away from the hearth of love, his heart will become cold and his mind darkened.[1]

6. WE SHOULD INCREASE OUR KNOWLEDGE OF GOD

After Holy Communion I prayed for the salvation of a soul. Our Lord showed me, it seemed to me, that many souls were saved, that they found peace and repose in Heaven but that they enjoyed the vision of God only imperfectly : that is to say, that they saw Him more feebly and less luminously (than others) ; and that the intimate union of the soul with God, the divine intoxication of love, and the ineffable delights of possession of God, were given according to the measure of the purity of love and of the desires which the soul had on earth.[2]

That is why we should endeavour to increase in the knowledge of God, not in the mere speculative and theoretical knowledge of Him, but in that practical knowledge which moves us to action, for the knowledge of God provokes us to love Him, love excites desire, and desire and love generate purity.

The more the soul loves God, the more it will desire to possess Him ; the more purified it becomes, the more it will enjoy the good things found in Him.

There will be, then, a return of the soul to its principle, an absorption of the soul by the Divinity from which it emanates, which on both sides will cause incomprehensible delights.[3]

---

[1] Intimate Notes : 30-11-1905.

[2] It suffices to read the whole of the passage to see that the imperfection of enjoyment of God in heaven of which Mother Louise here speaks does not refer to the essence of the Beatific Vision—all the blessed have the intuitive and immediate vision of the divine essence—but to the different degrees according to which this vision is realized. In heaven each of the blessed, according to the degree of perfection which he has reached on earth, will have an intuitive vision of the divine essence more or less intense and profound, without ever arriving at complete comprehension of it.

St. Augustine also holds that the more perfect contemplation of God on earth, brings the soul to a higher degree of virtue on earth, and disposes it for a more profound vision of God in Heaven.

[3] Intimate Notes : 26-9-1895.

7. TO KNOW GOD IN ORDER TO LOVE HIM

We have a duty to praise God, to conform ourselves to the will of God, and to aspire to see God and to be united to Him.

The desire for God is, on our part, a strict duty of justice. Does not the absence of the person loved produce almost naturally the desire to see Him?

Sacred Scripture offers us continual examples of the fulfilling of this duty. The Royal Psalmist exclaims : " Who will give me the wings of a dove and I will fly and be at rest ?" (Psalm LIV, 7). And again : " As the heart panteth after the fountains of water, so my soul panteth after Thee, my God." (Psalms XLI, 2).

In this same spirit of desire, St. Paul writes : " I desire to be dissolved and to be with Christ." (Philip I, 23).

The great Apostle formally indicates the desire for God as one of the fundamental dispositions required to merit heaven : " As to the rest, there is laid up for me a crown of justice which the Lord, the just Judge, will render to me in that day : and not only to me, but to them also that love His coming." (II Tim. IV, 8).

Doubtless, God does not demand from all such eager desires, which suppose particular lights ; but the Church demands of all Christians that they desire Him at least as their last end, and She demands of us, His spouses, His privileged ones, that we desire Him as the only object of our love and the only good of our souls.

Entering therefore into the sentiments of our Holy Mother, the Church, let us unite ourselves with the Prophets and Patriarchs, during the holy season of Advent, to desire, with an efficacious desire, that blessed coming which was the object of their sighs and their heart-felt prayers.

But we, who are much more favoured than the just of the Old Law, know what we desire. The Word made flesh has revealed God to us and, by His infinite amiability and by the superabundant love which He has shown us, He has also excited our desires and aroused our ardent aspirations.

Nevertheless, we are often indifferent to heavenly goods and, extending our desires and our thoughts over a multitude of exterior things and living too much the life of the senses, we neglect this duty, the fulfilment of which would be so sweet to the Heart of God.

But if we cannot love what we do not know or what we know only imperfectly, we cannot desire intensely what we love only feebly. Our desire will be according to the measure of our love, and as our love is increased by a more vivid and profound knowledge of the Divine Being, let us endeavour to know Him well in order to love Him ardently.

God has made Himself visible to us in Jesus Christ. Let us therefore study the Incarnate Word, let us meditate on Him, let us contemplate His Divine Perfections. Let us fix our thoughts and hearts in that Saviour Who is sovereignly desirable, Whom we shall possess in a higher degree in Heaven, according as we have desired more efficaciously to know Him and love Him during our mortal pilgrimage.

The fruit, then, of our knowledge of God is to conceive an ardent desire to love Jesus, to unite ourselves to Him and to model our lives on His. [1]

8. THE ROAD TO KNOWLEDGE : THE SACRED HEART OF JESUS

But how are we to arrive at a knowledge of Infinite Love ? Behold the secret : the devotion to the Sacred Heart, the wound of which is a door ever-open to allow us to acquire a knowledge of Love ; and the devotion to the Blessed Eucharist is the Light necessary to comprehend Love.

This morning before Mass, while I was in the choir reading a passage from the Epistles of St. Paul, Our Lord made His presence felt within me ; He said nothing to me, He merely showed me the place of His Heart on His breast.

At the same time a vivid interior light showed me that devotion to the Sacred Heart is the door by which to enter into the knowledge of Love (the Sacred Heart was open) and that devotion to the Blessed Sacrament is the light necessary to understand Love.

That is why Holy Church recommends these two devotions and insists on adoration of the Most Blessed Sacrament and frequent Communion.

Without the help of this light of the Blessed Sacrament we could not understand Love. I felt my soul filled with a new desire to know God-Love, to love Him, and to make Him known and loved.

---

[1] Conferences to the Sisters : 28-11-1910.

But what can I, miserable and ignorant that I am, do to realize this
desire ?

Oh ! how painful this ignorance is to express what I see and
understand !¹

9. THE STUDY OF THE DIVINE HEART

Jesus repeated to me the words of His Gospel : " No man cometh
to the Father except by Me." (John XLV, 6), and added : " No one
cometh to the knowledge and possession of Infinite Love but by
My Heart."

We must go to Our Lord, we must listen to the beats of His Heart,
and study Its movements of love.   Then we shall begin to love Jesus
in a new way ; the Holy Spirit will make an effusion of love into the
soul ; the Blessed Trinity will come there with its ineffable splendours
and Infinite Love will reveal itself, that is what Jesus has said : " If
anyone love Me . . . My Father will love him, and We will come to
him and will make our abode with him." (John XIV, 23).   " If
anyone love Me." that is the heart of man seeking the Heart of
Jesus . . . " My Father will love Him," that is the effusion of the
Holy Spirit, " We will come to him," that is the Trinity entering
the soul, " We will make our dwelling with him," that is Infinite
Love Which has revealed Itself and Which possesses the soul.²

10. THE CONDITIONS NECESSARY TO UNDERSTAND THAT GOD IS LOVE

If I could make but one soul understand clearly that God is Love !

In order to understand this truth, a person must be pure, very
humble, very charitable, very faithful to the inspirations from
the Heart of Jesus, very mortified, and very supernatural.³

---

¹ Intimate Notes : 21-9-1913.

² Intimate Notes : 2-5-1903.

³ Letter to Fr. Charrier : 5-7-1907.

CHAPTER II.

FAITH IN LOVE.

Faith in the love of the Sacred Heart of Jesus for us is, as we have seen, an essential element in the devotion to the Sacred Heart and, as all that Mother Louise Margaret has written is in complete harmony with the revelations made by Our Lord to St. Margaret Mary Alacoque, we find as we expect that Mother Louise Margaret makes faith in the love of God the foundation stone of the work of Infinite Love.

1. THE JOY OF FAITH

Yesterday evening at prayer, Jesus showed me how He Himself was taking charge of the Work, with what care and attention He was disposing all things for it. It is God Who does all ; it is neither Father Charrier nor I ; Jesus prepares everything with His adorable wisdom and His incomprehensible love.

It is Jesus Who, after Father's three years of trials, in the end, enlightened him and gave him the heart of a bishop[1] who is to serve this Work. O Master ! to feel, to know that Thou dost direct everything and that everything is in Thy hands, in Thy heart : how sweet that is ! [2]

2. I BELIEVE IN THY LOVE

It is not because I am good, it is not because I am humble, it is not because I am mortified, or faithful, or patient, or fervent, that Our Lord has granted me so many graces. Oh ! certainly not, for I have none of these qualities, but am miserable and weak and poor in virtue, even to being completely devoid of it.

If God has favoured me so much, it is solely because I have believed in His love ! Yes, in the simplicity of my soul, I have believed that God, Who had need of nothing, and Who alone was sufficient for Himself, had undertaken creation in order to have something to love outside Himself. I have believed that in this magnificent creation, man was the one most special object of His love.

---

[1] Monsignor Henri, Bishop of Grenoble, who helped to organize the Priests' Universal Union in France.
[2] Intimate Notes : 31-8-1904.

41

and I have believed that nothing could come forth from God for this loved creature that was not also from love. I have believed that in His dealings with me, God has acted only through love and I have recognized this Infinite Love, less perhaps in the sweetness and the lights received, than in the manifold sufferings that have crushed my soul, my heart and my body. I have believed in Love which consoles, which sustains, which inebriates ; I have believed also in Love which breaks, which crushes and which takes away.

My God, I have believed in Thy Love, and I believe in it with all the clearness of my intellect : I believe in it with all the precision of my reason, I believe in it especially with all the ardour of my heart. My God, I believe in Thy Love, and I wish always to believe in it, whatever sorrow Thou mayst send me, whatever cross Thou mayst lay upon me, whatever help Thou mayst deprive me of, whatever good Thou mayst withdraw from me, I will believe in thy Love !¹

3. OUR MISERY IS NOTHING WHEN PLACED BESIDE INFINITE LOVE

My good Father, our misery is nothing when placed beside Infinite Love. It is not even a little grain of sand cast into the ocean. Does a little grain of sand cause difficulty to the waves of the ocean when they wish to rise, fall, spread out, or submerge a vast extent of territory ? Thus, Father, your misery and mine will not be able to impede the work of Infinite Love.²

I cannot tell you what pain the latter part of your letter has given me. It is impossible for me to understand how your misery can be beyond the power of God. But, Father, your human misery, my own, and that of the whole world are but atoms in comparison with Infinite Love and divine Power. If I thought for a moment that my own misery was greater than the mercy of God, or could be an obstacle to His Power, I believe I would be committing the greatest sin of my life. It seems to me that with a little faith, a little confidence, and a little love we need fear nothing.³

---

¹ Intimate Notes : 24-9-1906.

² Letter to Father Charrier : 17-2-1908.

³ Letter to Father Charrier : 24-5-1910.

4. JESUS, GOD INCARNATE, IS MERCY

But truly, Father, why should you be so sad over your miseries? When we know that God is Love, and that Jesus, God incarnate, is Mercy, can we be sad? I believe that this state of interior sadness is willed by the good Master for your greater merit; however, it must not last too long, for in the end it would ruin your strength. You tell me, Father, that you will never arrive at the degree of sanctity which Jesus wished for you. And how do you know what this degree is? It seems to me that God has never said to anyone : " You are to arrive at this degree which I shall show you." No, He shows Himself to us and then He says to us : " Endeavour to reach Me " ; this involves labour. And when it is God's will to take us by death, if He finds us always at work, He is satisfied, and His mercy perfects in us what is still wanting. Is this not so, Father? Then let us speak no more of your miseries ; I place them all in the furnace of the Heart of Jesus and I see no more trace of them. Do you think that the fire of Infinite Love is not strong enough to burn out all that?[1]

5. CONFIDENCE IN GOD

I had committed a fault, and although I saw that it was not very grave, the matter being light and the cause of it being want of consideration, nevertheless I was a little embarrassed about appearing before the Lord, thinking that this stain on my soul might be displeasing to His eyes.

However, at the next meditation time He communicated Himself to my soul with extreme goodness, and instructed me about the confidence we should have in Him. He gave me to understand that what pleases God most is the confidence of His creatures in Him.

If the soul had sinned a thousand times, it should return to Him the thousandth time with that confidence which does not exclude either just fear or true sorrow.

The search for God, which the soul makes after its sin, neutralizes, as it were, the deadly effects of the poison, and disposes it to be cured. He showed me that confidence contains or produces the

---

[1] Letter to Father Charrier : 18-1-1908.

acts of all the virtues. It necessarily supposes faith ; it is so connected with hope that it seems to form but one single virtue with it, although it is a more interior and sweeter form of it ; it is by itself an excellent act of love, a real and sensible act.

It is an act of sovereign justice. What more just than that the creature should trust in Him Who has created him, regenerated him and redeemed him with His Blood ? If human prudence trusts in the abundance of riches and in the protection of the powerful, will it not be divine prudence for weak, miserable beings to trust in Him alone Who can enrich and protect them ?

Confidence is a power : " He who trusts in the Lord shall not be shaken," says Holy Scripture. The soul that trusts becomes strong with the strength of Him on Whom it relies, and because it counts on God, it can undertake mighty works.

Confidence is attached to temperance in so far as it is the well-regulated use of all things : it is right order, and the soul that expects all things from God, also uses all things solely according to God.

Confidence puts the soul in dependence on God ; and to depend is to wish and to obey. It is a very perfect act of humility : it is the recognition of its misery, it is the realization of its own weakness externally expressed, the confession of its own nothingness.

Finally, it is an act of sovereign homage rendered to all the divine attributes : the soul which trusts in God recognizes the Power of God ; it counts on His Wisdom ; it gives itself up to His Justice, it reposes on His Love. It is, then, an act of adoration which the soul makes, of adoration full of respect and love.

Who can tell the power which a soul that trusts, acquires over God Himself ! It so delights His adorable Heart, that it obtains more than it wishes for : it obtains the ineffable proof of His love, the pardon of its faults, and the inestimable grace of living in Him by the union of the one same spirit.[1]

6. WE SHOULD HAVE IMPLICIT TRUST IN THE SACRED HEART OF JESUS

I have not time to pray much for the souls that you are evangelizing, but it seems to me that what I am doing and suffering is a gift to the good Master, and this gift is my whole prayer. I do not even

---

[1] Intimate Notes : May, 1899.

wish to ask myself how I am going to manage ; I cast all that into the Heart of Jesus, and I wish to trust blindly in It. This evening I felt that I was like St. Peter walking on the waters ; if I failed in confidence, I would lose my footing, but it seems to me that Our Lord wishes such entire confidence from me as has fear of nothing.[1]

CHAPTER III.

LOVE FOR GOD.

Faith in the love of God is the foundation of the spiritual life of members of the Work of Infinite Love. The more the soul penetrates by faith into the mysteries of Love, the greater will be its desire to give a return of love. The object of its love will appear so worthy of love and so amiable that it will find its efforts to give a return of love puny and insignificant in comparison. This effort to make a fitting return of love, ever active and ever renewed, will be the expression of its Christian life, the duties of which are summed up in the precept of love.

1. THE TRUE LIFE OF THE SOUL

The true life of the soul is to know what God is ; the true life of the heart is to love God. Perhaps life is hidden under apparent death ? My God, I wish to believe so, and I abandon myself to Thee.[2]

2. MAN THIRSTS FOR LOVE

" Thou hast made us for Thyself, O my God, and our hearts can find no rest until they repose in Thee." (St. Augustine).

All the sentiments of the natural order are a reproduction, a sort of copy, very imperfect, it is true, of the sentiments of the supernatural order.

Divine love and human love have a thousand points of resemblance between them ; God created both at the beginning ; human love in the thought of God, was to be a very faithful, though pale reflection of divine love. Man, corrupted by sin, lost the right notion of love ;

---

[1] Letter to Father Charrier : 18-12-1908.

[2] Intimate Notes : 29-8-1895.

after the Fall, he forgot his origin and his end, and lived only the life of the senses ; divine love became obscure for him and appeared to him to be incompatible with his nature which had now become altogether carnal.

Human love, separated from the source from which it drew its life, was turned away by man from the path that God had marked out for it ; from being almost divine, it became a gross sentiment destined to give the senses the lowest form of enjoyment in which the soul has no share ; it became like the blind instinct of the beasts.

These two loves, by uniting and supplementing each other, were to give man perfect happiness almost like the infinite happiness of heaven ! Sin ! accursed sin ! Why did you come into our souls to wither them up and blight them?

Divine love was no longer understood by the heart of man ; human love appealing to the senses attracted him and seduced him ; he thought he found in it joy and repose of heart.   Strange illusion ! The heart, having tasted this love, was still hungry ; having drunk of these false delights, was still thirsty !

Happy are those who, having felt this thirst, have sought the spring of living water ; happier still are those who have found it and drunk from it.

How I pity those whose thirst is slaked by human love—but they are rare ; many feel that void in the heart which nothing earthly can fill, but many also remain with that void and that sadness, not knowing how ro remedy it.   Oh ! if they knew how to have recourse to the divine remedy ; if they knew that in the holy love of God all thirst would find its appeasement, all sadness its consolation, all langour its cure !

Is it not a sweet enjoyment to feel oneself loved by a mere creature, and the more beautiful and perfect that creature is, the sweeter also is the enjoyment.   But, what is a creature?   A heart that loves to-day but will not love to-morrow ; a head, very feeble, very cold very powerless, above all, very inconstant ; even if it might be constant, death puts an end to its love, but without waiting for the separation of death, the least estrangement extinguishes its poor flame.   One is forgotten so quickly !

But the love of God for a soul, the chaste love of a soul for God can last for eternity ; these loves commence and are formed in outline during life, but they are perfected only in eternity.

Eternity ! What mystery and what majesty this word contains !

We poor creatures of a day, cannot comprehend what eternity is.

Can we who see everything around us come to an end comprehend a duration which will have no end, and which never had a beginning? and it is perhaps this which amazes us most : eternity is for loving and being loved !

What poisons all our joys in this world is the thought that, sooner or later, they must end ; what tortures the heart that loves is the uncertainty of the duration of this love ; it is the fear of losing the loved being entirely or at least of losing his confidence or his heart ; but the love of God for the soul is infinite like the Being of the Divinity Itself.

If we are loved by God, we shall always be loved by Him, if we wish it ; if our heart attaches itself to God, it can remain always attached to Him, for all eternity !

O divine intoxication ! always united, always loved, always loving, always belonging to each other. Never put asunder, never at a distance, never separated ! For ever and ever. Amen.[1]

3. THE LOVE WHICH GOD DEMANDS FROM MAN

God loves. But He wishes to be loved ; love has need of a return and if, in the very bosom of the Divinity, the Father and the Word and the Holy Spirit give such a perfect return that They love each other with the same Love which is Their Being and Their Essence, so Infinite Love wishes to find outside Itself a reciprocity, relative, doubtless, and proportioned to the weakness of the created being, but nevertheless real. God pours out torrents of love upon the creature ; in his turn, the creature should love. By the fact of His creation God has deposited in each one a principle of love, not however in the same degree, or under the same form. In strict justice and as a necessary consequence of its condition, each creature is bound to love according to its nature and the will of its Creator. It has received everything from God, it ought to give everything back to God ; it is what it is only by God, it ought to employ its whole being for God.

This first love, this necessary love of the creature, has, as it were, two movements : the first, a movement of restitution ; the creature gives something to God, it returns it to Him ; the second, a move-

---

[1] Intimate Notes : June, 1891.

ment of submission ; it accomplishes the will of its Creator.

We see this manner of love exercised by the inferior creatures in a remarkable manner. The earth has received its fertility from God and it is always producing for its Creator. The flower has received from Him the brilliance of its calyx and the sweetness of its perfume ; it flowers each spring for its God and gives Him back its beauty and its fragrant odour. The bird has received its light wings and the sweetness of its song, and it flies and it sings in the presence of its God.

The wild animals of the forests have received from their Creator swiftness for running, strength for defence, and a beautiful coat of fur, and they increase before God, according to the laws of their nature, accomplishing the divine will and multiplying, according to the good pleasure of their Master. This regular fulfilment of the God's will and this renewed gift of what they have in themselves is the way in which the inferior creatures show their love.

God has formed superior creatures ; in them also He has deposited principles of love, and as they have received more from the divine munificence, they are bound to give more in return.

In their case, God is no longer satisfied with the love of nature and instinct which the inferior creatures give Him ; as He has made them rational beings, He expects from them a rational love ; as He has given them a free will, He expects from then a voluntary love ; as He has created them according to His image, He expects from them a love resembling His own.

God has deposited in man not only the principle of love which He has given to the inferior creatures and by which he was already bound, as if by instinct, to tend towards God and to submit himself to Him, but He has given him much more ; He has formed in Him a soul gifted with intellect, memory, and will, and by means of these three faculties, man can enter into the knowledge of His Creator and develop in his heart a superior love, sovereignly reasonable and truly worthy of God.

It is this enlightened love, this voluntary love which man owes to God ; why then does He not give this love to God ? Why then is love so little understood by the human heart ? I mean true love ; the pure love, the supernatural love demanded by God, which has descended from Him and which ought to ascend again to Him ; love, not such as the depraved senses of the accursed creature has conceived it, but such as Infinite Love expects from the rational being ;

a love finite and created like the creature himself, but enlightened, free, and strong. Nevertheless, few men love God as He wishes to be loved.

Man's senses, profoundly disturbed by sin, have lost the clear notion of truth. They go astray, they are deceived, they take the wrong road ; and of this beautiful and luminous intellect, of this firm and upright will which he had in the first days of his creation, only the ruins remain.

Thus we see him constantly turning away from the truth, changing the order of things, transforming good into evil, and often preferring evil to good. Man's judgment has no longer its primeval uprightness ; it is warped, and too often it goes astray. Since its first transgression, humanity has fallen into many errors, but perhaps on no point has it been so much deceived as on love.

According as man becomes more detached from God, He becomes more attached to creatures, and in an attempt to satisfy his heart which hungered after Infinite Love, he gave it as food this baneful attachment and called it love.

Man, forgetting God, no longer uniting himself to Him by love, not daring to hope for anything, found himself in the middle of the world like a poor shipwrecked man lost in the ocean. He endeavoured to seize anything that presented itself to him, he attached himself to the smallest floating spar and, clinging to it like a man in desperation, he pressed it to his heart and persuaded himself that he loved it.

But that was not love . . . True love, the only love which deserves that divine name, is the love which reascends to God, the only principle of love. Earthly lusts, carnal pleasures, are passions unchained by original sin ; they are the results of sin. They will never satisfy the intellect and heart of man, they will never be love ! The intellect and heart of man are two marvellous instruments created by God, touched by the divine breath of Infinite Love, they should, in perfect accord, give forth the most pleasing harmony, and, in a certain manner gathering together all the notes sent up to heaven by inferior creatures, they should form them into a melodious hymn of praise, gratitude, and adoration.

All the moral beauty of man, the human harmony which should go up from him to heaven, consists in this accord, in this perfect equilibrium which he preserves and sustains between his intellect and his heart. A single hand, a single breath, should make them resound

at the same time ; the Infinite Love alone is the divine Artist capable
of touching these harmonious instruments which He Himself has
created.[1]

4. INFINITE LOVE, THE DIVINE REMEDY WHICH WILL SAVE THE WORLD

> Like a river in flood, from its banks overflowing,
> I see divine Love from God's bosom escape,
> And mingling with the waters of Infinite Mercy
> Flow down on the world in an inundation divine.[2]

Jesus showed me the Infinite Love with which His Heart is filled
and which overflows from It, and He indicates it, if I am not mistaken,
as the divine remedy which alone will save the world.   It seemed to
me that perhaps the adorable Master has given me a little influence
over souls and liberty of action solely for the purpose of revealing
this saving Love and diffusing it everywhere.   Jesus showed me
the great heresies of the present day, the intellectual madness which
is directing its attacks against God, the general commotion which is
agitating all classes of society, the moral crisis which is disturbing the
world and shaking it to its foundations.   And I considered the causes
of all this.   I saw man created by God like a perfectly equilateral
triangle, animated by an all spiritual, and very pure soul.   One of the
sides of this triangle was the intellect or thought ; another was feeling,
the will, the heart ; the third was the flesh and the senses ; these
faculties and senses should be in perfect harmony, and it is from the
maintenance of this harmony that human equilibrium results.

The spiritual soul, living in this well-balanced being and remaining united to its divine Principle, constituted man such as he
should be.   In our times, humanity has broken this equilibrium.
In a great number of men the life of the senses and of the flesh
dominates ; in others less materialistic, thought dominates, but
thought unregulated and unbalanced.   In almost all, at least in a
great number, the life of the heart or of the will has become weakened.
The will has gone astray.[3]

---

[1] Intimate Notes : 20-12-1905.
[2] Intimate Notes : 1900.
[3] Intimate Notes : 10-8-1907.

5. LET US RETURN LOVE FOR LOVE

To-morrow we shall be beginning the month consecrated to honouring the Divine Heart of Jesus, the month during which we shall celebrate this year the three great Feasts of Love : the Feast of the most Holy Trinity, the ineffable mystery of the Love which goes from the Father to the Son and from which the Holy Ghost proceeds, the mystery of union which, by the strength and sweetness of an incomparable love, makes only one God of the three Divine Persons ; the Feast of Corpus Christi, of that mystery of faith, but above all of love, in which love, having arrived at its highest degree, multiplies *ad infinitum* the gift of divine munificence ; in fine, the Feast of the Sacred Heart, of that Heart Which is the symbol of the love of our Saviour and the living organ and tabernacle of Infinite Love.

Can we do else to-day than speak to you of love ?—of the love of God for us, for each one of us !

How useful it will be for each of us to meditate often on the love of God for us ! How necessary it is to understand well to what degree we have been loved by Jesus !

There is no more profitable occupation than to go over humbly in our own minds the innumerable proofs of love which God has given us from the first moment of our creation in the divine mind to the present moment. In spite of sufferings, sorrows and privations, we have nevertheless in our souls the marvellous gift of grace, and many other precious gifts of a secondary nature. The love of Jesus for us, His spouses, is immense : He has predestined us for His nuptials, He has surrounded us with His special graces, preserved us in the midst of the world, strengthened us in the combat, conducted us to the door of religious life, and preserved us in our vocation in spite of the efforts of persecution and of our own weaknesses.

We should meditate also on the love we owe to Jesus, on that love which we should give in return, if not in a measure equal to that which we received, which is not possible for us, at least in a more generous, more complete measure than hitherto given. Meditate well on these things during this month ; let everything be given to Love.

It is our urgent recommendation to you that, filled with the desire to love God, to render Him love for love, you give Him continuous proofs of that love ; interior proofs, by your fidelity, and exterior, by your charity. Let us have but one heart in the infinitely good Heart of the Master, let us have but one will with His, and let us live intimately united to Him in Love. ¹

6. LET US LOVE JESUS AS HE HAS LOVED US

Jesus was not content with inviting Judas to repentance, with calling him friend, with pardoning Peter for the denials that inflicted so much suffering on Him, but when suspended on the gibbet on which He was to expire, He pardoned also His executioners, His persecutors, His judges, the ungrateful people who had demanded His death, the agents who had bound Him, scourged Him and crucified Him; and His pardon was so efficacious that, in the weakness of the death-agony, He collected His remaining strength to pray for them and to excuse their misdeeds. When dying, He offered His Precious Blood, with unspeakable charity for their eternal salvation.

And it was not self-interest or fear that induced Jesus to pardon thus ; it was His love alone. Ah ! how profound and strong must then be the love of Christ for His friends, since His love for His enemies is so great and generous. " Jesus Christ has loved me," says St. Paul, " and has delivered Himself up for me."

And we all can say with the great Apostle : " Jesus has loved us." But if He has loved us, and still loves us with an ineffable love, should not we love Him in our turn, and do for Him what He has done for us ? He has given Himself for us, He has offered Himself for fatigue, for suffering, for death. Why then should we not generously embrace for Him the fatigue involved in our devotions or demanded by charity ? Why should we not endure patiently and courageously the portion of suffering which, in His mercy, He has reserved for us ? Why, in fine, should we not look forward to death with strong unshakeable confidence, trusting in the merits of Our Saviour ?

Let us do for Jesus what He has done for us, let us enter into the sentiments of His Heart.²

7. THE DESIRES OF JESUS

While the Divine Master, has tried us harder than others by

---

¹ Conference to the Sisters : 31-5-1908.
² Conference to the Sisters : 17-4-1908.

the rigour of persecution and has called us to follow Him on the way of the Cross—by which, doubtless, all Religious must pass, but which He has made narrower and more difficult to traverse in this land of exile—He has addressed to each one of us the words He spoke to St. Peter : " Lovest thou Me more than these ?" (John XXI, 15).

Jesus Christ wished to prove our love, to prove our fidelity. He wished to know whether our love would be equal to the sacrifice, whether we were ready to leave all for Him. By means of events, He has made known this desire to be loved and, fearing that some earthly attachment might come and claim a share in our hearts, He Himself has taken care to deprive us of all things.

The first desire of Jesus is therefore that we should love Him above all things and infinitely more than all things. He wishes to be loved by us, but loved even to the contempt of everything else, to the sacrifice of everything which we might have legitimately loved.

The second desire of our good Master is that we place under His Providence the care of everything, not only what regards us individually, but what concerns our Community, its conservation amidst the various events that are happening, and its future. The numerous proofs which He has given us in the past, and which He continues to give us of the loving care which His Providence has for our dear family, are a sufficiently clear indication of this desire of His Heart.

The third desire of Jesus is that, while loving Him above all things and trusting in His Providence, we adhere without reserve, without anxiety, and without regard for ourselves, to everything He wishes to do with us in the present and in the future.

It is by responding to the desires of our Divine Master that we shall console His Sacred Heart. He has so much need of finding in the souls of those who are consecrated to Him the comfort of an unshakable fidelity and of a generous, constant love !

Let us give Jesus what He demands of us with so much insistance. Let us courageously forget our own troubles, our sacrifices and our personal sorrows in order to remember only His and to bring to Him the beneficent balm of our faithful and fervent love.[1]

8. UNION, LOVE AND SUFFERING

I must make it my aim that these three words : union, love and

---

[1] Conference to the Sisters : 10-9-1910.

suffering, be the resumé of my life. I must strive to be constantly united with God by recollection and prayer, by having the eyes of my soul continually fixed on God by fidelity ; to be united to my neighbour by meekness, cordiality, friendliness of relations, sweet compliance, flexibility of will ; to love our Lord as my only and dear Spouse, to love Him as my greatest Benefactor, as my Principle, my End and my only Happiness ; to love my neighbour as the loved object of my Beloved ; to love souls as the most perfect works of my Creator ; to suffer for God, in soul and body, as sacrifice and as holocaust ; to suffer for myself, as expiation and necessary consequence of the faults of the past ; to suffer for my neighbour, as reparation, offering, propitiation, and as means of union between God and souls.[1]

9. OPEN YOUR HEART TO LOVE

I felt my soul more and more drawn by an invisible power ; then Our Lord said to me in a sweet accent of reproach : " Why are you resisting Me ?"

At these words I thought that my heart would melt and flow away in love.

Afterwards, Our Saviour gave me to understand that He wished my heart to be like a receptacle for His mercies and His love ; so many hearts are closed against Him that He needs to pour into mine the love which overflows from His own.

Since that time, all my days have been like an act of uninterrupted love ; at times, it seems to me that my miserable heart wishes to escape from my breast and to go and live in its God.[2]

10. PRAISE GOD IN THE NAME OF EVERY CREATURE

Yesterday, my adorable Master, after speaking sweetly to me, showed me how He wished that I should bring all creatures back to Him, how I ought to lend them my soul and my heart, in order that they might all love and glorify Infinite Love.

God is the unique Being ; all creatures have being only by Him ; they are all composed, if I may say so in figure, of two parts ; one part a piece of nothingness, the other, a creative will of God.

---

[1] Intimate Notes : 31-10-1892.
[2] Intimate Notes : 4-9-1896.

What is this creative will ? It is a flowing out of Infinite Love ; It is a spark from the great furnace of love. God has created because He has a superabundance of love. It would seem that this love, all shut up in Himself, was an embarrassment to Him. He had need of allowing it to issue forth by creation. But because creation is a work of love, all creation must love, and this love should return to God.

However, the greater number of creatures have neither heart nor soul ; these have being and form, they have a place in creation, an employment ; they do all that they should do according to this being, and they wait for man to lend them his heart to love the Love-Creator Who has produced them.

Many men, almost all, do not realize that they have a very ardent heart, a very great capacity for loving given to them for the purpose of being able to love God for themselves and also for the inferior creatures.

And God loses much love. Jesus said to me : " Lend your heart to creatures that they may love by you and that you may love in them ; make them glorify, exalt and love their Creator. Love with the bird that sings, with the cloud that floats in space, with the leaf which quivers in the breeze. Give a soul with intelligence, and a heart that beats to all these beings created by love."

Already for a long time, Our Lord has been leading me on to this practice. Formerly, in order to mortify myself, I would have turned away from creatures ; now that is no longer the impulse that I receive.

It seems to me that creation is like a musical instrument, a harp ; if no one touches this harp, it gives forth no sound ; the heart of man, like a skilful artist must touch the chords of this golden harp, then a harmonious sound goes up ; it is a hymn of love chanted by love in honour of Infinite Love.

I have often remarked that God takes a singular pleasure in that; He has so much need of love ! And then it is a sweet joy for the heart to be able to tell its love to God by different mouths. We cannot always keep saying to God that we love Him ; we have but one voice to tell Him we love Him. But by going to creatures, by lending them our hearts, a multitude of voices are raised, all singing of Infinite Love.

Oh ! this Infinite Love, this God-Love Who creates, Who gives life to everything, Who pours out His love on everything ! He is so sensibly visible to me that I have no longer need of faith to believe

in Him ; I touch Him in everything.   Oh ! how I would wish to
love Him ![1]

11. THE GREATNESS OF GOD'S LOVE

(*a*) Having had the happiness of receiving Holy Communion, I
consecrated myself anew to the Divine Heart with all the power of
my will, offering myself to Him entirely and without reserve in order
that He may operate in me according to His good pleasure.

The immense weight of the love of my Saviour overwhelms me
and confounds me ; to see oneself so much loved and to be able to
love so little in return is for the soul a suffering which the sight and
the caresses of one's Beloved only aggravate.[2]

(*b*) O my God, how great Thy goodness is !   What have I done, O
Lord, to be thus the object of Thy tender care !

When I look into the past, I see only faults, blemishes, and falls.
If I look at the present, I see only weakness, vain desires, coldness,
and yet Thou dost treat me as the spoiled child of Thy Heart.

O Heart full of love ! the more Thou dost overwhelm me with Thy
benefits, the more I feel ashamed of myself.   What can I do, O my
Jesus, to show my gratitude to Thee ?   Shall I give Thee myself ?
But can I offer to Thee as a gift what belongs to Thee already ?

Even my will does not belong to me ; by the number of Thy gifts,
by the abundance of Thy graces, it belongs to Thee by right.   Shall
I offer Thee my heart ?   But I have no longer any.   Thou hast
taken away this cold stone which has served me as a heart and Thou
hast put in its place a drop of Thy Divine Blood.   It is this divine
drop which gladdens me and inflames me ; since I have received it into
my breast, I am devoured with insatiable hunger, I burn with un-
quenchable thirst.

I am hungry for heavenly nourishment, I am thirsty for the Blessed
Eucharist.   I would wish that all souls should go to Jesus Christ.   It
seems to me that if I made Thee loved by many souls, O my God,
that Thou wouldst pardon me more easily for the many years which
I have spent away from Thee.[3]

---

[1] Intimate Notes : 1901.
[2] Intimate Notes : 27-2-1895.
[3] Intimate Notes : Oct., 1890.

12. THE DESIRE TO RETURN LOVE FOR LOVE

Oh ! how happy I was to receive Jesus in Holy Communion after three days' waiting (*she had been ill*). I did not speak to Him much, and He said nothing to me, but He was there living in me, hiding Himself in my misery, to purify me, strengthen me and raise me up. I see myself miserable to the last degree. I feel myself overwhelmed with graces, and so cowardly, so wanting in fidelity, gratitude and love. Infinite Love envelops me, fills me, bathes me in its vivifying light, nevertheless I am so wrapped in darkness, so bad, so indifferent ; I have no courage, I am afraid of suffering.

Is it fear ? Perhaps not, for I wish for and desire suffering. What then is the matter with me ? I have an immense desire to make a return of love to Infinite Love Which descends on me, by a love which I would wish to make infinite. And I am unable, my heart is too small, my soul is too weak. I suffer inexpressibly. I would wish to have millions of hearts in my hands in order to be able to open them to Infinite Love.[1]

13. IT IS AN IMPULSE FROM INFINITE LOVE THAT MOVES US TO LOVE GOD

I had an immense desire to make the little Pentecost Retreat well and then I· have not made it any better than other Retreats ; I do everything wretchedly, nevertheless, I would wish to love Our Lord so much ! It seems to me that by loving God we comfort Him, we take from Him a little of the superabundance of love which is in Him. We unburden Him in a certain manner, all the more so because we never love Him except with the share of Infinite Love which He puts into our souls. However, we love Him only with a finite and imperfect love, the love of a creature but all the same, it is the impulse of Infinite Love which moves us to love Him.[2]

14. THE LOVE OF GOD IS THE LIFE OF THE HEART

Love renders everything easy ; it makes us undertake with joy the most painful labours. In the human heart, it is a powerful lever which lifts easily the heaviest burdens.

---

[1] Intimate Notes : 30-9-1907.
[2] Letter from Father Charrier : 14-6-1895.

When divine love takes possession of a soul and remains there living and active, it enables it to perform superhuman works. Is not this proved from the lives of the Saints? Is not this what their writings teach us?

The love of God is the life of the Christian heart, it is above all the life of the heart of the Religious. It is the sole motive power which can give it that movement of ascent which is necessary for it in order to raise it from the shadows of time to the lights of eternity.

The love which ought to live in our souls is an active sentiment, full of strength and holy energy, supported by faith and illuminated by hope.

Love proceeds from the will, but the will is   its turn dominated by love. Our love is weak because our will is without strength. How could it, in that state of weakness, produce a powerful sentiment? Our will remains languid because we do not bring to bear on it the powerful motive of generous love.[1]

15. TRUE LOVE

It seems to me that true love for Jesus is the same thing as humility. To love Jesus is to wish that He be everything and, consequently, it is to wish to be nothing oneself. To love Jesus is to wish that He satisfy Himself in us and over us, and consequently to offer ourselves to all kinds of destruction, annihilation, and sufferings. To love Jesus is to wish to do His will whatever it may cost. To love Jesus is to wish to be united to Him with all our strength and to resemble Him, and for that, to take for ourselves His portion : His hidden life, the calumnies which have been uttered against Him, His crown of thorns, His mock purple, the scourges, the affronts, the mockeries, the insults, that lacerated His Body and pierced His Heart. To love Jesus is to be willing to keep Him company on His cross, in the horrors of Calvary, in the ignomonies of His death, in the cold abandonment of His sepulchre. To love Jesus is to be willing to console Him, to help Him in His work of Redemption, to gain souls for Him, and to do so, to take the means which He Himself has employed, that is to say, to sacrifice one's repose, one's honour, one's blood, one's life, one's whole being. To love Jesus is to be

---

[1] Conference to the Sisters : 13-7-1907.

willing to do all that for Him, without creatures knowing it, reserving for the Divine Eyes the secret of one's immolation.[1]

CHAPTER IV.

UNION WITH GOD.

*Love tends to union ; we tend towards the person whom we love. The
soul that loves God tends towards Him, and, on His part, God draws that
soul to Himself with irresistible force.*

*As the soul makes progress, it wishes to find the shortest and surest road
to God.   The shortest road is the straight road of the Gospels which makes
no detours and avoids no obstacles.   The surest way is the way of detachment, obedience and humility.   As the soul aspires to intimate union with
God, it seeks perfection and holiness.*

*No mere sentimental love will lead to this end ; the love must be strong
and virile, ready to make sacrifices.*

1. MY GOD, I AM HUNGRY FOR THEE

I had gone and sat beneath the cloister.   I was suffering in the
inmost depths of my soul.   I felt evil under all its forms rising up
like a flood and invading souls ; and I saw humanity, like a little
island scarcely raised above this sea of sin, being gradually covered
by its waters.

I saw evil in myself ; I saw it in others ; there was nothing pure
or just or holy.   The souls of men were so mercenary, their hearts
so cold and selfish, their minds so insincere.   Yes, I suffered ; the
weight of evil was crushing me, I had urgent need of the good, the
just, the true !

It was the end of a summer's day, a great calm reigned in nature.
On my right, the white pillars of the cloister and the curves of the
arches stood out in perspective ; on the left, a Bengal rose bush, still
in flower, contributed its joyous note of cheerful life.   Around me,
there was not a breath of air, but higher up a light breeze caused a
tremor in the leaves of the tops of the giant poplars.   The heavens
were of a pure, deep azure, and while my looks plunged into this
blue which stretched out to infinity, my soul ascended to regions

---

[1] Intimate Notes : 23-9-1906.

which were bathed in admirable light, but all silent and full of mysteries.

O God, I said to myself, when shall I be able to go to Thee? When will death be absorbed by life ; darkness by light ; evil, envy, and hate, by Love ?

O Infinite Love, source of life, divine food of souls, when shall I quench my thirst and become completely satiated with Thee ?

My God, I am hungry for Thee, for Thy Light without shadow, for Thy Justice without compromise, for Thy Eternity without end. I am hungry for Thy Love, so ardent, so pure, so faithful, and so strong ; I am hungry for Thee, my God, such as Thou art.[1]

2. DETACHMENT

God is Love and it is our love alone that He demands. Let us allow Him, then, to take out whole hearts.

Let us make for Him all the little sacrifices which our Rules require of us, not through compulsion or with a kind of regret, but with joy and without calculation.

Let us be firmly persuaded that the more we empty our hearts by entire detachment from earthly and created things, the more God-Infinite Love will pour into our souls the abundance of His divine gifts.[2]

3. WE SHOULD DIE TO ALL THINGS IN ORDER TO LIVE FOR GOD

Oh ! how happy one is to be nothing, to wish nothing, to desire nothing, not to trouble about small, contemptible things, and each day to sacrifice to God the purest aspirations of one's mind and heart ; how sweet it is to die to all things in order to live for God, to live in God !

This most lovable occupation is the lot of the Sisters of the Visitation ; as guardians and adorers of the adorable Heart of Jesus, we ought to live by love and for love, in meekness and humility. Our Blessed Father (St. Francis de Sales) said to me : " A Sister of the Visitation who is not meek and humble is not a true Visitandine ; she is a blot on the Institute."

---

[1] Intimate Notes : 1901.
[2] Conference to the Sisters : 31-12-1907.

The more we sink down into our nothingness, the more profoundly we shall penetrate into the abysses of Infinite Love ; the more charitable and meek we are, the more the Sacred Heart of Jesus dilates Itself to receive us and love us : the more sacrifices we make for God, the more of Himself He gives us.[1]

4. EMPTY THE HEART OF EARTHLY THINGS AND FILL IT WITH GOD

Sweet Jesus, here I am ; I have nothing, I can do nothing, I wish for nothing. How sweet it is to rest oneself from all one's cares with a friend such as Jesus ! How sweet it is to have one's spirit empty of all created things ! But my spirit and my heart are not empty ; on the contrary they are full, but full of Thee ; but this plenitude does not cause them trouble or oppression, for they are full of the Substance which suits them, Which is Thou, O my God.

Remain, O Lord, fill my mind and heart ; let nothing foreign to my nature, nothing created, intrude itself into them.

If anything enters there which is not of Thee, it is an unsupportable weight to me, it causes infinite pain ; however, if The good pleasure wishes that I should suffer for Thy love, be it done unto me according to Thy desire. For what do I wish but to please Thee, and if it pleases Thee better to see me struggle and suffer, I also wish it so.

However, I make bold to ask Thee to support me, to encourage me, to give me sometimes Thy holy consolation. I am so weak, I allow myself to be filled with grief and fear so quickly ; come, then, divine Friend, in Thy love I shall find strength and peace.[2]

5. INVITATION FROM JESUS

The winter has already passed ! The time of cold and sadness exists no more ; the North wind of the world which froze your soul has given place to the gentle zephyr whose cool breath comes from the heights of heaven. This frail flower of your soul, which the corrupt air of the world threatened to blight, can now open out. The winter is over ! The clouds laden with hoar-frost are scattered ; the sky has become blue again ; the warm Sun of divine Love is to give heat to your soul.

---

[1] Intimate Notes : 4-1-1900.
[2] Intimate Notes : Aug., 1890.

The winter has passed. The gloom of the night of error, of fear, and of doubt is scattered ; the Orient is lit up by the rays of the Sun of Justice ! The rain has ceased ! You need fear no more to dirty your feet in the mire, or to soil your robe in the mud of the road ; the dew alone will descend from heaven to fertilize your soul.

The rain has ceased ! Bitter tears will no longer flow from your eyes ; the holy tears of penance or the loving dew of gratitude alone will moisten your eyelids.

Arise, My beloved ! Arise, dear soul, that I have purchased with My Blood ; leave this dangerous repose which may prove fatal for you ; arise, take courage and come to Me.

During the year which is commencing, each one of your steps must bring you nearer to Me. Do not be alarmed if the road is rough and the distance long ; for each step which you take to ascend to Me, I will take one to descend to you. Be not frightened if you sometimes fall and if you feel yourself bruised ; in heaven above I have prepared in My Heart the divine balm which cures every wound and which gives marvellous strength.

Come, My beloved, come My sister. Come, you whom I have chosen among thousands in spite of your extreme misery and weakness ; come, I have pity on you and I open to you My Heart ; come and plunge into the infinite Ocean of My Mercy and Love ![1]

6. THE STRAIGHT PATH

O supernatural heavenly life, when one catches a glimpse of you, how desirable you appear ! What must I do to possess you ? What labour must I undergo to acquire you ? Tell me, O Lord ; in order to contemplate Thy face, and enjoy Thy sweet peace, I wish to undertake everything and do everything. I wish to go straight to Thee. O Lord, I will break through everything that stops me on the way ; if it be my friends, I will leave them ; if it be my goods I will give them away ; if it be my heart I will tear it out ; if it be my body, let it be destroyed ![2]

---

[1] Intimate Notes : October, 1891.

[1] Intimate Notes : Aug. 1890.

7. PURITY, SIMPLICITY AND CHARITY

I saw with sentiments of sweet and profound joy the pleasure which God finds in a pure and simple soul. The purity which is so pleasing to God is not purity entirely free from faults and imperfections ; no, but the purity which does not voluntarily tolerate in the soul any evil sentiment, either against one's neighbour or on any other subject.

The simplicity which delights the Heart of God is the simplicity of a soul which goes straight to God without caring about the effect which this may produce on creatures.

In order to possess this purity, we must not allow the smallest evil or imperfect sentiment to dwell in our minds. If the thought only passes through, it does not matter. However, great vigilance is required. In order to arrive at the simplicity which is so dear to God, we must go straight to what duty bids us to do through the motive of love, and consequently we must have courage and not be afraid of humiliation or of the judgements of men. Infinite Love delights in a soul that is simple and pure and, in such a soul, enjoys ineffable repose.[1]

8. WALK COURAGEOUSLY

Our Lord showed me that I should arm myself with great courage in order always to go straight towards Him, without seeing anything, or allowing myself to be hindered by anything, looking not at the past which saddens me, looking not towards the future, which terrifies me, not even dwelling on the present which often troubles me ; disregarding everything, leaving everything aside, fixing my eyes on my crucified Saviour and, without growing weary of failing, walking towards the divine goal.[2]

9. (a) THE ROYAL ROAD OF THE CROSS

During this Retreat, God has shown me religious life in its true light : a life of sacrifice ; I have counted one by one all the crosses which it will perhaps please Thy wisdom to place on my path, and

---

[1] Intimate Notes : 27-7-1912
[2] Intimate Notes : 18-12-1893.

which the continuous rebellion of my nature, corrupted by contact with the world, will render heavier to bear ; crosses of entire, absolute dependence : crosses of humiliations, of common life, crosses of corporal sufferings which the inflexibility of the Rule renders more painful ; crosses of mental suffering, temptations, repugnances.

On seeing all these crosses, if my nature has for a moment shuddered, my soul has not been shaken. This is my road ; Thou hast destined it for me from all eternity, O Lord ; were it a thousand times rougher to travel, I would be bound to follow it and I will follow it. Thy grace will sustain me ; the prospect of the struggles which I must keep up against myself and the evil spirit, does not shake my courage or make my soul falter ; I know, O Lord, that Thou shalt be with me.

And then, what is the use of trying to escape from the cross ? Shall we not find it everywhere when God wishes it ? And if it pleases God to lay His cross on me, in whatever place I may be, must I not carry it ? I embrace, then, firmly and resolutely, this life which for some is full of sweetness, but which perhaps for me will be full of combats and sacrifices ; I count on Thee, my Saviour, Thou wilt not abandon this soul which gives itself to Thee entirely, which trusts in Thee, and which, in spite of the crosses which Thou holdest in Thy hands and which Thou dost destine for me, does not cease to walk towards Thee and hold out to Thee her arms. Those who place their confidence in Thee and give themselves generously to Thee shall not be shaken ; have the pains of the martyrs ever been too much for their constancy ?

I am happy, O my God, to give myself to Thee, not in the joy and inclination of my nature, but by the fervent desire of my soul and the sole strength of my will.

After this Holy Communion which has purified my soul, the priest said to me : " Your sins are blotted out, think no more about them ; only remember that God wishes two things from you : penance and vigilance." Penance,—how can I better do penance than by embracing voluntarily and lovingly the life which the Lord has shown me to be so full of sacrifice ? Does not the blood which the martyr sheds for the glory of his God efface his sins through the merits of Christ, and does it not make him enter into glory ? If the blood of my body is not poured out, at least my life will be consumed, drop by drop, by crosses and sacrifices, and it will not be a martyrdom of a day or a year, but perhaps of twenty or perhaps of forty years, according as it may please the Lord. Vigilance : Yes, O Lord, I wish to watch, to watch over my heart in order that no earthly affection may there enter, for Thou dost wish it for Thyself alone ; to watch over my mind, in order that its foolish imagination may not draw it outside of Thee, O Jesus, Who art its way. wish to watch ! But alas ! Will not my indolent and feeble nature drag my will into this fatal sleep which has almost ruined me ?[1]

(b) THE REWARD

Who could ever tell the infinite sweetness which penetrates my soul when it feels itself loved by God ; what words can describe the divine delight which comes into it ? Human language has no words to describe this feeling. The understanding can with difficulty get a glimpse of only a very small part of it. This celestial sweetness remains in the higher part of the soul which, very rarely and very sparingly, allows a tiny portion to flow down to the other powers.

10. HUMAN WEAKNESS SHOULD NOT DISCOURAGE US

At times I experience a very strong inclination which draws me inwards ; I felt it in a very particular manner this morning after Holy Communion. I would wish to hide myself, to disappear from all eyes in order to leave all the place to Our Lord. It seems to me that He would do His work better if I were completely hidden, and I experience the need to enter some deep place where I could no more be perceived.

While I was writing these last lines, Jesus made Himself sweetly felt to my soul. He said to me : " Wrap yourself in humility and come and hide yourself in My Heart."

He is there quite near ; I wished to go on my knees ; He said : " No, write, write that your nothingness attracts Me, and that your weakness charms Me, and that I wish to transform your mud and make of it a magnet which will attract souls to My love." O Love, Love, I can say nothing, but I wish to love Thee, my adorable Master. He reproaches me for not having dared to write : " I love Thee," and to have put instead : " I wish to love Thee."

I love Thee, my Jesus, my God, my Saviour, my Mercy ![2]

---

[1] Intimate Notes : June, 1891.
[2] Intimate Notes : 17-8-1903.

The soul that aspires to union with God experiences an imperious need to sanctify itself. But the road to holiness is usually strewn with difficulties. We must struggle and labour in order to root out innumerable faults that are obstacles to our progress.

In the following pages, we shall see the generous efforts and unremitting struggle Mother Louise Margaret made to overcome herself, and that her victory was due to faithful co-operation with God's grace.

11. THE DESIRES OF JESUS FOR OUR SANCTIFICATION

(a) During my recent illness, I had some very vivid lights on the desire which Jesus has for the purity and perfection of the soul. I wish to labour energetically at this work of my sanctification. I ought to be holy for myself in order to render to Jesus the fruit of His graces. I ought to be holy for my priests, in order to merit graces for them and not to be unworthy of serving them. I ought to be holy for Jesus in order to console His Heart, to rejoice His divine eyes, and to accomplish His will. I ought to be holy, I wish to be holy; I cannot be so of myself, it is true, for I am misery, weakness, and imperfection itself, but I can do all things with the help of grace, with Jesus Who wishes it and Who can accomplish it.[1]

(b) " Be ye therefore perfect, as your heavenly Father is perfect." (Matt. V, 48). That is the commandment. It is not said, try to be perfect, but, be perfect; it is necessary to be perfect. But can man be perfect? Have we not this saying : " Perfection is not of this world," which appears to be an evident contradiction of the command of our Saviour.

How could our Lord Jesus Christ, Who knew men so well, and Who knows better than anyone else their inclination to evil,—how could He Who knows the weakness of our nature say to us : " Be ye perfect " ?

Yes, we have in ourselves a real attraction towards evil, and from our own corrupt nature we could do nothing but evil ; but by earnest persevering work on ourselves, aided by the grace of God which is never wanting to men of good will, we can, little by little, pluck out our vices, and plant some virtues in the garden of our soul, up to the last hour of our lives, when our bodies will succumb with fatigue and old age.

---

[1] Intimate Notes : 28-9-1905.

When our Saviour said : " Be ye perfect," it was not of our bodies, but of our souls, that there was question, and when we have laboured all our lives at our sanctification, when we have fought and struggled against our passions and our vices, when by dint of patience and violence to ourselves, we have broken down the wall of mud and of sin which separates us from God, at the moment when our bodies abandon us, by our victory over the last assault which our enemy will make against us, our souls will become really perfect.

That is why our Saviour said to us : " Be ye perfect " ; it is because we can really become so. But it is also true to say that perfection is not of this world : because perfection cannot dwell in this world ; we are truly perfect only for a moment, and this moment is the last one of our lives.

Let us, then, labour all the days of our short life at the work of our perfection, and let us preserve the hope, in order to sustain us in our combats, of becoming one day perfect, and of thus arriving at the eternal glory promised by our Lord Jesus Christ to His elect ![1]

12. THE SOUL OF SILENCE

Silence keeps our minds in proper subjection, because, although it is our mouths that express the words, it is our minds that think them and decide on their external expression.

It is the fertility of our minds which makes these words issue from our mouths in too great numbers ; it is the want of mortification of our hearts, which too often do not consider either the time or the place, that causes us to break the silence prescribed by our rule. It is the disorder of our minds that does not allow us to observe right measure, respect and meekness in our words.[2]

13. PURITY OF HEART

God unites Himself only to the pure of heart. Our daily warfare with sin should lead us to that purity of heart without which it is impossible to know, love and possess God.

To know God as far as he can be known in this life, to see Him with the eyes of the soul—which are a thousand times more piercing than those of the body—to understand Him by means of our

---

[1] Intimate Notes : 1890.
[2] Conference to the Sisters : 26-9-1910.

intellect and to unite ourselves to Him by means of love, we must
have a pure heart.

Our Lord has summed up all these advantages in one of His
admirable Beatitudes : " Blessed are the clean of heart : for they
shall see God." (Matt. V, 8).

Let us speak then of that purity of heart without which we cannot
make the first step in the science of prayer—that exercise which
should lead us to the knowledge of God, make us see God by interior
contemplation and unite us to Him by love—and much less can we
without it, make progress and obtain the fruits of sanctification
which it contains.

When we speak of purity of heart, we do not intend to speak of
that first degree of purity which consists in turning away from evil,
nor in that higher degree which consists in driving away carefully
from the mind all bad thoughts, and from the heart, all disordered
or culpable affections.

The third degree of purity which is necessary to obtain the grace
of prayer requires more. It will not tolerate in us the smallest
wilful thought, the least sentiment that can in any way be displeasing to God.

Ah ! we complain so often of aridity in prayer, of having no facility
for thinking of God, of being powerless to act, of being fatigued
by the multitude of distractions, of being without fervour, without
light and without spiritual relish.   But have we taken care to purify
our hearts ? Have we emptied them of the many imperfect sentiments which fill them every day, of the many human views, of all
mean susceptibility, of secret seeking after ourselves concealed
within, of so many interior faults, of criticisms formulated in our
minds regarding the acts, the words, and even the way of acting
of our neighbour ?

If we keep our hearts very pure, if we remove from them all the
dust of imperfections which obscures their transparency, we shall
enter into ourselves without difficulty, we shall be in the proper
dispositions to see the beautiful.

And then, the Divine Beauty, God Himself, will appear to us and
we shall see Him, whether in His works,—when in meditation we
recall them to our minds one after another—whether in His Divine
Essence,—when, by means of contemplation, we apply our thoughts
to consider His sacred attributes and His infinite perfections.   In
order to find God in prayer, we must watch with the greatest care

over the purity of our hearts ; we must not voluntarily allow the slightest shadow to enter into them.

Three things will help us marvellously to form in ourselves that luminous purity so much to be desired, which will reveal the divine Beauty to us :

The first is the renunciation of our own will in all things both temporal and spiritual, in our employments, in our labours, in things spiritual, in the practices of piety, in our finest undertakings ; not to be attached to anything, not to will anything with a tenacious, precise will, to seek only the will of God, to take account only of it, to fulfil it as soon as it is known, whatever it may cost us ; to be attached to nothing, to yield easily, to consent without difficulty, to obey without resistance, to make ourselves pliable and docile, in order that the least breath of the Divine Will may make our will incline sweetly.

This renunciation of our own will purifies our hearts quickly and opens them gently to God.

Attention to possess our souls in unalterable peace is not less necessary for us. Anything which disturbs us is not pure, even if it is good, like fear, the knowledge of our own misery, diffidence in ourselves, the thought of divine Justice : if any of these thoughts cause alarm or disturb our peace of mind, it is because they are mixed with something impure which causes the ferment : it is necessary to drive them from our minds because they attack the purity of our hearts.

Finally, the great means of purifying ourselves is humility ; simple, profound, true humility, by which one recognises one's own misery and sees Divine Mercy at hand, by which one does not fear to be raised up, or to be cast down before all, knowing that we shall always be the same nothingness before God ; purifying humility, because it is courageous and strong, above all because it reposes its trust in God.

Let us strive by constant renunciation of our own will and interior recollection to preserve profound peace in our souls and, by a generous practice of true humility, to purify our hearts more and more every day.

Let us not tolerate the smallest stain in ourselves. Let us constantly drive out of our minds those innumerable, petty, imperfect sentiments which our self-love produces in us and which we often allow to dwell too long within us, excusing them in our own eyes.

In a certain sense, we should be less afraid of bad thoughts, the evil nature of which is so evident, that it makes us detest them and flee from them. We should all the more fear small acts of cowardliness, the least disobedience, dislike for others which seems to us to be justified, little jealousies half consented to.

The Beatific Vision will be our eternal recompense. It depends on ourselves alone to enjoy its infinite sweetness in a higher degree.

Let us labour then unceasingly at this purification of our hearts which will merit for us a glimpse of God in this life and later on, the possession of Him in heaven with inexpressible joy.[1]

14. THE RELIGIOUS VOWS

The religious vows, if they are made with the necessary dispositions, should produce in our souls a change, a transformation which will give them in the eyes of God a new charm and a more powerful attraction to love them.

The vow of Obedience straightens our will that has been deformed and, as it were, twisted by sin, and renders it capable of uniting itself to the divine Will.

The vow of Poverty enlightens the soul and enables it to know God, to apply itself to Him by the power of its intellect, and in the same manner to see the infinite treasure of His perfections.

The vow of Chastity purifies the heart, dilates it, warms it, and gives it the means of loving God above all things, and of attaching itself solely to Him. This interior transformation is more or less perfect in us according as our dispositions are more or less perfect when making these vows ; but it is above all by the constant practice of these three virtues of Chastity, Poverty and Obedience, that it is operated in us and becomes more perfect every day.

Therefore, if after so many years of life in religion, we find ourselves so wanting in submission to the will of God, so easily, if not stirred up to revolt, at least terrified and dejected by the trials which He sends us, so inclined to ask God to render an account to us of His manner of acting towards us, let us be aware that we have not yet truly vowed obedience or truly practised this virtue.

And if we find ourselves so ignorant of the things of God, so dull in comprehending what He deigns to show to us concerning Him-

---

[1] Conference to the Sisters : 8-10-1907.

self, so incapable of raising ourselves up towards Him to contemplate what He takes so much pleasure in revealing to those who love Him, the reason is that we have not yet practised this divine Poverty: material poverty and poverty of spirit and absolute detachment not only from what is superfluous but from what is useful and even necessary.

Finally, if we feel our hearts so cold and languid in the love of God, so attached to creatures, so easily offended by their behaviour, so nettled by their egoism, let us know that we have not understood, and consequently, not practised the divine demands of the virtue of Chastity.

Genuine Chastity of the heart consists in loving God alone, seeking only Him in creatures, centering our affections on His immutable love alone, raising ourselves above created objects and leaving them behind us, not through haughty disdain, but by loving preference for what is higher than they ; seeing the infinite Love of God flowing down upon all beings, and cherishing them because they are all covered with it,—that is chastity of heart.[1]

As a condition for union with our souls, God wishes to find not only purity in them, but He requires also to find peace.

15. GOD WISHES PEACE

I saw that God does not find His complacence in the vain excited activity of men, but that He established His dwelling only in the peace and perfection of His own Being. In Himself He enjoys ineffable repose. This is neither immobility nor sleep, but a living active repose which proceeds from the plentitude of the perfection which is in Him. How far the action of God is from resembling the turbulent action of men !

The world is agitated and carried away in an incessant whirlwind, because the Spirit of God has withdrawn from it ; in order that God establish His special dwelling in a soul, He must find peace there ; that is why the soul should endeavour to establish calm in itself by the mortification of all the passions ; it is the passions that cause all the trouble and agitation ; the soul must exert itself to extinguish and diminish their activity ; then it must establish in itself the reign of the virtues, especially of those which bring peace, such

---

[1] Intimate Notes : 20-11-1899.

as indifference, submission to the divine will, confidence, etc.

When the soul is thus prepared, God comes to it and, to this peace which it has acquired, He adds a new peace, His own peace ; this is the peace which surpasses all understanding, because it is the reign of God in the soul.[1]

16. THE REIGN OF PEACE

Yesterday evening at prayer, Jesus filled my soul with a celestial peace. Communicating Himself to me in the inmost part of my heart, He said to me : " I wish to establish the reign of peace in your soul."

Then He showed me that He wished that no trouble, no fear, no anxiety should disturb my soul ; that He wished this profound calm in me in order to be able to act in me. I understood that the good Master wished my soul in great interior calm in order that it might be as a bed of repose for His love that is still so little known. He wishes that I receive suffering according as it presents itself, that I welcome it sweetly, without effort, in order not to disturb His love asleep in me. That is why He wishes that I endeavour to acquire meekness and to control my natural animation and impatience.[2]

17. JESUS WISHES US TO BE JOYFUL

Jesus wishes us to be joyful in soul in the midst of sacrifices and trials ; He has often given me to understand of late how much He loves souls free from agitation, fears, and human sadness. He loves souls transparent like fresh water, and never has He so much pleasure as when He can bathe and plunge the rays of His Infinite Love into their clearness, as the sun plunges its rays into the waters of a pure, transparent lake.

I have not much time to pray, but when I turn my heart towards Jesus, I always recommend my good Father Charrier to Him.[3]

18. AND NOT TO BE TROUBLED

He told me also that I would have to continue work to diffuse the knowledge of Love and that I should increase my confidence in

---

[1] Intimate Notes : 1-11-1899.
[2] Intimate Notes : 1-9-1905.
[3] Letter to Father Charrier : 15-1-1906.

Greater love than this no man hath, than that a man lay down
his life for his friends. (JOHN XV, 13).

"He was wounded for our iniquities : He was bruised
for our sins " (Isaias LIII, 5)

Him and not to allow cares and worries to get the better of me, for solicitude about the future causes trouble in the soul, and He does not wish my soul to be troubled about anything, because when the soul is troubled, it is no longer capable of receiving so easily and so clearly the radiation from Infinite Love.[1]

19. THE SIMPLE SOUL

God is not pleased at finding in the soul the continual troubles and fluctuating shadows caused by self-love, by human considerations ; the multiplicity of desires, wills, regrets, and fears.

The souls which God loves more than others are simple souls which have but one desire, namely, to please Him ; a single tendency, that of going to Him and becoming united to Him. These are the souls on whom He delights to confer his favours.

God, Who is Infinite Love, takes pleasure in reflecting into souls His divine perfections, the light of His Truth and the splendour of His Wisdom.

The simple soul is like a very clear mirror, like perfectly clear water ; it has the proper dispositions to receive in itself the reflection of the divine splendour.

Oh ! how pleasing in the sight of God is this clearness and transparency of soul ! It is by the reflection of God which the clear soul makes in itself that it becomes united to Him and communicates Him to others.[2]

20. THE REPOSE OF THE SOUL IN GOD

I see what pleases God most is the repose of the soul in Him, because this gives Him the means of communicating Himself to it. what divine Goodness communicates to my soul is ineffable. I find no words sufficient to express the greatness of the good things that are found in God and the desire which He has to communicate them to creatures.[3]

---

[1] Intimate Notes : 27-2-1911.
[2] Intimate Notes : No date.
[3] Intimate Notes : 4-10-1896.

21.   HUMILITY, THE SOURCE OF ALL VIRTUES

The soul meets with many obstacles on its path to God.   The one which hinders its progress most and prevents its union with God is pride.   It is also the most difficult to conquer, for victory over pride requires a very great effort and a very long struggle.

The fundamental virtue, therefore, for all, especially those who aim at perfection, is profound, sincere humility.

Humility towards God !   How easy it is to be wanting in it, and how that virtue is all the more necessary for us !

It is not only a virtue but a source of all the virtues ![1]

22.   JESUS THE MODEL OF HUMILITY

We shall enter to-morrow into that holy time of Advent, during which everything speaks of the depths of the humility of the Word made Man.

In the mysteries of His public life, in His Passion, there are indeed many humiliations for the Son of God ; but we feel His words full of grace and truth, we see His miracles, we admire the greatness of His patience, of His sacrifice, of His superhuman virtue.

On the contrary, in the mysteries which the Church proposes for our meditation during Advent, there is none of that.   It is abasement, the most complete humiliation,—the weakness of infancy, silence, apparent inaction.   In becoming man, God, in the words of St. Paul, "emptied Himself."   If, at the first moment of His life on earth, the Word had assumed the form of a perfect man with fully developed intellect, full of wisdom and knowledge, the humiliation would not have been so complete.

He has willed to descend to the lowest depths of humiliation in order to conquer our pride, and that through incomparable love and mercy.

In the beginning, God had made all things in the most perfect order.   In heaven above, God, the supreme Lord and Master, but also the Father infinitely good and liberal, reigned supreme ; on earth below was the creature, humble, grateful, under an obligation of obedience, of a filial, loving obedience.

---

[1] Conference to the Sisters : April, 1904.

The authority of God and the submission of the creature were but the expression of reciprocal love, an exchange of delights and of the purest and sweetest sentiments.

Pride and the spirit of independence came and destroyed this beautiful order.

God remained in His glory, but the creature, because he attempted to ascend too high, fell so low that he remained incapable of raising himself up.

Then, in order to restore all things, God decided to go in search of His creature in the depths of his misery. The Word " emptied Himself " in order to restore us to our original status by His grace. He abased Himself in order to raise us up. He made Himself little in order to make us great, He was silent in order to teach us to speak with wisdom ; He became weak to strengthen us, poor, to detach us from earthly goods. He became man, a Doctor of the Church has not been afraid to say, in order to make us gods, and that, in order to bring us near God, to establish us in His friendship, to regain for us the happiness which we had lost.

Do we think sufficiently that we owe the restoration of our nature and the just hope which we have of eternal rest and glory to the humiliations of a God, to His adorable condescension for our weakness and our misery?

If we meditated sufficiently on this, if this truth was a living force in our minds, our aversion to humiliations would disappear, we would understand that there is nothing more befitting us, as well as more glorious for us, than to enter on the way which the Word of God has trodden before us in order to save us.

Let us meditate well on this thought during Advent.

Let us enter with greater courage and generosity on that way of humility and abasement which is so repugnant to our ignorant nature, for the medicine which is to cure us is often distasteful to the poor, unconscious sick person.

Can we not do in little what God has done in such a complete and excessive manner for love of us, in order to show our gratitude?[1]

23. HUMILITY AND LOVE

Every day after Holy Communion I ask Our Lord to reveal to me His Heart, to teach me His divine humility, to tell me what

---

[1] Conference to the Sisters : 30-11-1912.

I must do to be humble, to know my misery. Yesterday I said to Him : " My Jesus, how hast Thou, eternal Wisdom, Infinite, Knowledge, Sovereign Holiness and Purity, been able to be humble, and how can I, profound misery, sin, ignorance, and weakness, not be so. Explain these two mysteries to me." He replied to me in something like the following terms, if I remember aright : " My humanity saw, by the light of the Divinity which was united to it, the extreme distance which there is between the creature drawn from nothing and the Creator, the only principle and source of being. It saw the subjection and dependence in which its state as creature placed it. The contrast between the power, greatness and wisdom of the Divinity, and the weakness, powerlessness, and insignificance of the humanity, was so striking that, by this sight, it remained in continual humiliation and confusion, and it could never get away from this condition, for the Divinity and humanity being inseparably joined together, this comparison and contrast would never cease."

I then said to Our Lord : " And I, what must I do to become humbler?" He replied to me : " The more closely you are united to Me, the better you will understand your weakness and the lowliness of your origin, which is nothingness."—" But how am I to unite myself so intimately to Thee?"—" It is love which produces union!"—Then I said : " My Jesus, my Director told me that humility is the road to love, and Thou, my adorable Master, tellest me that union by love will lead me to humility! What then must I believe?" Jesus replied to me with extreme sweetness : " Do not fear that there will ever be contradiction between what I teach you by My own mouth and what I have taught you by My brother. Love and humility increase and perfect one another in an admirable manner. Divine Charity, poured out into the soul by the Holy Spirit, enlightens it and shows it the necessity and justice of humility ; humility produces in the soul an increase of love, and this love in its turn produces still more self-annihilation and humiliation. In this continual movement which makes it descend by humility and ascend by love, the soul becomes dilated, enlarged and inflamed, and becomes always more capable of the Divinity."[1]

---

[1] Intimate Notes : 9-3-1904.

24. HOW TO PRACTICE HUMILITY

Our Saviour has given me to understand what was the humility He desired of me and of the daughters of the Visitation in general. This humility should be like a transparent tissue covering everything, or rather like a sweet, floating perfume with which our actions, thoughts, and words should be impregnated. This humility is not a humility of acts, but we must be so completely clothed with it exteriorly, that everything which proceeds from it should bear its seal ; in a word, it must be a state of humility.

I will practise great humility of faith towards God, abandoning myself without seeking to understand the operations of God in me.

I will accept with humble and loving resignation my powerlessness and weakness.

With my Superiors, I will be full of respectful and humble confidence, and I will humbly follow their direction ; with my Sisters, I will be humble, frank and cordial, and when they ask my advice I will give it to them with simplicity. With my relatives and neighbours, I will be humble, sweet and serious, with strangers, humble, grave and dignified.

Finally, this humility ought to consist in progressive effacement of all personality, gradually making personal action disappear to allow God to do and act.[1]

25. MOTIVES FOR HUMILITY

Yesterday morning, when my eyes fell on the copy book which contained the notes on the sacerdotal virtues, it seemed to be insupportable pride on the part of me, a wretched little sinful worm, to write on the virtues of priests who are my fathers, my masters ; I conceived an extreme disgust for myself and I annihilated myself under the feet of Jesus.

There, a sweet thought came to me which did me good. It seemed to me that Father Charrier was a fisherman and that he was preparing to cast out his line into the sea of souls and that he stooped down and picked up a little worm out of the mud to put on his hook.

This little worm was myself. Oh ! how disgusting a little worm

---

[1] Intimate Notes : 18-1-1893.

is ! However, it serves to attract the fishes, but in itself is nothing.

Well ! this thought that I was but a wretched little worm, calculated to cause disgust to everyone, except to Father who nevertheless makes use of me, for the fisherman does not consider whether the worm that he puts on his hook causes him disgust ; this thought, I say, filled my soul with peace, repose, and sweetness.

O Jesus, yes, I am nothing but that, a little worm, a hideous little worm, and I am happy to be so ; I do not wish to be anything else. I wish to be a little worm and to do Thy will always.[1]

26. HUMILITY IN CARRYING OUT ONE'S DUTIES

This morning, after Holy Communion, Our Lord, present within my heart, gave me His teachings and instructions. He showed me how necessary it is to deal with all matters pertaining to the religious life, according to His ideas, especially for those persons who have any charge, however small, in order not to introduce human considerations, which, in the end, infallibly ruin everything.

Religious should put aside all human feelings, divest themselves of all sympathy and antipathy and, listening to none of their own inclinations, place themselves before God like an empty vessel ready to receive what grace will put into it according as occasion demands.

They must not judge of anything humanly or according to its outward appearance, but they must judge according to God, that is to say, not according to their own inclinations, but according to the light which God has given the heart which presents itself before Him empty of itself and filled with the knowledge of its nothingness and of the injustice of its own thoughts. If they act according to their natural inclinations they cannot avoid mixing much passion with their acts and judgments. They must, therefore, by the destruction of their own spirit and by an ever closer union with God, put themselves in a state to allow Our Lord to think, speak, and act in them ; in that manner they will be able to carry out the duties imposed on them in a proper manner as Religious should, without injuring their own souls and without harm or disedification of their neighbours.[2]

---

[1] Intimate Notes : 28-12-1902.
[2] Intimate Notes : 18-2-1893.

27. HUMILITY IN OUR UNDERTAKINGS

Many people very easily believe themselves capable of everything, and others more easily believe themselves capable of nothing.

The first of these eagerly begin their undertakings and carry them on with great confidence in themselves, with great desire of success ; if they do not succeed as they wish, they are astonished and sometimes saddened.

The second, on the contrary, too conscious of their own incapacity, undertake their works with such trepidation that it paralyses the gifts of God in them and, by an excess of fear, they render themselves incapable of serving the cause of good, or at least of serving it usefully.

Both the one and the other fall into a harmful excess.

Without wishing to constitute ourselves judges of our talents, without vain presumption or exaggerated fear, let us abandon ourselves simply to the guidance of our Superiors, which for us is the very guidance of God. If God in His divine Goodness permits that we succeed in our undertakings, let us bless Him, if, on the contrary, He permits that we get only humiliations from them, let us bless Him still more. If we put all our confidence in God without ever relying on ourselves, we shall possess the power of God and we shall be able to do what humanly we would be unable to accomplish.

Let us, therefore, place ourselves in the hands of God, in these hands so good and so powerful ! Let us undertake the tasks given to us humbly and generously and, entrusting ourselves to the protection of the most Blessed Trinity and invoking the maternal help of Mary, let us lovingly submit ourselves to the Divine Will.[1]

28. SPIRIT OF DEPENDENCE

By the infinite mercy of God, we have sufficient knowledge of our own weakness and of our own profound ignorance not to have a spirit of independence in matters concerning faith and the great questions which are connected with it. But in other fields, and in the details of our daily life, do we not sometimes yield to that spirit of independence which is characteristic of our age? How easily we seek to reconcile the duty of religious obedience with our

---

[1] Conference to the Sisters : 25-5-1910.

own personal views ! How often do we not try, perhaps without even being aware of it, to diminish that blessed dependence which forms the basis of our holy rules ! In our relations with the Community, in the organization of our labours, in the way in which we carry out our undertakings, we wish to render ourselves, as far as possible, independent.

The spirit of dependence, so precious and so sanctifying, is often wanting among people in charge and their assistants. They take on themselves to pass judgment on definite decisions and insist on getting them modified, they easily criticise measures adopted by authority, when they have not been thought out by themselves, or when they do not at first sight understand their usefulness. These are little infiltrations of the modern spirit, they are a little breath of that dangerous spirit of confidence in oneself and of independence from authority.

Let us be humble in heart and spirit ! Let us submit ourselves easily to the will of legitimate authority, let us love those precious acts of submission which are walls of defence that will protect us from external and internal enemies.[1]

If we had a greater spirit of faith, more humility of heart, and a little less self-love, we would certainly have greater obedience and submission of spirit.[2]

29. DESIRE FOR HUMILIATIONS

(*a*) I am so wretched and so ignorant of how to correspond with the graces of the good Master that I cannot reflect on myself without being confounded at the sight of the goodness of Jesus, Who endures me and seems to hide my profound misery from others, in order that they may not turn away from me.

God is accustomed to draw His finest works out of nothing. Praise be to His goodness and His power for drawing His glory out of real nothing, which I am.

I beg your Excellency to treat with me according to my deserts, that is to say, as a nothing which I am, and to reprove me and correct me well, and especially not to be afraid to humiliate me, for that is necessary for me.[3]

Conference to the Sisters 27-10-1907.
Conference to the Sisters : 24-2-1909.
Letter to Mgr. Filipello : 8-2-1911.

(*b*) You are very good, and I am very pleased when you put before my eyes the picture of my profound misery and all my past faults. It is true that the Providence of God in my regard is very mysterious ; that is why, it seems to me, that I should more and more leave Him absolute Master of everything in me and apply myself to allow Him alone to act.[1]

(*c*) I see that Father has attributed an evil thought to me, or at least a vain and foolish thought ; I am satisfied that he does so. There is such evil in me which he does not perhaps see, he may well suppose that I have an evil sentiment which I have not. That will make compensation. I have been pleased that he should believe me still capable of a thing so vain. It is not that from a human view-point I have not suffered a little from it, however not much, because the gratification which the humiliation has given me has absorbed the natural feeling.[2]

(*d*) It seems to me that the will of Jesus in my regard is that I forgot myself always more and more to allow Him to reign in me and to allow Him to act in my place in everything, and then that I have humility founded on the knowledge of my past and present misery. To love and cherish humiliations, abjection, contradiction, that is my true part ; the rest, the grace of Jesus, the lights, those things pass through me but they are not for me ; they are for my Director, for souls, for priests.

For myself, nothing but suffering and humility ![3]

30. PRAYER

O Word Incarnate, Eternal God, Infinite Love eager for union has made Thee go out of Thyself and descend even to our lowliness ; so great had been Thy love for Thy creatures that Thou hast not feared to clothe Thyself in human nature and take on Thyself the weight of its miseries. By the self-annihilation of Thy Incarnation and the humiliations of Thy entire life, grant us to understand both the love which Thou hast for us and the necessity which obliges us to keep ourselves humble before Thee.

---

[1] Letter to Father Charrier : 26-6-1907.
[2] Intimate Notes : Aug., 1905.
[3] Intimate Notes : 28-10-1908.

We have been raised up only by Thy abasement, we can glorify Thee only by our own ; grant, O adorable Jesus, that by uniting ourselves always more and more to Thy divine goodness, we may understand also better and better the weakness of our nature and the power of Thy merciful grace ; and that by humiliating ourselves at Thy feet in the knowledge of our nothingness, we may merit to be eternally united to Thee in the participation of Thy glory. Amen.[1]

CHAPTER V.

DONATION OF OURSELVES TO INFINITE LOVE

Love tends to union, to a union which is a reciprocal donation. To love is to give oneself.

To love God is to give ourself to Him ; it is to respond by the poor gift of ourselves to the gift of infinite value which God makes to us of Himself.

To give ourselves to God is to give ourselves to Infinite Love ; is there anything difficult or terrifying in giving ourselves to God Who has loved us so much ?

This act of donation is also an act of faith. What have we to fear from putting ourselves in the hands of an infinitely good and wise Being. The use that God will make of that gift will be to pour more abundantly His love into our souls.

1. GOD DESIRES TO UNITE HIMSELF TO HIS CREATURES, BUT THEY MUST OPEN THEIR HEARTS TO HIM

Our Lord has again condescended to unite me to Him by suffering between two and four o'clock this morning. The exterior pains were less violent, but I had such an extreme desire to love God to make up to Him for the want of love of other creatures that it caused a most painful kind of suffering and langour.

At Holy Mass, I began to feel the presence of Our Lord. During None when I went into the chapel, my divine Saviour made me feel the delights of His love.

---

[1] Intimate Notes : Oct., 1906.

In spite of my unworthiness, it seemed to me that Our Lord took pleasure in uniting Himself to me ; it was as if two hearts touched together and became melted into each other. During this time and a little afterwards, I felt that piercing pain in my heart from which I sometimes suffer.

During evening prayer, I contemplated deeply the love which God has for His creatures.

If people understood this, if they knew the desire which God has to unite Himself to creatures, they would not delay in opening their hearts to receive the treasures of love which flow incessantly from the bosom of the Divinity.[1]

2. LOVE WISHES TO COMMUNICATE ITSELF

It seems to me that Our Lord suffers because there is no one who is willing to receive His gifts ; all hearts are contracted, faint, and, in a manner, closed.

God wishes to communicate Himself, and He finds no entry. What marvels would not God work in souls, if they allowed Him to act, but they will not open their souls to grace, so they remain imperfect and miserable.

If they allowed the Lord to act, He would raise them up even to the divine union, and, even in this world, the creature would be, in a manner, divinized, so that God would do everything in him, and he would do everything in God.

I have endeavoured to open my soul very wide, and I have surrendered myself completely to His action.

I felt that even though I am weak, if I allowed Our Lord to act, all would be well ; everything would be His work ; of myself, there would be nothing but the first act of consent given. Nothing pleases God so much as to be able to act as Master in a soul. When He comes to the soul, He commences by pulling up everything by the roots, by taking away everything found in it, and then He purifies the soul.

Sometimes this is done by fire, and the pain is intense ; sometimes He purifies the soul from its stains with the delicacy of a mother who washes the frail body of her little child. The soul suffers because the purifying action always causes suffering, but the soul feels

[1] Intimate Notes : 20-9-1896.

that it is the hand of the Lord and the suffering is sweet to it.

Afterwards when it is very pure, it will be able to unite itself to God, to lose itself and be merged in God.

O sacred and most desirable Union, why is it that so few souls seek Thee?

In order to give God entry into the soul, two things are necessary: never to resist grace, and not to stop after falls, but to throw oneself with loving repentance into the arms of God.

Since I have resolved to do what is most perfect according to the lights of the moment, I feel in myself a quite distinctive expansiveness of heart and an entire confidence that Our Lord will do all, and that my weakness, my misery and my corruption will not be obstacles.

I feel a kind of assurance that Our Lord will do all that He wishes, and that nothing will prevent Him. How good God is to the soul! He makes it suffer only to render it capable of uniting itself to Him.[1]

3. GOD IS EAGER TO POUR OUT HIS GIFTS, BUT MAN REFUSES THEM

The day before yesterday, being before the Blessed Sacrament, I did nothing else but open my heart very wide to receive the graces of my Saviour and to expose myself to Its vivifying rays.

Oh! how great the abundance of blessings in God! What we need is to be disposed and to receive them. The necessary dispositions, it seems to me, are blind faith and fidelity.

The riches of the Divinity have not been exhausted; the Holy Spirit still pours all His gifts into souls, but few give Him sufficient entry.

What admirable and sacred communication is that which takes place between the Creator and the creature, between the Divinity and the humanity; it is a perpetual flow and counter-flow.

I feel that God wishes to give Himself to many souls, but He withdraws Himself, because they do not surrender themselves sufficiently to Him. Therefore, to make up for them I find an ever-increasing need to give myself to Him; this I do by acts of abandonment and love; it is by acts of love that I try to dilate and enlarge the capacity of my heart.

---

[1] Intimate Notes: 1894.

Our Lord does not wish that I look at His action in me or that I seek to get a clear idea of it, but He wishes me to look at Him, to be faithful to Him and to turn away from all else.[1]

4. GOD IS PLEASED AT SEEING THE SOUL GIVE ITSELF TO HIM

For the past three years Divine Goodness has been attracting my soul to Itself in a very special manner; when I have to come away from prayer I feel my soul rent asunder, as when one wishes to separate two things which are closely united and stuck together.

This morning at the beginning of meditation, it seemed to me that Our Saviour said to me interiorly: " You must belong completely to me ; but in order that you may not be elated over the intimacy which I wish to have with your soul, at other times I will show you, in a way known to Myself, your misery and your nothingness."

Sometimes Our Lord urges my soul to suffer for Him; because now He can no longer suffer in His humanity as His love would wish to do, then He asks me if I would be willing to suffer in place of Him.

But, Lord, Thou art the Master; Thou canst do what Thou wishest in my body and in my soul, why should Thou ask me?

I feel that He asks this, because His love takes pleasure in seeing the soul give itself again, and surrender itself to Him voluntarily.[2]

THE NEW AND SPECIAL DONATION TO INFINITE LOVE

The meaning and obligations of the act of donation of oneself to Infinite Love may be gathered from the following brief extracts, and especially from the text of the Act of Consecration and Donation to Infinite Love.

The act of total donation of oneself to Infinite Love is the response to the desire of Our Lord to communicate Himself to the world through those souls who are disposed to receive His gifts.

This act of donation must be made by all those who wish to participate in the Work of Infinite Love.

---

[1] Intimate Notes : 6-10-1895.
[2] Intimate Notes : Nov. 1893.

6. JESUS DEMANDS THE ACT OF DONATION

This morning after Holy Communion, I asked Our Lord to give
Father Charrier all the light and all the certainty which he desires.
A little later, when I was in the refectory, I continued to speak
interiorly to Jesus and I received the following reply : " What has he
to fear in announcing My love ?" Again, a little later, I insisted
anew with my Saviour, asking Him to give Father Charrier the sign
which he desires ; it seems to me that He replied to me : " I have
already given him so many !"

Just now when I was in the garden and was praying to Jesus to
aid and enlighten Father, the thought occurred to me that this
absolute donation to Love which, it seems to me, Jesus demands of
Father Charrier and of myself, had not been made.   I know well that
Father has given himself completely to God by his religious vows,
and I also ; I know that he has given himself in a special way by his
vow of servitude as I have by the vow of abandonment ; but what
Our Saviour has shown me, and what I saw very clearly just now,
is His desire for a new and special donation made by us to Infinite
Love, in order to be consecrated to Its service ; to be dedicated to
procure Its glory, and finally to be the instruments of the reign of
Infinite Love over the world.   This thought occurred to me again
in the month of May, but I waited to speak of it until Father Charrier
should have made his solemn vows.

Besides, this would not be a vow, but rather an offering, a total
consecration of himself to Infinite Love, living in the Heart of Jesus.[1]

7. WHAT THE ACT OF DONATION REQUIRES

Just now at prayer, I asked Our Lord how the donation to Infinite
Love should be made.   He said to me : " It should be made in the
form of a sacrifice ; you should offer yourselves as holocausts to be
consumed in the fire of love, in order that this love may be diffused
throughout the world and inflame souls."[2]

---

[1] Intimate Notes : Sept. 1903.
[2] Intimate Notes : 10-10-1904.

8. WE SHOULD NOT BE AFRAID TO MAKE THIS ACT OF DONATION

You speak to me of the act to be made to Infinite Love and you give as objections : (1) that you were not prepared ; (2) that you were too unworthy ; (3) that you have not yet seen sufficiently clearly what obligations will result from this act.   Father, when Our Lord asked St. Peter : " Lovest thou Me more than these ?" (John XXI, 15), there were many unknown mysteries of suffering for the Apostle in this question.   He did not make so much preparation, he did not make long reflections on the import of his reply, he did not insist on seeing just to what he was going to bind himself, he did not put forward his own unworthiness.   He replied straight out in a generous outburst from the heart, without calculating and without fear. Jesus had said to you : " I have chosen you to propagate My Infinite Love, I entrust to you Its treasures ; are you willing to love Me more than others, are you willing to do more than others for My love ?" He expected you to reply to Him by a total and absolute consecration of yourself to this Love.   Because you have not done so, my dear Father, our souls will not be separated in the love of Jesus, I do not believe so ; but perhaps, because you have been wanting in confidence in God, He has deprived you of necessary lights and of the joy of giving this first book (*The Sacred Heart and the Priesthood*) to priests yourself.[1]

9. ACT OF CONSECRATION AND DONATION OF ONESELF TO INFINITE LOVE

O Infinite Love, Eternal God, Principle of being, I adore Thee in Thy sovereign Unity and in the Trinity of Thy Persons.

I adore Thee in the Father, omnipotent Creator Who has made all things.   I adore Thee in the Son, eternal Wisdom by Whom all things have been made, the Word of the Father, incarnate in time in the womb of the Virgin Mary, Jesus Christ, Redeemer and King.   I adore Thee in the Holy Ghost, substantial Love of the Father and the Son, in Whom are light, strength and fruitfulness.

I adore Thee, Infinite Love, hidden in all the mysteries of our Faith, shedding Thy beneficent rays in the Blessed Eucharist, over-

---

[1] Letter to Father Charrier : 23-12-1909.

flowing on Calvary and giving life to the Church by the channels
of the Sacraments, I adore Thee throbbing in the Heart of Jesus
Thine ineffable Tabernacle, and I consecrate myself to Thee.

I give myself to Thee without fear with the fulness of my will ;
take possession of my being, penetrate it entirely, I am but a nothing
powerless to serve Thee, it is true, but it is Thou, Infinite Love,
Who hast given life to this nothing and Who dost draw it to Thee.

Behold me then, O Jesus, come to do Thy work of love : to labour
to the utmost of my capacity in bringing to Thy priests, and through
them to the entire world, the knowledge of Thy mercies and of the
sublime and tender love of Thy Heart.

I wish to accomplish Thy will, whatever it may cost me ; even to
the shedding of my blood, if my blood be not unworthy to flow for
Thy glory.

O Mary, Immaculate Virgin whom Infinite Love has rendered
fruitful, it is by thy virginal hands that I give and consecrate
myself.

Obtain for me the grace to be humble and faithful, and to devote
myself without reserve to the interests of Jesus Christ, Thy adorable
Son and to the glory of His Sacred Heart !

Indulgences (for members only) : 300 days toties quoties ; plenary once a month
for those who recite it daily. (Pope Pius XI).

10. THE ACT OF DONATION MAKES US THE POSSESSION OF INFINITE LOVE

I do not know how to express in words what I realized to-day.   I
felt myself to be the possession of Infinite Love.   I belong to God,
Infinite Love, in an unbelievable way, like an object designed solely
for His use, like an instrument made to execute His work.   What
is the work and what must I do ?   I do not know ; nevertheless I feel
myself being employed.   I feel that I am being operated by the hand
of the Divine Agent.

If the lifeless metal could feel, it seems to me that, when it is
being hammered and chiseled by the goldsmith, it would have
impressions similar to mine.[1]

---

[1] Intimate Notes : 3-5-1906.

11. THE FRUITS OF THIS DONATION TO INFINITE LOVE

This morning during Mass, I told Jesus of my weariness ; I begged Him to bring me away somewhere into profound solitude where I might converse alone with Him. After Holy Communion, in spite of my unworthiness, He manifested Himself to my soul. He said to me : " When My servant and you will be completely given to love by the consecration which It have demanded of you, I will not merely draw you to My Heart, but I will make you penetrate into It. I will introduce you into a mysterious dwelling of which you do not yet know. You will be enlightened on the nothingness of your being and of your own actions by a living light. Then, elevated above what is sensible, you will understand the mysteries of love of which you are now ignorant. You will see that I am everything in all things and everything in you. Sorrow may be able to reach you, but in suffering you will know a plenitude of peace which you have not yet tasted."[1]

12. THE RECOMPENSE FOR THE DONATION

I am not astonished at what you said about the inward graces which your consecration to Infinite Love is obtaining for you. It is at times a very crucifying love, but also infinitely sweet and liberal towards those souls who give themselves completely to It. How I would love to find souls who are capable of understanding and to whom we could reveal Infinite Love. I feel my soul full of ideas on all that and, if it please God, I will speak to you in June about it. Yes, I would wish, if it be the will of Jesus, to imbue souls with this life-giving Love and then send them or lead them to sow it on all sides everywhere.[2]

13. THE POSSESSION OF INFINITE LOVE

I find myself in presence of several painful crosses : Father Charrier's health makes me uneasy ; the future is for me full of poignant uncertainty ; whatever turn things may take there will be immense suffering, I am sure of it, I expect it ; I have a very precise view of that ; I feel all that in a very penetrating manner and never-

---

[1] Intimate Notes : 21-9-1904.
[2] Letter to Father Charrier : 12-3-1914.

theless my soul is in peace, in repose, in calmness that astonishes me. I have sunshine in my soul. There is something warm, sweet, life-giving and strong enveloping my soul which keeps it separated from all that is of earth. I think, if I am not mistaken, that it is an effect which the taking possession of my soul by Infinite Love has produced.

It seems to me that I am conscious that there is in my soul a supernatural power which is not merely grace, as has often been given to me. Perhaps it is grace of a higher, stronger degree, or a special gift, a special indwelling of the Spirit of Love. I am confounded in presence of the infinite goodness of God towards His poor creature ; but I understand very clearly that in all this, I am of no consequence ; that God does not give me this because He is under any necessity to give it to one of His creatures ; that it is solely for His own glory, for the purpose of the reign of His love. If He did not make use of me for His Work of Love, He would make use of another. A bridge is needed for divine Charity to pass over ; I am that bridge, that humble plank, that poor trunk of a tree thrown from one bank to the other, that is all. My God, help me by Thy divine grace not to place any obstacle to Thy passing. Do not permit that I should impede Thy work of love.[1]

CHAPTER VI.

ABANDONMENT TO THE WILL OF GOD

If we love God we will be willing to give ourselves to Him. But what does this gift of ourselves involve? To give ourselves to God is to lose our will in the will of God ; that is the end to which our donation of ourselves to God leads us. This sometimes seems hard to our human nature, but when we consider that the will of God is nothing else than the expression of the love of God, acquiescence in this will becomes easy and sweet.

" He that loses his life for My sake shall find it," says Our Lord. Thus, he that loses himself in God by sacrificing to Him all his own inclinations will find the fruits of union with God ; these are peace and contentment of soul ; the vicissitudes of life will not be able to disturb them.

---

[1] Intimate Notes : 7-10-1906.

1. SUBMISSION TO THE WILL OF GOD

God demands docility to His known will and absolute confidence in His Paternal Love.[1]

Our Lord showed me that the life of a Visitation Sister ought to be a life of very exact dependence on the inspiration of grace ; to accomplish this, a Visitation nun should be constantly listening to the inspirations of our Saviour, Who at each moment speaks to her.

She should desire nothing, seek for nothing, and wish for nothing, in order to be every moment disposed to acquiesce perfectly and lovingly to the designs of God.[2]

RESOLUTIONS OF RETREAT, AUGUST, 1894

To be careful to do at each moment what I believe to be most perfect according as the Rule or my duty indicates, endeavouring to perform acts of virtue as they present themselves ;

to see one thing only, namely, God ; and to walk without looking to the right or to the left, to the future or to the past ;

to sink down into, to be immersed, and to lose myself in the Divine Will, to see its direction in every event.[3]

2. I WISH TO LIVE BY THY WILL

O my God, my Creator, and my Father, I wish to live by Thy Will, I wish to act only through Thy Will, to think only in Thy Will, to speak only according to Thy Will, to desire nothing outside of Thy Will.

In submission to Thy Holy Will I wish to be what Thou wishest me to be, and, at each moment to take from Thy Will the portion of nourishment necessary for the life of my soul.

I wish to love Thy adorable Will above everything else, immolating my will in order to offer a sacrifice of adoration and praise.

The will in man is his most private and personal possession ; a man's will is the man himself ! In like manner Thy Will, O my God, is what is most elevated and divine in Thee ; Thy Will is

---

[1] Conference to the Sisters 6-7-1907.
[2] Intimate Notes : 1-10-1892.
[3] Intimate Notes : Aug. 1894.

Thyself ; it is Thy most intimate possession.   It is this most personal and most divine possession of Thine that I wish to love and adore, to which I wish to sacrifice myself.

I wish to love Thy Will under all the forms in which it clothes itself, I wish to search for it and to discover it in everything.   I wish to love it, no matter what way it may manifest itself to me, whether in suffering or in joy.   I wish to approve of it always, to make it accepted by others, to defend it, to embrace it with all the affection of my soul, to seek to make it loved, respected, approved of and praised.

O most sweet Will of God, what pain it causes me, and how I suffer when I hear Thee blamed, when I see creatures born of Thee, formed and sustained by Thee, who seem to doubt Thy wisdom and Thy goodness !

My God, I believe that Thou art Love, I believe that Thy will is the expression of Thy love ; I entrust myself to Thy love.   By withdrawing everything from me, Thou dost multiply around me occasions for sacrificing myself ; but where would my confidence in Thee be, if, when Thou takest away from me the helps which, in Thy bounty, Thou hast given to me, I were to be troubled and uneasy !   Thou dost, it is true, take away from me human support and I remain alone, afflicted by fear, assailed by temptation, but there still remains for me a divine support !   Yes, Thou remainest with me, my God, and if sometimes it seems to me that my infidelities drive Thee away, that my weakness disgusts Thee, that my sins repel Thee, then, O Thou Who art Holiness itself, Thy Mercy cometh to me !

Mercy incarnate, loving Mercy, Jesus the Faithful, is there ; what have I to fear ?

The more bonds Thou breakest in us, O my God, the more our liberty increases ; the more Thou dost strip us of creatures, the more Thou dost clothe us with Thyself, O God-Love, O Will of love, I wish to love Thee in life and in death, to love Thee when Thou dost lavish Thy gifts on me, to love Thee when Thou dost withdraw everything from me.

I wish to love Thee when Thou dost break my heart, to love Thee in tears, always to love Thee ![1]

---

[1] Intimate Notes : 13-5-1901.

3. THE WILL OF GOD IS ALL GOD

To our first duty of praise is joined that of perfect submission to the divine will. And this is the praise of God by means of acts, praise much better than that of words and sentiments, praise, without which, the preceding will have no value. To say : " Lord, Lord " is good ; but it is not sufficient, we must do the will of our Lord and Master. This is true praise, because it leads us to the most irrefutable proof of love and even to sacrifice. In the holy disposition which triumphs over selfishness, the only incentive to our determination is the wish to please God by the complete submission of our will to His. The use of the things of this world is regulated for us in the divine law and is always directed to the service of God and to His glory.

A certain author has said : " The will of man is all man." In the same way we may say :" The Will of God is all God." God lives interiorly in each act of His adorable Will, and each time that His Will is manifested to us, it is for us a living manifestation of God, before which we should fall on our knees.

But the divine Will, because it is infinitely holy, just and right often runs counter to our human nature. It imposes sacrifices on us, it crucifies us by putting itself in opposition to our own will and our own natural attractions. That is why our lower nature resists it and sometimes even rebels against it, although our souls illuminated by faith recognise this Divine Will to be worthy of homage and of our interior submission.

But if we are fully persuaded that the Will of God is God Himself, God with His power, His wisdom, and His infinite goodness, how can we fail to welcome it with respect, with joy, and with love ? With respect, because God being omnipotent, I cannot do other than submit myself to Him ; with joy, because the Divine Will being the will of uncreated Wisdom, I am sure of being on the right path in following it ; with love, because this will being the will of the Being Who loves me with an infinite love, it cannot be other than beneficial for me.

Let us then love the Will of God, let us love only it. Let us learn to discover it under the veils with which it often surrounds itself in order to test the firmness of our faith and the clear-sightedness of our love.

In the events which affect us, in the acts of our neighbour which,

as it were, strike against us, in the sufferings of body and soul which
break our hearts, let us recognise the Will of God always just, always
holy, always infinitely good, because it comes from the heart of the
best of fathers.

We make this praise ascend to God, we render this glory to Him,
as often as, raising ourselves above ourselves and our human judgments, we adhere lovingly to every act of the Divine Will.[1]

4. NOT TO WISH FOR ANYTHING ELSE BUT THE WILL OF GOD

We should love suffering principally for three ends : in the first
place, because it quells the revolts of the flesh and weakens the force
of our passions ; in the second place, because it expiates our sins and,
through that, obtains for us eternal life ; in the third place, because
it renders us conformable to Jesus Christ and thus pleasing to His
heavenly Father.

Now, if we love suffering for the effects it produces, which are
to repress and conquer the passions, we should love the suffering
which comes from sickness as much as that which is produced by
hair-shirts and disciplines, because it weakens the strength of the
body to the same degree and even more. If we loved it because it
is a just expiation, the suffering from sickness, being very much
opposed to our will and very humiliating, would expiate our sins as
well as voluntary suffering.

Finally, we should love sickness because it renders us conformable
to Jesus Christ. Oh ! how we should love the sufferings of sickness
which by afflicting all our members, making them endure violent
pain, and making us walk with tottering step, renders us truly like
Jesus Christ crucified, crowned with thorns and bending beneath
the weight of the cross.

But if we loved the adorable Will of God above all things, and if
we knew the value of sacrifice and humiliation, how much we would
cherish this state of suffering which comes to us so directly from God,
which inflicts so many privations on us, and which places us in such
a humiliating state of powerlessness.

The greater part of our griefs and vexations and annoyances come
from no other source than that we have a personal will with very
positive likes and dislikes. If we could only arrive at this happy

---

[1] Conference to the Sisters : 12-10-1910.

point of having no likes and dislikes, we would, with one stroke, dry up the source of all our miseries.

To wish for nothing but the sovereign Will of God, to desire only that it be accomplished, to see in everything the palpable, direct action of God, to believe that this invisible and divine Mover acts always under the influence of incomparable love ;—these are the sentiments which should replace in us the operations of a will without light and without power.

If I wish to accomplish the Will of God alone and please my God, why should I be less happy in the isolation, humiliation and suffering caused by sickness, than in the activity of a life filled with works of zeal and in the exact practice of the Rule? If I prefer one state to the other, it can only be from some natural motive, from dislike for suffering, from horror of all that humiliates me or from the natural eagerness for action and movement.

What matters it to be here or there, what matters it to be doing this work or that, what matters it to have a life filled with useful works, or devoid of all that appears to the eyes of men? One day, soon, the voice of the Spouse will come and whisper in my ear : " Arise !" He will come and take me from a bed of sorrow as well as from a feast of joy.

The last act of the Will of God over my being, body and soul, will be my death ; in this, the Divine Will will affirm its rights over me ; it will show in that the supremacy which it has over my weak creature-will ; it will show the power it has to command me ; and if I have not loved the Divine Will during life, if I have not submitted myself to it, it will exercise its just vengeance over me.

O Will of love, O amiable Will, I wish to love Thee before being able to understand Thee, in order that, one day when I meet Thee face to face, Thou mayest recognise in me Thy faithful servant.[1]

O my God, Thy Will, nothing but Thy Will ! I wish for nothing, I desire for nothing but only to obey Thee in all things.

Do with me according to Thy good pleasure, take complete possession of my heart and of my whole being ; by this Communion I put myself without reserve in Thy hands ; command as Master in Thy own domain ; destroy, break, uproot, act with me according to Thy Divine Will ; all my endeavour shall be to follow the inspiration of Thy grace and to obey Thee and my Superiors in all things.[2]

[1] Intimate Notes : 18-6-1895.
[2] Intimate Notes : 23-3-1893.

5. O JESUS, I WISH TO LOVE ALL THAT THOU WILT DO

I kiss lovingly this divine hand which to-day gives me joy; to-morrow, if it contains sorrow, I shall kiss it again !

O my sweet Mercy, O Jesus, I do not know what Thou wishest to do, but I wish to love all that Thou wilt do. I love to see Thee command, arrange and dispose all things. I love to see Thee act as my Master ; my Jesus, that is Thy divine right, exercise it, exercise Thy holy Will all full of love over me and for me and around me.[1]

6. IF WE FOLLOW THE DIVINE WILL, WE SHALL NOT GO ASTRAY

I will first fix firmly in my soul the certainty which I have obtained in this retreat that I am certainly following the Will of God in leaving the world and embracing the religious life : by this firm certainty about the Will of God, I will repel with all my strength, temptations of discouragement, repugnances, fears, and this thought which the devil puts so often in my mind that I am incapable of devoting myself to the perfect life, that I am commencing a work of sanctification which I am not able to finish, and that I would do well to abandon all.[2]

7. WE SHOULD FULFIL AT THE PRESENT MOMENT WHAT GOD WILLS

What matters it whether we are this person or that, whether we do this thing or that : God, Whose eyes are ever upon us, takes account only of the interior dispositions of our souls.   And while He occupies Himself in giving us the grace necessary for what we are doing at the present moment, we should occupy ourselves in fulfilling what is commanded.

It is extremely painful to see that we often lose a good part of the merits of our labours, of our mortifications, of our works, because, in part, we substitute our own wills for the Will of God.   How much more advantageous it would be for us if, in every act we perform

---

[1] Intimate Notes : 29-3-1893.
[2] Intimate Notes : May 1891.

under obedience, we put ourselves in that disposition of detachment
and of religious indifference to which our vocation calls us.[1]

8.   LET US AWAIT GOD'S WILL IN PEACE

I am not troubling myself about anything, I assure you, either
about what people may say or what they may think about me.

Let us allow the storm to pass, Father; whatever is from
creatures, whatever is merely external, lasts only for a time and can
do very little against the works of God.   If this foundation is willed
by Our Lord, He will be able to preserve it, and if it is not willed by
Him, we do not want it either.   I am completely tranquil about all
that comes from the exterior, but for the interior of our little foundation, I wish that the pure spirit of charity and humility be established
there.   Accordingly, I am inflexible in certain cases and I think
that it is my duty.[2]

" May the good Master do what is His holy Will; whatever it
may be, we will bless Him for everything.   The more He deprives
us of everything, the more He will become our only riches, and the
more we wish to love Him.   After two and a half years we find
ourselves without a roof to shelter our dear family, but we will
always have His Sacred Heart to lodge us all.   I have before me,
Father, to the end of my three years of office, a future of cares without number, and sometimes I feel the weight of my burden.   Happily,
Jesus is with me and I count on Him,—and on your good prayers
also, Father."[3]

9.   I WISH TO DO THY WILL IN ALL THINGS IN ORDER TO GIVE PROOF OF MY LOVE

O Jesus, my beloved, my Saviour, and my Master, I put myself
completely into Thy powerful and merciful hands.   I wish to do
Thy holy Will in all things, in order to give Thee a proof of my love.
O Lord, since Thou art my Saviour, Thou knowest better than I
what I must do to be saved; and then, since Thou art my Master,
I wish to obey Thee in all things, like a perfectly faithful servant.
I will take away from my soul all the desires that I may have, whether
they appear to me holy or profane; I do not wish even to ask of

---

[1] Conference to the Sisters : 14-9-1907.
[2] Letter to Father Charrier : 12-5-1914.
[3] Letter to Father Charrier : March 9th, 1908.

Thee the only grace which I desire eagerly, and that is to consecrate myself entirely to Thee. Do with me and in me as Thou
wishest, O Lord.[1]

10. I ACCEPT THY WILL IN EVERYTHING WITHOUT RESERVE

I have felt myself attracted to the practice of exact obedience
not only to Thee, O my Master, but to Thy creatures, to those
especially who represent Thee in my regard.

I am powerless to bring forth any good fruit, or to direct myself ;
enlighten, O Lord, those whom I wish to obey as if it were Thyself ;
teach them what is necessary for my soul, in order that when obeying
their voice, it may be Thine that I will obey. O Jesus ! I would
wish to sleep, to sleep on Thy Heart ; to sleep long in Thy arms ;
no more to see evil, no more to see the world, no more to see my own
corruption ; to see Thee alone so divine, so loving, so pure, so great,
so generous ! I would wish to see only Thee, to occupy myself
with Thee alone ; everything else is a burden to me and makes me
suffer ; draw me to Thee, O Lord !

If Thou wishest that my body should suffer, expiate and merit
for a long term on the earth, at least let my soul and its powers
abide in Thee, but rather do what Thou wishest. I accept all,
O Lord ; I give myself to Thee without reserve, renouncing every
desire and every request.[2]

RELIGIOUS OBEDIENCE IS A PERFECT SACRIFICE

*The following beautiful conference on religious obedience was addressed
to the Sisters of the Visitation in exile, but everyone, even people in the world
can adapt it to their state of life, for all, from children up, have superiors
both in the natural and supernatural order, and obedience to them, because
they represent God, is the most pleasing holocaust that they can offer God,
and the most sanctifying practice for their souls.*

11. RELIGIOUS OBEDIENCE IS A PERFECT SACRIFICE

The obedient man, says the Sacred Scripture, will gain the victory.
It is a well-known truth that the devil can have no power over an

---

[1] Intimate Notes : 1890.
[2] Intimate Notes : 1892.

obedient heart, provided the obedience is perfect. The soul of a Religious, if it wishes to belong to God, must allow itself to be formed and sculptured by obedience, which is for it the will of God ; it must, so to speak, be cast in that divine mould, in order that it assume the form which the divine Artist wishes it to have.

Obedience should be the distinctive and necessary characteristic of the consecrated soul. The soul cannot belong to God if it belongs to itself ; now it still belongs to itself if its obedience is not perfect, if it is attached to its own judgments, its own tastes, its own views, if it gives only half obedience, if it limits the obedience to make it fit its own ideas, if it reasons according to human standards. The divine will manifested by means of obedience wishes to be followed without restriction. It is easy to obey when the obedience is pleasing and when the reason approves of it ; but such obedience, measured in this way and submitted to human reasoning, is the rejection of the interior life. This virtue, in order to be supernatural and heroic, must be above reason and often against reason.

The sacrifice of the human judgment and the human will to the Divine Wisdom and the Divine Will is the most perfect gift that a creature can make to its Creator, and this complete renunciation of oneself often works prodigies. Supernatural obedience, like an emanation from heaven, elevates the soul, develops its faculties and even augments its capacity ; in fact, people of very ordinary minds and intellects who would have remained all their lives in the state of mediocrity, once they have surrendered to grace and obedience, begin to expand and to develop their faculties and become capable of carrying out most difficult and arduous works, so powerful is the divine, reforming action to operate new creations.

To practise humility in its highest form, we should never consider the creature directly, but always God. If we act differently, human reasoning will very quickly weaken obedience, and it will then become something vulgar and common in spite of the grace of the first order which we have received and which should raise us to the perfection of total renunciation. The centre of life is God : Life can only come from that centre ; it is from Him that come the activity and vigour which diffuse themselves in the members. In the hierarchical order, God is the first Superior ; your Superioress, who derives her position from God, is a consequence of that hierarchial order and should represent God Himself in it. It is the Superioress, it is her words, which are the living rule, and it belongs to her to explain it and make it understood by all, and have it practised by all according to the will of God. If this were not so, there would very soon be chaos in religious communities. How easy it would be for every particular mind, for every particular person to give to the rule his or her own personal colouring according to his or her own tastes and inclinations. True unity would be destroyed and each one would try to make himself or herself right and all the others wrong.

And let us take careful note of this : was it not private judgment that has given rise to all the heresies in the Church? It was erroneous interpretations, peculiar ideas, wrong ways of viewing and explaining the truth, which have adulterated the Divine Truth.

But is it not also heretical in matters of religious life to try to give to our own rules the interpretation which pleases us, to wish to interpret them according to our own tastes, to attempt to adapt them to our own thoughts?

Now to keep ourselves removed from that evil, it is necessary to see only God in our own Superiors and to act with blind obedience without considering anything and without discussion.

When I say discussion, I mean not only discussion in words, but also interior discussion. And indeed what is the use of a docile and submissive exterior if, in the bottom of the heart, there are discussions and judgments passed on what is commanded? Often there is apparent obedience because what has been commanded has been carried out, but the interior conflicts and agitations that result from human reasoning, human views and considerations prove clearly that the obedience is not perfect.

To render our obedience perfect, we must have interior docility, we must give our hearts ; we must, I repeat, see God and none other in our Superiors. If you seek God you will find God. If you seek man you will find only man. Your Superioress will act vainly towards you in a supernatural manner if you yourselves are not inspired with those divine sentiments ; you will again find man, miserable, and weak. Seek God : do with regard to obedience what you do with regard to the Blessed Eucharist : when you receive Holy Communion you do not look to see whether the Particle which is given to you is big or small, complete or broken ; you do not look at its form, you look at God. And in like manner, in the sacrifice of the Mass, you do not consider whether the priest who celebrates is learned or unlearned, you consider only God. So therefore do not consider whether those who command you are pleasing to you or not, whether they are talented, capable, charming or such like ; again I say, consider only God.

Obedience practised in this manner adds such greatness to the soul that, of beings of the most ordinary kind, it makes heavenly beings, because it is the property of this virtue to make divine. It may be said of an obedient soul that it is like the tree of which the Prophet speaks that being planted on the bank of a running stream: it never ceases to send forth branches and bear fruit in season. Thus this soul never ceases to grow in stature, to raise itself towards heaven, and in season bears the delicious fruits of most eminent virtue ; it progresses ever from conquest to conquest, from victory to victory, even to perfection, to the consummation of love in eternity.[1]

Love for the will of God leads the soul to abandon itself completely to the designs of God, to lose itself, as it were, in the divine Will, sacrificing its own desires and preferences.

The act of abandonment to the Will of God is most pleasing to God, for it opens the heart to Him so that He can pour into it the abundance of His love, and the soul allows itself to be loved by God, Who takes more pleasure in loving than in being loved.

12. WE SHOULD ALLOW OURSELVES TO BE LOVED BY GOD

The light which I received on this question gave me an ardent desire to increase in myself the little love which I have for my God ; but I feel that He wishes me to be more passive than active in love, more free to receive than to exert myself to give ; all the more so because what I would be able to give is nothing, and would not be capable of giving satisfaction to God, while He finds His contentment in pouring out into souls what abounds in Himself.

To love God is very sweet, to allow oneself to be loved by God is sometimes very hard for our human nature to bear ; but God takes more pleasure in loving than in being loved ; we must give the pleasure to God of allowing ourselves to be loved by Him, and of remaining motionless in His arms, ready to receive everything, to do everything, and to endure everything.[2]

---

[1] Conference to the Sisters : Undated.
[2] Intimate Notes : 26-10-1895.

13. LOVE WHICH REGARDS GOD IS ABANDONMENT TO HIS WILL

Humility towards God consists in receiving troubles, sufferings, contumely as things that are due to us, as things which we expect, and which we receive without astonishment or revolt; and in receiving consolations, graces, favours, joys and prosperity as pure gifts which God is in no way bound to give us, which He can withdraw when He pleases, without taking from us anything that is our own, or without our having the right to complain. Our whole spiritual life should be impregnated with humility towards God, and meekness of heart towards our neighbours. Humility towards God corresponds to abandonment; meekness of heart is charity with all its sweet and delicate attention.

All virtue can be summed up in abandonment and charity, because these are two forms of love, and lead to perfect love. Yes, love has two faces; the one which regards God is abandonment, the one which regards creatures is charity.[1]

14. THE ACT OF ABANDONMENT GIVES GOD, NOT NEW RIGHTS, BUT GREATER LIBERTY OF ACTION OVER US

I understood that the voluntary act of abandonment gives God, not new rights over His creatures, but greater liberty of action; that the creature should, therefore, rely on God for everything, see God in everything that happens, and not only acquiesce in the Divine Will, not only make its judgment confess that the Will of God is always equally good, but even to turn oneself away from the visible event to see God alone.

I understand that the soul which abandons itself should not voluntarily dwell on worries, regrets, anxieties about the future, or desires which might arise over the past, the present, or the future, but at each moment, remain under the divine action, without formal act of the will, without ardent desires, simply waiting for the Divine Will.[2]

---

[1] Intimate Notes : 1899.
[2] Intimate Notes : July, 1895.

15. VOW OF ABANDONMENT

Before and during the retreat I had the idea that I might be able to make a certain vow of abandonment to God in my troubles.

My divine Saviour, in order to correspond with the inspirations of Thy grace, to enter on this crucifying way that Thou hast pointed out for me during this retreat, and in order to allow my love to exercise its action freely in me, I make, with the authorization of the Rev. Mother and for the time marked out for me by obedience, a vow of total abandonment to the mercy of Thy Sacred Heart.

This vow will consist in turning away my mind and making an act of abandonment immediately I perceive that I am in one of the four following states ; and in renewing this act as many times as it will be necessary : (1) When feeling my passions stirred up in the depths of my soul, and knowing my weakness, I see hell opened up before me and drawing me towards its abyss ;

(2) When I receive some special lights, consolations or graces whether at prayer, or at other times, and when I am afraid of illusion ;

(3) When I am in a state of destitution, of darkness, and of interior anguish : When God seems to be very far away ;

(4) When, before Holy Communion, I am seized with fear at the sight of my own corruption ; with fear that in eating this adorable flesh, that I am eating my own judgment and condemnation .

This vow will not bind me under pain of sin ; it is a vow of love, made through love to love.

If it happen that in some extraordinary circumstances, this vow causes me trouble and uneasiness, increases my pains, or gives rise to scruples of conscience, my Superioress in whose hands I make this vow, can relieve me of it.[1]

16. FORMULA OF THE VOW OF ABANDONMENT

O My God, prostrate in Thy divine presence, I adore Thy infinite perfection, I adore Thy Will always equally good, I adore Thy sovereign dominion over all Thy creatures, and in order to recognise Thy dominion over me, I make a vow of total abandonment of my whole being into Thy hands, allowing Thee to dispose

---

[1] Intimate Notes : Nov. 1893.

of me according to Thy good pleasure, for time and for eternity.

O Jesus, I abandon myself without reserve to Thy divine Heart giving Thy love entire liberty of action in me and around me, wishing to see only Thy action in all things and to adore every disposition of Thy will.

Receive this vow, O my Saviour, as a profession of my love ; receive the abandonment which I make to Thee of every formal exercise of my will, of everything that concerns myself, of every anxiety about the past and the future, and grant me the grace to be faithful in accomplishing it all the days of my life. I place this vow under the protection of the Blessed Virgin Mary, of our holy Founders, of my special protectors, of my holy Angel Guardian and I ask them to obtain for me from the divine bounty the grace of perfect abandonment to His adorable will.

Made today, with the permission of my confessor and the approbation of our Rev. Mother, who can dispense me from the obligation which I contract if they judge it useful for the good of my soul so to do.[1]

17. THE WAY OF LOVING ABANDONMENT TO THE WILL OF GOD

The way which Thou dost point out to me, O Lord, is holy indifference and loving abandonment to Thy Holy Will. I feel that this is the way along which Thou wishest to lead my soul. I see the proof of this in the endless resistance made by my rebellious nature, and especially in the constant opposition of the devil. If he raises such opposition and endeavours in so many ways to turn me away from this path, it is doubtless because it is the path that leads to the salvation and life of my soul.

All my faults are the result of my resistance to the inspirations of God. If a trifle discourages me, if a fault astonishes me, if a humiliation disconcerts me, the reason is that I have not holy indifference for all the creatures and vanities of this world. By indifference, I shall conquer pride ; by it I shall overcome discouragement, by it I shall live for God, with God, and in God.[2]

---

[1] Intimate Notes : 2-8-1895.
[2] Intimate Notes : May, 1891.

18. I KNOW THAT THOU HAST A WORK FOR ME TO DO

O Jesus, how admirable and holy are Thy ways ; all that Thou dost in us and for us is for our good !   We need only allow Thee to act ; we can close our eyes and abandon ourselves to Thee without reserve.

When it pleases Thee, O Lord, to reveal to me some of the secrets of Thy Providence and to uncover to my eyes the hidden wheels which rule Thy divine movements, my soul can only admire and adore in silence.   Oh ! how I desire at such times to remove the obstacles which might hinder Thy divine operations in me !

What are Thy designs over me ?   I know not ;   I know, however, that Thou hast a work for me to do, I know that I shall find salvation and life in accomplishing it ; but I know also, and I feel that if a single act of infidelity were to stop Thy work, and suspend, even for a moment, the course of Thy grace, I might fall miserably.

O Jesus, Jesus, help me !   Thou dost ask much of me and I feel myself so weak.   I appear before Thee devoid of everything, without strength, without will.   That is the very source from which my courage springs ; the less I can do of myself, the more Thou wilt do ; the less will I have of my own, the more Thou wilt reign over me.   The void attracts ; the more I shall be deprived of all things, the stronger and more powerful will be Thy grace.

O my God, I renounce every act of my own will, in order that Thy Will may dominate and direct everything in me.   I renounce all personal desires and inclinations, in order to follow the interior inspiration of Thy grace.   I renounce all worry over the state of my soul, placing the past, the present and the future in Thy Sacred Heart.

I renounce all indiscreet eagerness about attaining to perfection, resigning myself to imperfection and powerlessness for good, if Thou dost permit it thus.

I renounce all natural activity and the desire to act, and I accept all the physical powerlessness and weakness and abjection which Thou mayst be pleased to send me.   I renounce every desire to be or appear something of consequence, whether by virtue, or by talents, or by employments, and I consent to be a useless person, a burden to all, and unwanted everywhere, if Thou dost demand that of me.

I put the direction of my soul into the hands of my Superiors and Confessors, and I renounce every idea I have about the way my soul should be directed.

I accept in advance all the states through which it may please God to make me pass, and I abandon myself completely both in body and in soul, for time and for eternity, to the infinite mercy of our Lord.

O Jesus, My Saviour, tomorrow the sun of the radiant day of my profession will arise. Tomorrow I shall become really and publicly Thy spouse. Thou wilt be all mine, and I shall be all Thine. Yes, grant that I may be completely and entirely Thine ; do not permit that I should give to creatures what belongs to Thee ; do not permit me to become attached to anything earthly and to become separated from Thee.

During these holy exercises I understood that God had special designs over my soul. What were these designs ? I knew not. I was troubled by the thought of what these hidden designs might be, and I went forward trembling. However, I abandoned myself to Jesus, and I offered myself for all the sufferings and trials which He had destined for me. I renewed my confidence in His infinite goodness ; I felt confident that, since God Himself had led me into the religious life, He would certainly give me the graces necessary to be faithful.[1]

19. TO SEE ONLY JESUS

In the divine Being there is neither change nor the shadow of vicissitude. What consolation, what repose for the soul amidst the incessant changes and the upheavals which are constantly recurring in this world ! Amidst the uninterrupted succession of various events, it can repose on the Immutable and the Eternal !

Our dear Religious Family is on the eve of one of those changes which, although periodic and foreseen, is, in a human sense, none the less full of uncertainty and painful for many.

Let us ascend in spirit to the Father of light in Whom there is never any change for us, and let us reanimate in ourselves the spirit of faith. Let us consider that all legitimate authority comes from God, that it is God Himself Who will rule us by means of the visible instruments which He will use, and the external form will disappear

---

[1] Intimate Notes : Oct., 1892.

to our eyes and we shall see in the person chosen by God only " Jesus alone."

There will then be for us no more vicissitudes : Jesus yesterday Jesus to-day, Jesus to-morrow, Jesus always, under a form more or less attractive to our human nature, under an appearance more or less perfect, but Jesus, God and Man, living under a poor disguise, Who directs us Himself, by the ways that are most advantageous for us, towards the perfection of virtue, the possession of eternal glory.[1]

20. I ABANDON MYSELF TO THE HEART OF THE GOOD MASTER

I believe that it is Jesus Who had permitted all and arranged all for His glory and for the realization of His Work of Love. For my part, I will have suffering and humiliation ; it is indeed the part that I should desire, the only part that suits my misery and my weakness.

All this is good and I would not wish to have things or persons otherwise.

You have found Monsignor well disposed towards the Work ; that is something to make our hearts glad. For as to what is to happen to me in the future, I abandon myself to the Heart of our dear, good Master. It is a little hard for poor human nature to see oneself thus without refuge and without roof, in the most complete uncertainty for the morrow ; but for the soul this is excellent, and conduces powerfully to detach us from earthly things and to sanctify us. It is a kind of poverty to which I had never thought before that I would be called, and which delights me. You know that poverty has always been the virtue dearest to my heart ; I would never have dared to hope for this form of it. You see that Jesus is very good to serve me according to my taste. Help me, however, with your good prayers to make good use of this favour from the good Master.[2]

21. GOD WILL ACCOMPLISH IN ME WHAT I AM INCAPABLE OF DOING

I am making this retreat in profound peace, in complete repose of soul in God. This, however, is not due to the fact that sources

---

[1] Conference to the Sisters : 25-4-1913.
[2] Letter to Father Charrier : 3-9-1913.

of worry are lacking; on the contrary, I can see in the not
distant future many troubles and labours and crosses waiting
for me; it is because I feel so vividly that Our Lord is with me!
I cannot help entrusting myself to Him, abandoning myself to Him.
It seems to me—I do not know whether I am mistaken—that this
profound calm which my soul enjoys is given to me by Our Lord
as a preparation for a multitude of cares, business worries and complications of every kind which are to follow; but even this thought
does not trouble me in the least.   I have a great inward certainty
that it is God Himself Who has placed me in this position of authority
which I occupy, all the more so because, according to all human
probabilities, this could not have been. God knows well my pitiable
plight, my ignorance, my physical and moral incapacity, my powerlessness of every kind.   If then He has given me this office, it is
because He Himself is to see to the accomplishment of what I am
incapable of doing, and that the end which He has in view cannot
be other than His own glory.[1]

22. IT IS JESUS WHO HAS DONE IT; IT IS THEREFORE GOOD

When the election was finished, the good Father said that he was
going to announce to us with joy the choice of Our Lord; then he
mentioned my name.   Ah! Father, how can I describe to you what
passed in my soul; my breast heaved and I gave three sobs; I thought
that I was going to die.   Soon the tears burst forth, without my being
able to stop them.   Scarcely had I begun to read the Profession of
Faith, when I felt that God had taken possession of me completely;
my soul was filled with strength; I continued the holy words of the
Profession of Faith in a firm voice, without seeing anything around
me. Our Lord was present!   But at the end, when I came to the
last words: " So help me God and these Holy Gospels," this divine
presence veiled itself and my tears began to flow again.

My inner feeling was this : It is Jesus Who has done it ; then it is
good.   I wish it also.   I have confidence in Him and I abandon
myself.   At a quarter past nine all was finished; Jesus had made
me the Mother of this dear family.   My heart was and is from that
hour, filled with this maternal tenderness which I feel descending
from the adorable Heart of Jesus into mine.   It is by the Heart of

---

[1] Intimate Notes : 10-8-1907.

the Master that I love each of these souls, and I understand that He has placed me in this position in order to make these souls ascend to His Heart by bearing them in mine. Help me, Father, to do in all things this work of Love for which alone I exist.[1]

23. ABANDONMENT TO GOD'S WILL

This evening at prayer, Our Lord made me taste the bitterness of the sacrifice which He is preparing for me. No matter how things turn out, the cross awaits me at the end of the year.

The upper part of my soul adheres to God and finds peace in constantly renewed abandonment, but the lower part is in agony. I see nothing, I can do nothing, I walk in the dark ; everything seems to me to be full of dangers.

My God, I would have been happy if Thou hadst given me the aid of Thy very faithful servant, but I do not wish for anything but what Thou hast willed ; I know that Thou art pleased at seeing souls making themselves independent of all created things and repose in Thee alone ; therefore, I shut my eyes and abandon myself to Thee in suffering, in fear, in anguish, in uncertainty, and in tears ![2]

24. HOW CAN WE BE AFRAID ON THE BOSOM OF LOVE AND MERCY ?

The day before yesterday, I received a special light about the detachment of heart which Our Lord requires of me ; on seeing the effort I would have to make to arrive at it, I could only abandon myself to God, and pray to Our Lord to work the change in me.

Since it has pleased divine Goodness to restore me to life, I ought consecrate my life to holy love. Even if my heart were melted and immolated to love, that would not be sufficient to express the gratitude which I owe to God for the love which He shows me. In the midst of the sufferings of that illness, when I could not pray, nor hardly think, I felt the Infinite Love of God enveloping me on all sides like a mantle.

It seemed as if God were saying to me : " I am now free to deal with this creature of Mine as I desire." And, when renewing my vow of abandonment, I found inexpressible peace and sweetness in

---

[1] Letter to Father Charrier : 23-5-1907.
[2] Intimate Notes : May, 1900.

always giving to God more liberty and in lending myself to His divine projects without resistance.   At the time when scarcely a quarter of an hour separated me from death, I saw my misery to be so profound, so incurable, I saw myself so completely powerless to do the least thing for my own salvation, that I had no other thought or inclination but to throw myself into God's arms ; there I had no fear.

How could we be afraid on the bosom of mercy and love ?   If our eternity depended on any other but God, we might indeed fear, but with Him !   Would He have created us that we might be lost ?   How wrongly we judge of the Heart of God if we think that He could take His pleasure in making us suffer eternally !

The whole scheme of the Redemption rests on the foundation of the love of God for men ; the love of the Father Who immolates His only Son, the love of Jesus Christ Who voluntarily made Himself a Victim.

There should also be a love in the creature to correspond with this ; now love does not fear, it trusts.[1]

25. I ACCEPT IN ADVANCE THE KIND OF DEATH THAT GOD HAS DESTINED FOR ME

I was meditating on death yesterday, and I thought that there were two kinds of death which I would like.   The first would be to die of some malady in our dear monastery, surrounded by our Sisters ; having Father beside me in order to teach me to die, to absolve me, to bless me and at that moment to offer me to Jesus as a little victim, very unworthy, it is true, but completely given and sacrificed for my dear priests.

The second would be (I would like this kind also, I would even prefer it) to die under the axe or by a bullet in a time of persecution, after the rigours of prison, and in the midst of a crowd who would heap insults on me.   I feel myself completely unworthy of this death so like that of my Divine Master ; but I would like it, I desire it, I would wish it, in order to be like Jesus.   After considering these things, I thought that, perhaps neither of these deaths would be given to me.   Then I made the sacrifice of all these desires to Jesus, and I accepted in advance, with my whole will and heart,

[1] Intimate Notes : 21-11-1895.

and wished for the kind of death which it will please God to ordain for me. Yes, I wish for, and I love, all that Thou wishest for me, Divine Jesus ; but with the confidence of a little child towards its mother, I tell Thee what I would like ; it would be sweet for me to pass from the hands of Father into Thine : it would be good for me to pass from the ignominy and abandonment of the scaffold into the joy of seeing Thee face to face. What is sweet to me what is above all good for me is to abandon myself to Infinite Love and to live only by love, in order to die for Love and in Love :[1]

26. " OUT OF THE DEPTHS I HAVE CRIED TO THEE "

I come to Thee, my Jesus, I trust myself and abandon myself to Thee, have pity on me, help me ; the night envelops me, I am afraid of myself, I am afraid of everything ; do not abandon me.[2]

27. MAY THE DIVINE WILL BE DONE IN ME

On the day after the retreat, I remained under this impression of desire for love, but afterwards I felt that I had entered on the way which Our Lord had pointed out to me : a way of self-annihil-ation ; I saw nothing ; I felt nothing ; I did not suffer as during the retreat ; however, I had not this sweet interior feeling that suffering gives ; it was annihilation, death to everything sensible, a kind of interior want of all things. Since that time, my disposi-tions have been : to abandon myself, to apply myself to the rule, to the practice of the virtues as occasion demands : May the divine Will be done in me ![3]

28. NOTHING CAN COME FROM THE LOVING HEART OF JESUS BUT GRACE AND MERCY

O my adorable Master, I bless Thee and I love Thee in Thy severity, for I believe that nothing can come from Thy loving Heart but grace and love.

I offer Thee my sufferings, I offer Thee these privations so pain-ful to the soul, this state of separation which goes on increasing,

---

[1] Intimate Notes : April, 1904.
[2] Intimate Notes : August, 1894.
[3] Intimate Notes : Nov. 1893.

hollowing out as it were, an abyss by which I see myself isolated from every creature.

Thou Thyself, my Saviour, seemest to me so far away in these infinite heights where I cannot reach Thee, that cold envelops my heart and sorrow strangles it. The more I am surrounded with creatures, the more solitary I feel, and this impression of isolation is never so strong as in the midst of people enjoying themselves or engaged in conversation. In the solitude of the cell and in the silence of prayer I feel it less keenly.

O my God, I adore Thee, I adore Thy hand which rends and burns and I abandon myself to Thee.[1]

29. WE SHOULD BE LIKE CHRIST, RESIGNED TO SUFFER FROM OTHERS

Our Lord showed me how we must allow God to act in us ; in His Passion He endured everything, but He did not do anything by Himself. He did not crucify Himself ; He did not tear off His garments which adhered to His wounds, but He allowed them to be torn off ; He consented to experience all kinds of weakness, bitterness and anguish : He did not give to Himself the extraordinary ardour of love which He gave to some of the martyrs, and which, prevented them from feeling their sufferings.

In order to be like God, we must allow what happens to us to be done by Him and by His instruments ; we must suffer in fear, in weakness, and by acquiescence in the will of the Father only.[2]

30. WE SHOULD ALWAYS WELCOME THE CROSS WITH A SMILE

I wish you always to receive everything from My hands with a smile, and to accept without murmur the crosses that yiu meet with on your path of life. I wish you always to preserve peace of mind and holy joy and to trust in Me always. Whether the day brings sorrow or joy, be always found faithful to duty. I wish you to place yourself completely in My hands like a little child. I will know how to trace out your path for you and guide your hesitating steps.

---

[1] Intimate Notes : Dec. 1900.
[2] Intimate Notes : Aug. 1895.

Finally, in days of sadness as well as in days of joy, I wish you always to keep a smile of victory on your lips.[1]

31. WE SHOULD PUT OUR WHOLE TRUST IN OUR SAVIOUR, AND NOT DWELL TOO MUCH ON OUR OWN IMPERFECTIONS

I said to Our Lord : " My Jesus, must I examine myself more ; must I consider my imperfections more attentively ? " My most sweet Master replied to me : no, remain like a little child in my arms, on My Heart, in the hands of him to whom I have given you. "

Then He gave me to understand that although consideration of one's miseries, one's weakness, and all the details of one's actions, is a good means to acquire humility and contrition, nevertheless for me it would be better not to dwell on myself but rather to look at Our Lord. Looking deeply into myself might disturb the action of Love in me. It seems that Our Lord wishes that I be nothing at all, and that He do everything ; that is why I must not look at what is nothing ; I must not dwell on what is, so to speak, an accident without value.

Besides, if I were to dwell on myself ever so little, I would never have the courage to do, or say, or write what Our Lord wishes, and then I would not be faithful, and I would be still more miserable.[2]

32. I FELT MYSELF ENVELOPED BY THE SUPERNATURAL VIRTUE WHICH GOES OUT FROM JESUS

I have passed these four days of retreat in most sweet repose beside Jesus ; although invisible and almost completely silent, the adorable Master made His presence felt by me ; He was there quite near, and I reposed in Him with infinite confidence and abandonment full of love.

I felt myself enveloped by the supernatural virtue which goes out from Jesus ; I look at the past and I see so much love lavished by my Saviour on the multitude of my miseries, that my heart, pressed by the excess of divine Charity, seems to stop its movements and remain mute in adoration.

I look at the future and, without illusion as to the possible sufferings

---

[1] Intimate Notes : Dec. 1894.
[2] Intimate Notes : 18-10-1902.

and sacrifices, but without any fear or shadow of trouble, I embrace
the Divine Will always full of love and mercy.[1]

33. THY GOOD PLEASURE WILL BE MY ONLY JOY

Divine Infant, I wish to place myself in Thy hands as a toy, Thou
canst take me, O dear little Master, as Thy plaything. Whether
Thou shouldst press me between Thy little teeth or give me divine
caresses, all will be acceptable. At times Thou canst take me in
Thy arms to embrace me, at times Thou mayst stretch me under
Thy feet and tread on me. I am become Thy toy to satisfy Thee,
to make Thee happy. I will allow Thee to treat me just as Thou
willest and I will offer no resistance. Thy good pleasure will be
my only joy, my only happiness. It is Thou, dear Master, Who
hast taught me the way of abandonment, the way dear to Thy Heart.[2]

34. WE SHOULD BE PLIABLE AND DOCILE IN THE HANDS OF GOD

As for me, I am nothing and can do nothing; it is God-Infinite
Love which is all in all and which will accomplish His work of re-
generation and salvation. Shall we not allow Him to act, and shall
you or I place any obstacle to His designs? It seems to me that Our
Lord wishes that we should remain pliable in His hands and docile
to His wishes, in great simplicity and without allowing ourselves to
be stopped by cowardice or any human sentiment.[3]

35. GOD, WHO IS INFINITE WISDOM, DISPOSES ALL THINGS ACCORDING TO HIS WILL

I have come to understand, especially during these last two years,
that God, Whose wisdom is infinite, disposes all things that happen
according to His will, and that it is only our poor action which
prevents Him from attaining His ends strongly and sweetly. If we
could only will what God wills; if, pliable in His hands, we entered
into His designs for us, however painful they might be, without
resistance or fixed personal wishes, our sufferings would become
sweetened and transformed.

---

[1] Intimate Notes : 18-10-1902.
[2] Intimate Notes : Dec., 1895.
[3] Letter to Father Charrier : 10-12-1907.

As for me, I endeavour to go on from day to day according to the Divine Will, without knowing whither I am going. I expect still many sufferings and trials, many unexpected happenings, many complications and humiliations ; but I count on the grace of God for each occasion, which Jesus, Infinite Love, will not refuse to His spouse.[1]

36. PEACE OF SOUL IS THE FRUIT OF ABANDONMENT TO THE WILL OF GOD

On the first two days of the retreat, Divine Goodness established me in great peace.

I saw that I had not yet loved God, but I resolved to commence in earnest. I could see nothing in myself free from stain, but I was not troubled by that.

Our Lord showed me that this peace was the fruit of abandoning myself to Him, and that He would have left me no repose until I had made this vow.

This time I did not feel the indefinable need, as I had formerly, to take a decisive step, to throw myself with my eyes closed into the gulf ; I felt only an interior movement urging me to become indifferent to everything, in order that, when leaving the retreat, I should be content either to be stretched on a bed of pain, or to take part in works of zeal.[2]

37. HOW SWEET IT IS TO ABANDON ONESELF TO THE ADORABLE HEART OF JESUS

The adorable Heart of Jesus wishes to take possession of everything in me and to do everything ; that is why all human sentiments embarass Him. His wish is that there be nothing human in the heart in order that He may put into it what is divine.

I felt something in me which went forth from me and rushed with force towards God as towards its principle.

I would wish, in order to unite myself to the sovereign divinity which attracts me, to destroy this corrupt nature which is an obstacle, but my Saviour stops me and does not permit me to do any of these acts of loving folly.

---

[1] Letter to Father Charrier : 30-11-1911.
[2] Intimate Notes : 27-8-1895.

He is there in the centre of my heart, as a divine Regulator, imprinting on my soul the love of His own supreme perfection.

Oh ! how sweet it is to abandon oneself without reserve to the amiable Heart of Jesus ! what superabundant peace enters the soul when it adheres without resistance to the Divine Will !

I feel the hand of God operating in me ; it destroys and crushes the depraved instincts of nature ; it tears out, slowly but relentlessly, all such as are still attached to the soul, and reduces to impotency and annihilates my insupressibly proud nature.

As the sight of its suffering caused me joy, how I would wish to see it die in order that no obstacle might come to stop the flight of my soul towards God !

At meditation Our Lord showed me that all the troubles, uneasiness, suffering and anguish that are usually felt, come entirely from our resistance not only to the Divine Will, but also to the desires of God.[1]

38. CONFIDENCE IN GOD AND ABANDONMENT TO HIS WILL ARE SOURCES OF GREAT PEACE OF SOUL

With regard to my interior life as I have told you, I enjoy profound peace mingled however with many sufferings. Abandonment, entire abandonment, boundless confidence are, it seems to me, the sources of this great peace which human language cannot express, and of this repose in God.[2]

39. A MOMENT OF REPOSE IN INFINITE LOVE CAN REFRESH THE SOUL AFTER YEARS OF SUFFERING

I have found in Infinite Love the repose of soul of which I had need after two years of trials such as those throught which I have passed. A moment of repose in Love can refresh the soul after, many years of struggles and sufferings. What I have seen, it seems to me, is that we must be faithful to the desires of Love. Yes Father, what Infinite Love has given us must not be left unused ; it must pass on to souls. You and I should remain hidden in God and unknown, without our personality appearing ; then other priests will come who will draw from us and diffuse around them.[3]

---

[1] Intimate Notes : 19-5-1895.
[2] Letter to Father Charrier : 14-8-1907.
[3] Letter to Father Charrier : 20-11-1909.

CHAPTER VII.

LOVE OF SUFFERING.

*The Will of God does not always bring us sweetness ; on the contrary,
it is very often a crucifying Will which despoils, takes away, annihilates.
But the soul which has learned to recognise in the Will of God, the expression
of His love, and believes that even when it strikes, the hand of God is the
hand of a Father, that soul welcomes with joy the gift of suffering.
I say with joy, because it is the love of God for it that brings it, a love
infinitely wise and tender which gives suffering, sometimes because it is necessary.*

1. SUFFERING IS A SIGN OF GOD'S LOVE

The good Master is giving us a large share in His cross these
times ; it is a sign that He loves us since He associates us with the
mystery of His Infinite Love. In the midst of all these difficulties
and all these crosses my soul is in peace.[1]

2. SUFFERING IS SALUTARY FOR THE SOUL

Oh ! how salutary is suffering for my soul ! It purifies it,
it strengthens it, it strips off from it the earthly dross that is pressing
it down ; it makes it ascend towards Love.

My God, my Christ-Love, pardon me if I sometimes shrink
from suffering and if sometimes, because of not knowing its value
sufficiently, I reject it.[2]

3. SUFFERING IS THE CRUCIBLE IN WHICH OUR SOULS ARE REFINED

To the suffering of my soul, Jesus joins that of my heart. How
good Thou art, my adorable Master, to unite me thus to Thee.
I was not expecting this suffering, I did not think I would find so
much bitterness from that direction.

It is Thou, my Jesus, Who permittest all, Thou directest all.
Thus without dwelling on the secondary causes, on the instrument

---

[1] Letter to Father Charrier : 17-2-1908.
[2] Intimate Notes : 9-1-1907.

with which Thou dost rend my heart, I come to Thee and kiss the hand which strikes me.

But how I love Thy hands, my Jesus, these hands, divine and so humanly charitable, which heal by their touch, which dry our tears, which bind up our wounds, which make incisions also and which despoil, which sometimes crush as well as caress ; but which always operate for our good. I thank Thee, my sweet Master, for making me suffer, I have so much need of it ! I have so much need of it for myself to refine this nature still full of pride, of natural sensibility and of cowardice. I have so much need of it for others, for those whom Thou hast given me. I have need of it for Thee, my Jesus, for Thee Who wouldst wish to be able to suffer still, and Who dost finish in us, Thy faithful, the work of Thy dolorous passion.

Take all then, O my Master, my soul, my heart, my body ; pardon me for my weakness and for the impulse which would wish to reject Thy Cross. I belong to thee ; do then in me, without regard for the tears which I sometimes shed, Thy divine and loving will.[1]

4. SUFFERING FANS THE FLAMES OF LOVE

Last night, I was witness to a violent conflagration ; the fire was intense ; the enormous flames which devoured hay, straw and grain issued out from all openings. A brilliant light lit up the heavens all around, casting its sparkling reflection on the most distant buildings. Sometimes the fire seemed to be under control ; the brightness became shrouded. It was not, however, that the fire was about to be extinguished, but because another part of the building had caught fire, and the flame which was soon to be rendered more active by this new fuel, was gathering itself together, so to speak, before devouring its prey, and because thick smoke for a moment veiled its brightness.

And I reflected : something similar sometimes happens in the human soul ; in the Christian soul which knows Christ and loves Him, suffering is a fuel for love, it serves marvellously to increase it. But at the moment when it makes itself felt in the soul, there is produced a sort of diminution of the loving forces. The light of love becomes veiled in a dark cloud, a cold feeling sets in ; it

---

[1] Intimate Notes : 11-7-1904.

seems to the soul, steeped in its suffering, that it no longer loves God as much as formerly. In prayer, at Holy Communion, every time that it approaches God, all that it is able to say to God is a resigned but sorrowful *fiat*. Love seems to be becoming extinct; it is not so, however; on the contrary, it is feeding itself on this suffering, and when the shadows which veil the light are dispelled, it will show itself to be stronger and more ardent.[1]

5. NOTHING IS SO PLEASING TO JESUS AS SUFFERING LOVINGLY ACCEPTED FOR HIM

Oh! how good Jesus is! This morning while our Sisters were chanting the Office, I was hidden away in a corner of the choir; Jesus came to me and said to me : " I come to My daughter, My sister, and My spouse. " And at the same time He made me understand why He gave me these three names : " His daughter, " because as Creator, He has created me and as Saviour, He has remade my soul ; " His sister, " because He wishes to give me a share with Him in the inheritance of His heavenly Father, and because, through His mercy, He wishes to establish a little equality between Himself and me ; " His spouse, " because I belong to Him and He to me, and because He wishes to associate me with both His states, of sufferings now, and of glory above.

Dwelling on this title of spouse and looking at our Sisters I said to Him : " These also are Thy spouses " He replied to me : " Yes, but you are weak and little and you suffer for Me. " And He gave me to understand that nothing was so pleasing to Him as this suffering lovingly accepted for Him.

Our Lord does indeed love actions done for His love and glory, but action is a thing natural to man. To live is to act. In action a man has always a little personal contentment. That is not evil ; it is a satisfaction arising from the nature of his being. In suffering, nature has no contentment ; the soul alone is satisfied if it loves.

Sometimes it has not even the enjoyment of this satisfaction. Its will, moved by love, wishes for suffering, because it knows that it is thereby making to God a gift which is pleasing to Him, but it has no personal pleasure in making this gift, I mean no human or natural pleasure. In this gift of suffering the soul regards only God's pleasure without considering itself : it is purer.[2]

---

[1] Intimate Notes : 9-1-1907.
[2] Intimate Notes : 30-8-1903.

6. THE VISION OF JESUS CROWNED WITH THORNS, WITH A SMILE ON HIS DIVINE COUNTENANCE

I made the two o'clock meditation in our cell ; I was meditating on the benefit of a religious vocation when I seemed to see the figure of Our Lord in an interior vision. He was crowned with thorns and torn by the scourges, but a divine smile appeared upon His lips : it was when He was given the cross on going out of the Pretorium ; His smile was so full of joy and love, and His look was so sweet ! I understood that I am to receive the pains which my Saviour will send me, from His divine hands with great interior joy, with a smiling countenance, always the same, always joyful.

Jesus was smiling at the thought that now He would be able to give us the greatest proof of His love.[1]

7. WE ARE MYSTICAL MEMBERS OF CHRIST ; WE SHOULD BE VICTIMS WITH HIM

This morning at holy Mass, I understood and tasted the mystery of Jesus Victim ; I saw Him born only in order to die, become incarnate only in order to have a body to sacrifice, form for Himself a sensitive, delicate Heart only in order to suffer, through It, the immolation of His whole being.

In all these roles of King, Priest, Legislator, Advocate, Friend, Brother, Jesus is divine. But when my soul applies itself to Jesus Victim, it seems to drink an inebriating liquor which enchants it, and makes it go outside of itself. This morning, transported out of myself, I contemplated Jesus stretched on the altar ; I exerted myself to the utmost to become united to Him, to give myself up to Him ; I clasped Him with force in order to be immolated with Him. His look, so gentle, made my heart melt with sorrow and with delight, and my soul, inundated with light, burning with ardent fire, relished ineffable pleasures in indescribable suffering.

We are all mystical members of Christ, we should be victims with Christ ; the nobler and more delicate a member is, the more it participates in the state of victim of its divine Chief. Many souls, many hearts, many bodies suffer, which are victims in a sense, but not victims immolated on the altar with Christ.

---

[1] Intimate Notes : August, 1894.

To enter into the state and spirit of Jesus-Victim, one must blend one's will with that of Jesus ; one must share in all His desires, in all the thoughts and intentions of His Heart, and remain under His hand, offering oneself willingly for all that He wishes for one's soul.

For the past year I have been vainly endeavouring to resist the attraction urging me to unite myself with Jesus-Victim ; at times I feel this desire so strong that I suffer at not being able to follow it.

It is not that nature is not troubled and does not cry out, when occasions for immolation offer themselves, but the soul enlightened by Jesus makes no compromise with nature, and Jesus does not regard as a refusal the tears which the eyes sometimes shed, the fears which precede the struggle and the weariness which follows it.

Did not the adorable Victim of the Garden of Olives say : " My Father, if it be possible let this chalice pass from Me." (Math. XXVI, 39). Yes, the soul itself in its lower part may be frightened when sacrifice is demanded and may ask to be relieved of it, while in its higher part it remains immovable and serene, in a permanent state of immolation, always offered, always given.

To be victim with Jesus is not precisely to ask for suffering, but it is to offer oneself freely for all sufferings which it may please God to send, to receive them with peace full of joy and love, and to relish them as a want satisfied.[1]

8. THE FOLLOWING OF JESUS

Every time that an act of renunciation of self or a sacrifice is put in our way, it is Jesus Who asks from us an act of love.

When meditating at the feet of Our Lord on the year that is coming to a close, it will be well that we should consider what has been our attitude towards sacrifices

God has permitted trials, fatigues, cares of all kinds, opportunities for self-denial and sacrifices to present themselves to us in great numbers during the year that is ending. Have we always received them as coming from the hand of God? Have we bent down submissively and humbly under the divine hand? Have we grasped clearly that every sacrifice of earthly things will be an enrichment of our souls ; that those acts of renunciation and those sacrifices were ladders which were intended to make us ascend to God?

---

[1] Intimate Notes : 1899.

" If anyone wishes to be My disciple," and do not we all wish to
be ? " let him deny himself." (Matt. XVI 24) or   (Luke IX, 23)
Do we not, alas ! too often wish to satisfy ourselves, to obtain what
is agreeable to us, to fly from what is distasteful ?   Have we not,
perhaps, adopted every means to attain our own ends, to do our own
will ?

" And carry his cross daily."   And this cross which God presents
to us every day, by means of events or the arrangements of our
Superiors,—do we carry it courageously, lovingly, with resignation
and humility, counting ourselves honoured ?

" And follow Me."   To follow Jesus is to go to labours, to sufferings, to exile, to Calvary, to death !

Let us ask pardon of Our Lord for not having followed Him where
He wished to lead us this year, for having often followed Him at a
distance, and as if by compulsion, for having frequently allowed
Him to go alone on the road of self-renunciation and sacrifice.

And for the new year that is about to begin, let us arouse our
courage to follow Jesus wherever He wishes to lead us.   Let us
imitate those holy women who, with their humble, modest, persevering self-sacrifice, followed the Master to provide for His wants.

In following Jesus, what can we fear ?   He is not going to deceive
us !   By following Jesus faithfully by means of renunciation and
sacrifice, we shall find peace and joy of heart.[1]

9. THE PRESENTATION IN THE TEMPLE : LESSON OF SELF-SACRIFICE

The mystery which we are about to celebrate to-morrow, like the
other mysteries of the life of Christ, affords us many lights and pious
considerations.

Jesus, Mary, Joseph, the pious Guardian of their apparent weakness ; the holy old man Simeon, whose serene, grand figure closes
worthily the long series of Patriarchs of the Old Law ; Anna, the
Prophetess, who, under the weight of years, still preserves the fervour
of youth, appear one after the other in the majestic square of the
Temple, of that Temple in which so many powerless victims had been
offered, and where Jesus, the only Victim acceptable to the Father,
will come to announce the truths of His doctrine, before pouring

---

[1] Conference to the Sisters : 1-2-1909.

out on the cross on Calvary the life-giving streams of His redeeming Blood.

Everything in this mystery is capable of affording us instruction and it will be useful to meditate on it attentively. But to-day, we shall only stop to consider one very simple detail. We shall speak of those two white doves carried to the Temple by St. Joseph and destined to be offered in sacrifice in place of Jesus and for Jesus.

That little detail has not been omitted in the Gospel, where so many other more important facts have not been narrated. It was because it could be the subject of sweet meditation, and because souls would be able to find in it salutary lessons and precious consolations.

It appears to me that we have in those two doves a gracious symbol of Religious souls. They were selected by God from among a great number, without any other reason but the divine preference, which is always inexplicable. They were bound and brought to the Temple in order to be offered in sacrifice as a substitute for the divine Child.

Is not the case of Religious souls the same? They have been selected out of the multitude of other souls by God as His special portion and solely through the liberality of Infinite Love throbbing in the divine Heart. Conducted to the house of the Lord and bound by the chain of three vows, they are offered in sacrifice and immolated as pure victims.

On the day of the Presentation, Jesus could not yet immolate Himself by suffering and death, His hour has not yet come : the white doves then took His place. Now, Jesus risen from the dead, can no longer suffer or die. The day of His great sorrows is passed, and it is Religious who offer themselves in His place, continuing and completing in themselves the sufferings of His Passion which remained to be suffered by Him (in His members).[1]

But how much more fortunate those select souls are than the doves, devoid of reason, that were carried by St. Joseph to the Temple ! They offer themselves to God voluntarily ; it is love which immolates them, and the grace of Jesus, Who has already been offered in sacrifice for them, envelops them with supernatural strength and illuminates them with divine brightness.

The spirit of sacrifice dominates this great mystery of the Presentation in the Temple. Let us imbue our hearts well with this

---

[1] Col. 1-24.

spirit, for sacrifice is the soul of religion and the highest expression of love.

Let us go to-morrow like white doves and offer ourselves to the Lord with Jesus. Let us endeavour to imitate their lily-like whiteness, their lovable simplicity and fascinating gentleness. These are the ornaments with which Our Lord wishes to see victims offered to Him adorned. Let us be the doves of Jesus, pure and gentle, but above all, let us learn to sacrifice ourselves to love and by love. Let us learn to walk with Our Saviour on the path of immolation. Let us be glad to continue His works of salvation and redemption. We have been brought to the Temple for the sole purpose of becoming holocausts of pleasing odour, of being substituted for Jesus Who can no longer suffer. Far from us therefore be that fear of everything which despoils, of everything which destroys. It is thus that Love immolates Its victims.

But, if Love immolates, It recompenses and consoles also. To-morrow we will allow the Virgin Mary to go out of the Temple, her soul pierced with sorrow, carrying in her arms and clasping to her breast her adorable Son. We will remain to be sacrificed in her place, not only carrying Jesus, but remaining immolated with Him in the Tabernacle, and as white doves united to the White Host, we will allow ourselves to be consumed by Love in the holy joy of sacrifice and loving abandonment.[1]

PRAYER

10. " FOLLOW THOU ME " (John XXI, 22)

O Jesus, Victim of love, divine ransom for sin, I adore Thee in Thy sufferings without number.

I adore Thee in the pains of Thy sacred Flesh, all bathed in the blood of the agony, torn by the scourges, pierced by the thorns and the nails. I adore Thee in the martyrdom of Thy Heart, overflowing with love, broken by the ingratitude of men, by their jealousy and hatred, and cowardly abandonment. I adore Thee in the unspeakable tortures of Thy soul, in its sadness, its fears, its mortal anguish.

I adore Thee and bless Thee !

---

[1] Conference to the Sisters : 1-2-1908.

I bless Thee because Thou hast permitted me to mingle my tears with Thine, to join my sufferings to Thy sufferings, and to unite my martyrdom to Thine.

I bless Thee and I love Thee !

I love Thee because Thou hast permitted me to walk by the same sorrowful way as Thyself ! Sometimes, it is true, I tremble when placing my feet in Thy bloodstained foot-prints, and my hand rejects the chalice which Thou offerest to me, after drinking from it Thyself. But Thou . . . Thou hast known our faint-heartedness and our resistance, and Thou knowest that this instinctive gesture of terrified nature is not instigated by the will or authorised by the free soul. My will, with full determination, seizes the bitter chalice, and I abandon myself to Thee, to suffer Thy agony and Thy martyrdom.

Allow me only to draw a little strength and life from the chalice of Thy wounded Heart and then . . . accomplish in me Thy work of sorrow.[1]

11. IT IS THE LOT OF MAN TO SUFFER ; GOD ALONE CAN CONSOLE US

The love of the Cross does not prevent the soul from feeling its own human weakness ; but if it feels its own powerlessness, it knows also that Jesus is with it and that He will be its strength.

Every time the soul loses an illusion, that it comes up against the nothingness of the creature, it suffers ; this, it seems to me, is not very strange. God should suffice for it, but it sees itself enveloped in the flesh, subject to a thousand wants, in necessary contact with other creatures whose help it cannot do without. What wonder is it that it forms bonds between itself and what surrounds it ? And when one of these bonds breaks, when it sees itself disappointed in a creature that it had thought it could lean on in case of need, it cannot help suffering. It does not complain, it does not rebel, it knows well that everything that detaches us from creatures is good, and that it conduces to our sanctification and brings us nearer to God. Thus, it suffers in peace, sweetly, in the hands of God ; it blesses Him, but it suffers all the same.

---

[1] Intimate Notes : May. 1904.

I am leaving this retreat more detached, it seems to me, and stronger to bear suffering, the suffering of uncertainty, of isolation, of entire absence of human help in which it has pleased Jesus to place me.

Abandonment to Him brings peace.[1]

12. THE HEAVENLY BREAD OF SUFFERING IS SALUTARY FOR MY SOUL

O Jesus, my divine Master, I wish to bless Thee and to thank Thee, Thy most sweet hand is liberal to me in sufferings and humiliations, and that is what is necessary for me.

This heavenly bread, almost as salutary as that of Thy sacred Body, suits my soul. I feel its bitterness, it is true, my nature rejects it ; give it to me, nevertheless, my sweet Master ; my soul desires it ; not only do I accept it, but I ask Thee for it.

For the last four years, since Thou hast manifested the riches of Thy adorable Heart to me in a more particular manner, Thou hast discovered to me a new source of sufferings and humiliations.

I should kneel down and kiss Thy hand which presents these sufferings to me ; on the contrary, my weak and proud nature shudders painfully before them.

Pardon me, my Jesus, pardon me for being so sensitive to censure and so cowardly in presence of suffering.

I have given myself to Thee, poor, little, unworthy victim that I am, to be sacrificed by Love and for the glory of Thy Love, and when Thou, Jesus-Love, my divine Priest, dost perform the immolation, I groan beneath Thy hand and I endeavour to thrust it aside. Pardon me, O sweet Sacrificial Priest, strengthen me, enlighten me, sacrifice me by Thy divine hand on the altar of Thy Sacred Heart.[2]

13. JESUS SAID : " I WILL BE YOUR STRENGTH "

Yesterday at prayer I was seized by an interior pain of soul, the cause of which I can not understand. I began to examine myself to see whether I had been guilty of any fault, or whether I had been unfaithful, I discovered nothing serious ; but it seemed to me that

[1] Letter to Father Charrier : 14-8-1907.
[2] Intimate Notes : 22-12-1904.

Our Lord gave me to understand interiorly that it was not only for myself that I must suffer, but for those who seek only their own pleasure, as I had done for a long time.

Then, I said gently to Our Lord that I felt that I was very weak, that corporal suffering frightened me and that suffering of soul unnerved me, and that I was not capable of suffering for others. Our Lord replied to me interiorly: " I will be your strength." Afterwards I said to Him : " My Saviour, I am still more afraid of my pride than of my weakness. I fear that it may ruin me if Thou shouldst give me such a grace as to allow me to suffer a little. " It seemed to me that He replied : " I will know how to humble it. "

Then I said no more, but a strange fear came over me that what I believed to be the inner voice of Our Lord might only be an art-tifice of the devil or just simply the effect of my imagination.

I abandoned myself to God for everything ; I offered myself to do what He wished. I surrendered myself like a piece of inert matter, without even thinking, without having any wish, always suffering, but feeling the presence of Our Lord.[1]

14. " I WILL BE WITH YOU "

I had passed a Lent filled with so much exterior work and dis-turbance that I was thirsty for retreat and solitude ; I shut myself up in my cell as much as possible during this Holy Week, seeking Jesus crucified and turning away from everything else. I suffered much, not so much corporally as interiorly. I had begun to suffer like that on Passion Sunday, and the suffering went on increasing up to Holy Saturday which I passed entirely on the Cross. A terrible weight seemed to be crushing my soul that day and I was in unspeakable anguish. It seemed to me that all the sins of the world came to me and enveloped me in a poisonous vapour which was suffocating me. However, I could not meditate either on the passion of Jesus, or on sin, or on anything. The strain was not released except just for a moment after Holy Communion on Saturday. It was like a moment's repose, very sweet, taken on the breast of Jesus. And my adorable Master said to me in low tones : " I will make you suffer, I will deprive you of support

---

[1] Intimat Notes : 15-12-1893.

and help, you will feel yourself alone in difficulties and troubles, humiliation and suffering will press you on all sides, but I will be with you, " and I felt something sweet and strong which gave life to my soul. It was like a strengthening potion taken on the road to Calvary ; during the rest of the day I suffered unspeakably.[1]

15. THOU HAST MADE ME UNDERSTAND THE DIVINE CHARM OF THE CROSS

The time had come when Mother Louise Margaret, aided by divine grace, intimately united to Jesus Who sustained and strengthened her, and entirely taken possession of by Infinite Love, began to find an unexpected source of joy in suffering.

I have again surrendered myself completely to Our Lord, to do and suffer all that it may please Him for poor sinners, and for the extension of His reign. I asked Him for the grace to continue suffering, to suffer more ; it is as a need which I feel ; it is only in suffering that I feel assurance. Some time ago I was seized by a strange fear ; I found myself too happy, and it seemed to me that it is not thus that Our Lord usually treats His beloved ; I found myself surrounded with very great affection, everything was going too well ; I was afraid, and I besought Our Lord to make me suffer and to humiliate me.

He has heard my prayer ; He has cut a thread in this heart which He wishes to be detached from everything, and to belong to Him alone.

If He has heard my prayer, it is because He loves me ; and if He loves me, what more can I need ?

O Love, O divine Love which tortures and breaks, but which makes Thy friends find in suffering a happiness unknown to this earth, O Jesus, Who at my last retreat, hast made me understand the divine charm of the cross, I offer Thee my body, my heart, my whole being ; I can neither pray, nor love, nor suffer, but come, and do all that in me.

Come, annihilate my own being, and operating a kind of divine transubstantiation, come and suffer in me.[2]

---

[1] Intimate Notes : 4-4-1904.
[2] Intimate Notes : 1894.

16. HOW GOOD JESUS IS!

How good Jesus is ! He wishes for suffering and He sends it to me in order that I may be able to offer it to Him. This morning my headache was more painful than it usually is ; the longer I have it, the more the pain increases ; just now during the Chapter, I was not able to open my eyes. I strove during the recreation not to let anything of this appear, in order that I may be all for Jesus, for my priests. It is good to suffer in body and in soul when no one knows anything about it.[1]

17. ABYSSES OF SUFFERING

You tell me, Father, that you would wish to gaze into my soul and to see its depths. Alas ! what would you see there ? Abysses of suffering, heart-rendings renewed unceasingly ; most painful acts of abandonment to divine Providence ; acts of blind faith, and, with all that, profound peace and at times joy, supernatural and sweet, from the humiliations which I receive. Finally, Father, an immense desire for charity, an impulse for complete pardon which urges me to cover up everything and to love all.[2]

18. I ABOUND WITH JOY IN ALL TRIBULATIONS

All that people say about me, some of which is being written to you, is good for me ; I assure you I am profoundly happy over it, and were it not on account of the Foundation, I would not wish to clear myself of any of it.

Jesus had united me to His hidden life during the first years of my religious life ; to His public life during the six years when I was Superioress, and now He unites to His Passion, and everything is on a little scale,—suited to my person. What goodness on the part of the good Master ! Help me to thank Him. I can truly say with St. Paul : " I exceedingly abound with joy in all our tribulation. " (ii. Cor. VII, 4.)

However, at times, I suffer much, Father, and my poor heart is penetrated with the most intense sorrows.[3]

---

[1] Intimate Notes : 25-2-1905.
[2] Letter to Father Charrier : 9-1-1914.
[3] Letter to Father Charrier : 10-3-1914.

19.   I HAVE OFFERED MYSELF AS A VICTIM TO INFINITE LOVE

After passing through the most painful inward sorrows, I commenced my retreat. My heart became more and more broken and sorrowful, but my soul was in a state of abandonment and peace. I am not surprised at the heavy crosses and crushing trials through which I have passed, especially for the last six months. It is Jesus Who wills and permits all that. I have offered myself as a victim to Infinite Love : it is His Love which performs in me His work of immolation. I ask but one thing of Jesus : to have the strength and fortitude necessary to support, without flinching, and without offending the Sacred Heart, the weight of so many sorrows. At the beginning of this painful crisis, my poor heart was so sorrow-stricken that I gave way to complaints : I said things which I should have had the strength to keep back. I humble myself once more before Infinite Love and I thank Him once more for having permitted these weaknesses which have humiliated me before creatures, and discredited me in their eyes. Yes, I am happy not only to suffer, but still more to be humiliated.

I suffer at feeling myself without family or permanent abode, a burden to all the monasteries which receive me as I pass, and as if for charity ; and I am happy on account of this sorrow, of this humiliation. Jesus also had not a stone on which to lay His head.[1]

CHAPTER VIII.

CHARITY TOWARDS OUR NEIGHBOUR

When the Doctor of the Law asked Our Lord what was the great commandment of the Law, He replied : " Thou shalt love the Lord thy God with thy whole heart and with thy whole soul and thy whole mind " (Matt. xxii, 37) but He added : " The second is like to this : " Thou shalt love thy neighbour as thyself" (Ibid 39).

The commentary in the following selections shows the perfect love of the neighbour to be an indispensable condition for arriving at the perfect love of God. This is but a summary of the teaching of Sacred Scripture on the relation between the love of our neighbour and the love of God which is given special prominence in the Epistles of St. John.

---

[1] Intimate Notes : 23-10-1913.

1. CHARITY TOWARDS OUR NEIGHBOUR INDISPENSIBLE FOR ATTAINING TO LOVE.

I have not had a moment for the past month to finish writing what I had commenced about a visit from our holy Founder (St. Francis de Sales,) which was full of sweetness and comfort for my soul. There remains to me from it a most sweet perfume, and if I cannot write exactly the words which he spoke to me, I am able however to note down the substance of them.

Our Blessed Father said to me that we had been established especially for the service of Infinite Love, but that no soul could arrive at the love of God unless it had also great and true charity for its neighbour. He gave me to understand that only rarely are souls raised to a higher degree of love for God because they do not carry their love for others far enough; that is not enough to serve them and merely to fulfil the commandment of charity, but it is necessary to have very exquisite delicacy in one's interior sentiments.

In many souls there are vindictive sentiments and evil intentions which are not voluntarily cultivated, but which are not sufficiently combated; these being only venial sins, do not kill charity in the soul, but prevent the development of Infinite Love. He taught me that delicacy and meekness of interior sentiments which renders the soul so pleasing to God that the gift of Infinite Love is then given to it in very great abundance. He told me that we must pardon everything and always render good for evil; then He told me that, if I always did so, Infinite Love would make its sojourn of repose and delight in my soul.[1]

2. A SINGLE ROAD LEADS TO INFINITE LOVE : CHARITY

The divine Will, which is the rule and form of our sanctification, on the part of God is nothing else but love for His creatures, and in exchange, the will of the creature should be nothing else but love for God. It is towards the increase of this heavenly love in ourselves that we, my Beloved Sisters, should work together, continually endeavouring to give more strength and activity to this double current of sacred love which descends from the Heart of God to souls, and which goes up from our souls to God.

Love is the great need of our hearts; in these sad times which

[1] Intimate Notes : 23-2-1907.

are troubled by so much dissension and frozen by so much egoism, love is the constant, ardent desire of souls who, knowing God, are aware of what He deserves and what is due to Him, but which, alas ! is almost everywhere refused to Him. Let us love this God Who is so good and so worthy of being loved. Let us go to Jesus Christ, God made man ; let us seek His Heart, the source of love ; let us study It ; let us give all our affection to It ; and we shall come to the knowledge of the Divinity by entering into contact with His adorable Humanity.

But, my beloved Sisters, a single way leads to Infinite Love, a single door gives access to the divine temple ; this door, this royal way is love of the neighbour, it is charity ! Aided by grace and always attentive to the desires of the adorable Heart, we shall endeavour to remove the obstacles which might come to impede the exercise of this divine virtue.

We shall strive to the best of our ability to unite our hearts, to bind them together, so that they will form but one.

Community of suffering brings hearts together more perhaps than community of life. It has been God's will, doubtless in order to cement still better the love and union of the members of our dear family, to make them pass through most painful trials. Each of your souls, my beloved Sisters has had its own particular sufferings and anguish of heart. Several of you have had to leave works dear to your heart, which had for you all the attraction of an apostolate ; many of you have seen mothers, sisters, loved families weeping, and have had to impose on them a sacrifice as painful as that of their profession ; all of you have had to leave your native land, unfortunate and much loved France, and take the road for exile towards the uncertainty of the morrow and the unknown of the future. The Divine Master has seen the fidelity of your hearts and the generosity of your courage and He will recompense you.

But your souls, fatigued by the struggles and exhausted by the sacrifices, have need of peace, repose, and joy. Together we shall seek all that in love, Infinite Love, the source of light and of generous ardour, in fraternal charity, the source of serene peace and of trusting joy.

For myself, my beloved Sisters, my sole ambition will be to aid the Master in doing His work of love in this dear family.[1]

---

[1] First Instruction to the Community after her election : 16-5-1907.

3. CHARITY, A MEANS OF ATTAINING TO UNION WITH GOD

All our happiness and well-being come from union with God. This union is our life and our joy on earth, and it will be our happiness in heaven.

What must we do to arrive at this union, which is so much to be desired ? We must advance in the love of God and our fellowmen. All our interior efforts should consist in making this progress.

Change your spiritual life in any way you will, alter your practices, fatigue yourself with numerous reflections and exercises : all that is nothing and leads to nothing ; one thing alone is necessary to lead you to union with God : progress in His holy love and in the love of your neighbour.

If this were well understood, how the interior life would be simplified, how quickly an end would be put to perplexities and troubles of mind, and how wills would be brought in unison in one same movement towards a common end : to strive towards union with God by one sole means : progress in charity !

Let us endeavour to realise this progress in ourselves, let us spare no effort to attain it, and you shall see that our union with God will become closer day by day. When we have developed charity in ourselves, when love will reign supreme in our souls, Jesus Christ, God-Love will live truly in us and we in Him.[1]

4. TO LOVE LIKE JESUS

The charity towards our neighbour, of which Mother Louise Margaret speaks, should be charity according to the precept of Our Lord : " Love one another as I have loved you."

Jesus will then be our divine Model. We shall learn from Him how to practise this virtue in its perfection.

Alas ! very often instead of giving ourselves to Jesus, we resist Him, instead of participating in His sentiments, we nourish in our hearts sentiments completely opposed to His. The sentiments of our adorable Master when He hung expiring on the cross were all sentiments of forgiveness, of infinite tenderness and of charity.

How many times have we not, on the contrary, harboured in our hearts sentiments of aversion but weakly combated, of rancour not weeded out, of coldness deliberately entertained, of inconceivably childish susceptibility.

Is that the way that we give ourselves to Jesus, Whose Heart overflowing with charity poured out only forgiveness and love on His

---

[1] Conference to the Sisters : 3-8-1912.

enemies ? At the foot of the Cross, we should empty our hearts of all sentiments of bitterness and resentment, of all seeking after our selfish interests which close our hearts and render them arid.

Let us love God, let us love Jesus Who has loved us so much, but let us love Him with a love like His own, all-embracing, generous, trusting ; with a love that pardons everything, which overflows on everyone, which believes that it can never do enough, with a love which gives without calculation, without reserve, and which, when there is question of sacrifice gives even to complete immolation.[1]

5. AID ME, O JESUS, TO ADOPT THE SENTIMENTS OF THY HEART

During this retreat I felt two inclinations ; the first was to hide myself, to disappear, especially in this Work of Infinite Love. The second, to give myself more and more to Love, bringing all creatures, as far as it lies in me, to glorify Infinite Love, endeavouring to live only for love, opening wide my heart. Thou wishest, my Jesus, that my heart be dilated and that it be opened wide in order to receive the currents of love which descend from Thy Heart.

Father gave me as resolutions : recollection, humility, and continual annihilation of myself. It seems to me that the humility which, Thou, O Lord, wishest me, is a sweet and loving disposition to receive all the humiliations which Thou wilt send to me either directly or through Thy creatures, with a sweet " still more " spoken to the ear of Thy Heart. I will add also, my sweet Jesus, charity, tender and profound charity towards the persons who make me suffer, who do me disservices, and judge me. Not only do I pardon them, but I wish to do them all the good that depends on me ; and as the greatest good, my Saviour, is Thy love, I ask of Thee and beseech Thee, not to impute to them as a fault what they may do against me, but on the contrary, to recompense by Thy love all that they will do and say to humiliate me or to cause me pain. Aid me, O Jesus, to adopt the sentiments of Thy Heart ; grant that I may be all love, since Thou hast created me and conserved me only to be employed in the service of Thy most holy Love.[2]

6. THE NEW PRECEPT OF LOVE

Jesus said : " A new commandment I give unto you : that you love

---

[1] Conference to the Sisters : 17-4-1908.
[2] Intimate Notes : 6-9-1903.

He that seeth Me seeth the Father also

(JOHN XIV, 9)

" And Jesus, making His priests repose on His divine Breast,
gave them His adorable Heart, the pledge of His incomparable
love."   (See *Book of Infinite Love*, page 106).

one another, as I have loved you." (John XIV, 34).

Is it not strange that He was obliged to command love ? It is so sweet to love our brethren, and there is such a need in the human heart to attach itself, to devote itself, and it is so natural for love to give itself !

However, the divine Master did not think it superfluous to demand our love, and to make a new precept of love. It is because He knows the depths of egoism in us, which are the result of sin. He knows how many passions hostile to charity surge within our poor hearts, and for this wretchedness and misery which is ever being born again from our poor human nature, He sees Himself obliged to apply a constantly-renewed remedy : the precept of Charity. It is God-Infinite Love Who gives us this ever-new commandment of mutual love. And it is not mere common love, mediocre charity, which He prescribes for us ; it is not that barely-sufficient, common charity which consists in not doing or wishing evil to our neighbour, in rendering him strictly necessary services, in obliging him in a small way, in pardoning him his offences. Oh ! no, He is not satis-fied with a love of that kind from us. He wants a love of preference, full of exquisite sentiments, of affectionate dealings, of delicate attention ; it is the purest charity, the most disinterested, the most perfumed, if I may use the expression, of all the perfumes of Infinite Love.[1]

7. GENTLENESS AND EQUANIMITY

We should give our virtue an external form of serene equanimity and lovable, religious courtesy.

Our exterior acts and words generally express the sentiments of our souls. If the soul is well-balanced, constant, always the same in the midst of the vicissitudes of life, the humour, the character will not change.

The great secret of this balance of soul and of this evenness of humour and character which results from it and which is so much to be desired, is above all union with God and contempt for all earthly things.

When the heart has become detached, when the spirit has become elevated above the ever-changing events of this life, the soul estab-lishes itself in that lofty region in which sorrow and suffering have

[1] Conference to the Sisters : 14-9-1907.

their abode, but serenity reigns supreme.

Let us labour therefore to acquire this most amiable quality of evenness of soul, and let us join to it that perfect affability which makes relations with others so full of sweetness and charm. A little violence to ourselves is required to speak sweetly always, to have always suavity of manner without affectation, and unvarying gentleness. But if violence is required, it is sweet violence, because it is done for God, and there is virtue in it : we should therefore not neglect it.[1]

8. I BLESS THEE FOR HAVING GIVEN ME A SHARE IN THY CROSS

My God, I thank Thee for making me suffer, I bless Thee for giving me a share in Thy cross ! O Master, it is hard . . . but no, I wish that this bitterness be sweet to me, since Thou wishes it for me. I wish to love still more those who make me suffer ; I wish to sacrifice myself still more for them, since they give me a blessing superior to all blessings, that of suffering with Thee and like Thee.

The words which Thou hast spoken to me one day, many years ago, come back to my mind and I understand them now. Thou hast said to me : " I will perfect in your heart the faculty of loving and the faculty of suffering in order that you may be able to understand and feel the sorrows of Mine."

Yes, my sweet Master, when I suffer thus, I understand better, it seems to me, the tortures of Thy divine Heart ; I feel them in myself, I see them by my own sorrows, and my broken heart unites itself to Thine by sorrow and love.

It seems to me that I do not suffer merely by my own suffering, but also by that which Thou Thyself dost feel in the inward depths of Thy sovereignly loving Heart ; I suffer by my own suffering and by the infidelity of those who make me suffer.[2]

9. THE LAWS OF INFINITE LOVE

As for us, shut up in our little nest, we wish to bless those who speak ill of us, love those who hate us, and do good to those who

---

[1] Conference to the Sisters : 31-12-1907.
[2] Intimate Notes : 17-7-1905.

injure us. These are the laws of Infinite Love, and we should practise them here more than any place else, for this is the house of Infinite Love.[1]

10. WE SHOULD SACRIFICE EVERYTHING FOR CHARITY

Let us live by charity and in charity. That is our last word. Let us sacrifice everything including ourselves to preserve charity.

" God is Charity, and he that abideth in Charity abideth in God, and God in him. (I John, IV, 16).

By means of charity we shall attain happiness, and we shall make our Superiors and our Sisters happy ; our heavenly Mother, the Virgin Mary, the Mother of beautiful Love will be consoled by us, and the Heart of Jesus will be fully glorified by our means.[2]

CHAPTER IX

THE DESIRE TO MAKE LOVE KNOWN

Love is by its nature diffusive ; it cannot remain inactive in the soul. When a soul advances in the love of God, its keenest and most profound suffering is to see that Love is not loved. It seeks to sanctify itself still more and to fill itself with God in order to become a channel by which the love of God may pass to the world. For this end, it gives itself to God by greater fidelity in His service and by sacrificing its own interests to the interests of God. It offers itself joyfully for suffering and humiliation, for it knows that these are the principal weapons by which it can attain its dearest ambition, to conquer souls for God.

Now, since priests are God's chief instruments for the salvation of souls, it is for them that the soul consecrates itself to God, it is to help them in their ministry that it prays and suffers, and when it can, it gives its humble, generous collaboration which is always respectful, always dictated by disinterested zeal.

1. GOD IS LOVE, AND LOVE WISHES TO BE LOVED

During this whole week, my soul found itself in an almost continuous state of adoration, praise and gratitude. This divine invention by which God has united Himself to human nature in the Person of Our Lord, has aroused in my soul sentiments of ever-

[1] Letter to Father Charrier : 26-4-1914.
[2] Conference to the Sisters : 25-4-1913.

renewed admiration and delight.

I saw the immense desire which God has for union with man, a desire which proceeds solely from His love for him. This Infinite Love, so strong, since man's sin has not been able to weaken it, so ardent, since it has made Him go out of Himself, so disinterested, since it has made Him sacrifice Himself for us, this Love which is God, this bottomless, endless, boundless sea of Love which is the Divine Essence, as it causes its waves to descend on me, submerges my soul and leaves it without speech and without any other movement, except a sort of ardent, incessant aspiration towards a union becoming ever more complete. I would wish to be able to convey to all creatures how great this desire of God is ; I would wish to open my arms and take hold of the whole world, to clasp it to my breast, and throw myself with it into the Ocean of Infinite Love in order thus to satisfy the desire of God.

God is Love, and Love wishes to be loved, and Love is not loved enough. It is in vain for me to open my heart in order to receive this overflow of love from the Heart of God ; my heart is too small, and, besides, it is only one heart.

What God looks for and demands are hearts which love Him even to the contempt of everything else, hearts so given up to Him, so divested of their own interest, that He can find His pleasure in them.[1]

2. I HAVE AN ARDENT DESIRE TO MAKE GOD KNOWN

Oh ! how can people help loving this great God ? He is so beautiful, so good, so just, so holy, so powerful !

What a grace ! what goodness on the part of God to have given us an intellect capable of knowing Him and a heart capable of loving Him ! It seems to me that if people do not love God, it is because they do not know Him. If they knew Him even a little, they could not help loving Him. I have an ardent desire to make this great God known ; not indeed as He is, but at least as I myself know Him. If everyone only had the knowledge of Him which I have, all hearts would open to Him, they would not be able to resist Him.[2]

---

[1] Intimate Notes : 16-10-1899.
[2] Intimate Notes : 26-8-1905.

3. O JESUS, I GIVE MYSELF ENTIRELY TO THEE FOR SOULS

I give myself to Thee for the salvation and conversion of souls ; I give myself to Thee, undivided and without restriction, ready to suffer in my soul, in my body, and in my heart, in order to expiate, and to merit the salvation of sinners.

I do not even wish, O Jesus, for death, for death which will unite me to Thee for ever, which will separate me from the flesh which weighs me down.

If by suffering and toiling on earth, I can obtain the salvation of some poor souls, that is enough for me, O my Lord.

I give myself entirely to Thee for souls,
I give myself entirely for Thee and for souls,
I give myself entirely to souls with Thee ;
I wish for nothing but Thee for my soul, nothing but my soul alone and Thee.[1]

4. THE ETERNAL JOY OF MY SOUL WILL BE THY GREATER GLORY AND THE ACCOMPLISHMENT OF THY WILL

Jesus ! my love ! in this state of adoration in which Thou dost place my soul, I find peace, light and a divine satiety ; but I suffer also, I suffer from the coldness of my heart, from its smallness, from not being able to fill myself as I desire with these treasures of love which are disclosed to my eyes.

I find my satiety in Thee, O divine Sweetness, and I have an ever-increasing hunger for Thee. I find my repose in Thee, and my soul rushes forward towards Thee and pants after Thee.

To love Thee ! How sweet it would be, O divine Goodness, to be able to love Thee ! Equally sweet it would be to see Thee loved ! I am neither capable nor worthy of causing Thee to be loved, which would be too sweet.

If all that were needed that Thou might be loved was to give my life, it is already given ; if it were necessary to give the eternal sweetness of the final union of my soul with Thee O my God, could I find it in me to give it? **Yes, I would give it, for Thy joy will be all my happiness ; my heaven will be the entire satisfying of Thy Heart ; the eternal joy of my soul, Thy greater glory and the accomplishment of Thy will**[2]

---

[1] Intimate Notes : Oct., 1892.
[2] Intimate Notes : 16-10-1899.

(b) ALL GOD'S WORKS ARE WORKS OF LOVE

Oh ! Infinite Love, Principle of life, of light, and of strength, I feel Thee within me sustaining me and vivifying me. Without this divine strength what would I be able to do ? My God, may Thou be blessed for having revealed to me Thy Love ; would that I could, in my turn, reveal this divine secret to all souls, and plunge them into the living ocean of light and of truth in which Thou hast plunged me !

My God, I adore Thee in the perfection of Thy works ; they are all works of love ; all that Thy Wisdom decides, all that Thy will ordains, all that Thy Power accomplished,—all that cannot be other than good. Do then, O my God, Thy works of love. If it be necessary that my heart be broken, if it be necessary that my soul weep, what matter ? Too unworthy that I am to labour for the glory of Infinite Love, would that I might at least be able to suffer and to be immolated by it.[1]

5. A MOMENT'S GLIMPSE OF INFINITE LOVE SUFFICES FOR A PERSON TO BE RAVISHED WITH JOY

Christmas night has been sweet to me. This sweetness did not last very long, but in a few moments Jesus gave repose, peace, and joy, sufficient to make up for all the sufferings, anguish, and humiliations of the year. I tell you this in all simplicity as to my most dear and good Father. At the Communion of the midnight Mass, Infinite Love manifested Itself to me abridged, condensed, and enclosed in this divine Infant in the crib. A moment's glimpse of Infinite Love suffices for a person to be ravished with joy and filled with peace. The impression it made was so strong and so sweet that it has remained with me and as I am writing to you, the memory of it still touches me profoundly.

Ah ! if souls could but understand Infinite Love ! It is incredible how few there are who know it ; and this is Our Lord's pain ; this is His sadness as man, to see that Infinite Love is unknown. I cannot express to you how great my desire is to die. Here on earth, I do nothing but foolish things and then I see sc

---

[1] Intimate Notes : 27-12-1906.

much evil. I wish to go and get lost in Infinite Love ; but before doing so, I wish to do something to make it known, at least as I know it. I wish to give Our Lord the pleasure of manifesting His Infinite Love. I feel more and more that I was born only for that object. I was not born to be a Religious, or to be a Superioress ; according to the will of God, I am to be both, but it is not the reason for my existence. My raison d'etre is to be a nothing, a feather flying in the wind, a grain of sand heaved up by the sea ; but this nothing, this grain of sand are messengers of Infinite Love.[1]

6. THE TRIUMPH OF MERCY

Our Lord impressed His will anew on my soul : My Director (Father Charrier) had given himself to Him absolutely and irrevocably seventeen or eighteen years previously, he had given himself to Jesus as to a Master, in order to devote himself to Him and to serve Him, and placing Jesus on his heart, he surrendered himself to Him as a slave to his Master.

But what Jesus wants now is that he should make a new donation of himself to Love and that, instead of placing Jesus on his heart, he should put himself in the Heart of Jesus.

Oh ! Jesus has already placed him on His Heart, but He wishes a new, voluntary act, an act which will be the principle of a more profound and intimate, and also of a sweeter union with the divine Master.

God would wish to purify and renew the world by a deluge of love. He cannot ; not that He has not always the power to execute all His designs, but His justice opposes itself to His goodness, and it is necessary that His mercy come and contend against His justice in order to make Love triumph.

And while in heaven Mercy wrestles for the cause of love, on earth, souls who have surrendered themselves to Love must give aid to Mercy. That is why God wants such souls, for He passionately desires to make His Mercy triumph.

Oh ! how well Jesus does His work in a heart that has surrendered itself to Love ; all that comes forth from that heart is almost divine and does the work of Jesus.[2]

---

[1] Letter to Father Charrier : 27-12-1908.
[2] Intimate Notes : No date.

7. APOSTOLATE OF PERSONAL SANCTIFICATION

We have no other apostolate (but how fine that apostolate is !) but
that of our own personal sanctification which, as it were, overflows
and influences others, and that of the accumulation of merits which
ought to carry the good odour of Christ to the hearts of the faithful.

Let us therefore make an ample provision of merits and graces in
order to enrich souls.   It is for this end that we have entered the
Visitation : it was our ambition and it ought still to be the incessant
aspiration of our lives.

Thus we shall help Holy Church and, at the same time, contribute
to the salvation of our neighbour.[1]

8. WE SHOULD CARRY OUT THE WORK MARKED OUT FOR US BY GOD

Our Lord is content to see us act faithfully under His inspiration,
taking the proper means to promote His work, but He certainly does
not want either natural eagerness or inconsiderate haste ; it
suffices for Him that we go forward gently, without wishing to antic-
ipate His hour.   The hour chosen by God is always the best.   However, our good Master is not pleased, if we remain entirely inactive
and, through our own cowardice or lack of confidence in God, or,
from some other natural motive, oblige Him in some way to delay
His hour.   For my part, Father, I shall die content whenever Jesus
calls me, even though I should see nothing accomplished of what
seems to me He wishes done, provided that, on my side, I have employed myself faithfully in doing the little that I am able.   Indeed,
it matters nothing when we die, whether we have accomplished a
work, whether we have succeeded or failed.   It suffices that we
should have carried out courageously the part of the work that has
been marked out for us.[2]

9. THE CROSS IS JESUS

The most efficacious means for the salvation of souls will always
be that employed by Jesus : the Cross.

Yesterday, in the parlour, I was asking my little niece questions to

[1] Conference to the Sisters : 11-5-1912.
[2] Letter to Father Charrier : 5-11-1907.

make her speak, and showing her the little silver cross which we wear on our breast, I said to her : " Tell me what is that?" She looked at me carefully and replied with the smile of a cherub : " That is Jesus." However, the image of Jesus crucified was not on it, but for this child, the cross was Jesus.

Oh ! would that we had the clear-sightedness of this child, and when suffering comes to us, when some cross weighs down upon us, would that we might say : " That is Jesus !" Yes, the cross is Jesus ; Jesus is the Saviour ; the cross saves us also.

The cross is expiation for our sins ; it purifies us continually from those stains which we contract by contact with what is not pure.

And not only does it save ourselves, but it helps us to save souls. Prayer is, doubtless, all powerful over the heart of God, for Jesus has said : " If you ask the Father anything in My name, He will give it to you." (John XVI, 23). But suffering ! Not suffering of man alone, but suffering of man united to that of Jesus,—what does it not obtain ? When a creature that is loved by God, when a spouse of Jesus suffers voluntarily for a soul, that soul is saved. And if that soul through diabolical hatred were to reject salvation, the sufferings of a spouse of Jesus would go to save another soul, for suffering voluntarily endured for the salvation of a soul cannot be lost.[1]

10. SUFFERING, A MEANS OF SHOWING OUR LOVE FOR GOD

I was not able to tell you anything on the day before yesterday ; however, I had ever so many things in my soul, and so many things of so many kinds I said nothing because I was suffering, and when I am suffering, I shut up everything inside and I suffocate. To-day it seems to me that if you were here, I should be better able to open my soul to you ; but perhaps it was better that I said nothing ; in that way the suffering was greater ; there was then more for souls and for priests. I feel the divine hand, and its weight causes pain ; but it is the hand of Jesus.

When I have suffered like that, I feel in myself afterwards such a great and ardent desire to love God that I am consumed by it ; nevertheless, I am unable to do anything to show my love, and I suffer painfully. I would wish to suffer and to love immensely in order to form, as it were, an immense store of sufferings and of love from

---

[1] Intimate Notes : 10-11-1900.

which God could draw for souls and especially for the souls of priests.[1]

11. GOD WISHES TO GIVE US THE JOY OF BEING USEFUL TO HIM

The good Master has sent me the blessing of suffering these days, but I have been able to keep going and now I am better. Perhaps Jesus has need of something for a soul and He has taken it. How amiable the adorable Saviour is to deign to have need of something from us, from me in particular, who am so wretched.

It is like when He said to His disciples that He had need of the little donkey of Bethphage for His triumphal entry into Jerusalem. He loves to depend on His smallest creatures ; it is because He wishes to give us the joy of being of some use to Him. However, we are nothing, and we are no use whatever to our great God, except that we give Him the opportunity to exercise his love.[2]

12. I WOULD WISH TO BE ABLE TO ENVELOP THE SOULS OF PRIESTS IN INFINITE LOVE

To pray, immolate herself, and suffer for priests, the instruments of Infinite Love, was the mission of Mother Louise Margaret.

I have noted down nothing for a whole month. My interior disposition has been constantly the same : dilation of the soul in Infinite Love ; sufferings, in the sensitive faculties, but sufferings in some way absorbed by Love. I have prayed much for my dear priests ; I have given them all that I have done and suffered. At times I experience immense sorrow at seeing their souls, their faith, their fidelity in peril. What I am going to say is perhaps not proper, it is perhaps not in order, but I seem to feel that intimate, sorrowful sensation which mothers feel when they see their children exposed to great danger. I would wish to be able to protect them, to defend them, to guard them,—these sacerdotal souls that Jesus has taught me to love so much ; I would wish to be able to envelop them in Infinite Love, to hide them in the Heart of the Divine Master in order that they may escape from the dangers which threaten them.

Not being able to do anything for them, I go to Jesus ; I tell Him

---

[1] Letter to Father Charrier : 21-2-1906.
[2] Letter to Father Charrier : 4-3-1906.

that I love Him, that I wish to love Him with my whole heart, with all my strength ; I endeavour to snatch from Him by my tender love, by my loving supplications, the grace necessary for my priests.

In the midst of this inward maternal sorrow which tortures my heart, Infinite Love, living in my soul, diffuses a peace, a sweetness, a most celestial repose.

I fear for the souls of my priests taken individually, but I have no fear for the priestly body, for the Church. I have absolute, strong, serene confidence in the triumph of Christ and the reign of His Infinite Love. All the present agitations, all these conflicts of ideas, all these struggles of contrary principles, this universal deluge of errors which is inundating men's minds and withering up their hearts—all this is going to die at the feet of Christ as the waves, when finally stilled after a great tempest, expire gently on the strand.[1]

13. WE CAN MERIT GRACES FOR OTHERS BY SUFFERING

When I suffer or when I am humiliated, in spite of the natural feeling of aversion it causes, I feel in the inmost depths of my soul a most sweet satisfaction. This inward satisfaction is caused by the thought which comes to me immediately, that it is something which I can give to God for my dear priests, for souls ! I feel myself so strongly urged to give to them, to merit graces for them, and to obtain gifts for them.[2]

14. A WORD FROM JESUS REPAYS FOR FORTY YEARS OF SUFFERING

Jesus communicated Himself to me this evening with divine abundance : He said to me : " I am content." How sweet these words were to me ! The adorable Master deigns to be content with my poor work for the little book. To see Jesus content and to hear Him say so is more than sufficient recompense for forty years of suffering and twenty years of martyrdom. I do not know whether this inward joy may not be the prelude of some great sorrow. Provided He is content and that He obtains His glory, that is sufficient for me ![3]

---

[1] Letter to Father Charrier : 14-11-1906.
[2] Intimate Notes : Aug. 1905.
[3] Intimate Notes : 19-2-1910.

15. GOD WILL HAVE ALL HIS GLORY

If I look at the earth, a profound feeling of sadness takes possession of me, for the evil is great and my God is very much offended ; if I look up to heaven, I see God triumphing in glory and loved, and my soul superabounds with joy. Yes, God will have His glory, all His glory ; the evil which seems to prevail for a time will perish and the last word will remain with Love.

I, we, what do we matter ! Little atoms, revolutions that last but for a day, sufferings that will pass in an hour, all are as nothing, for eternity belongs to God and His glory is for eternity.[1]

CHAPTER X

THE INTERIOR LIFE

This life of faith, love, self-sacrifice, abandonment to the will of God, cannot be lived without continuous, humble, trusting recourse to God, from Whom every blessing comes.

Consequently, whoever wishes to consecrate himself to Infinite Love should be a man of prayer and have a profound interior life.

For the man that loves God, prayer is not a burden. It is sweet to converse with Him Who loves us with infinite tenderness, and to pour out our hearts' desires into His adorable Heart, always favourably inclined towards us.

The following pages are for the most part taken from the conferences given to the Sisters by Mother Louise Margaret during the years that she was Rev. Mother. They are all the more valuable because they are the expression of her own fervour and reflect the communications which she received from Our Lord.

1. THE INTERIOR LIFE

The interior life does not consist, as some people wrongfully think, in the suppression of all activity ; if that were so, it would be incompatible with good works, which are the fruit of charity. The interior life can be established and maintained in the midst of the most exacting employments, and many Saints who have added lustre to the Church have proved this by their lives which were filled with holy works and, which were at the same time, altogether interior.

---

[1] Intimate Notes : 18-10-1902.

The interior life is synonomyous with the union of the soul with God. It requires not merely that necessary union which is the supernatural life of the soul, but a closer, more intimate and more profound union which is maintained continuously and forms the basis and, as it were, the principle of all the operations of the soul.

This union, which is so desirable, this interior life which should be our life, encounters many obstacles, and it is our duty to combat them and surmount them by the aid of grace.

These obstacles do not arise from the activity and the multiplicity of our actions, but they are often encountered in the ill-directed activity of our minds and in the multiplicity of our thoughts.

Let us endeavour therefore, during this holy season of Advent, to collect all our thoughts interiorly for the Word Incarnate ; let us direct to Him all the outbursts of our hearts and, by means of meditation, let us fix our minds on that divine subject.

Let us unite ourselves with the Virgin Mary and, like her, completely recollected in our interior, let us seek Jesus, Who reposes there in silence and in peace.

Let us think of the sentiments of Mary, and like her, detaching our souls more and more from the exterior, passing things of time, let us live with the divine Master that interior life which will be for us a prelude of the life of happiness in heaven.[1]

2. JESUS, THE MODEL OF PRAYER

Our Lord has given us the model of every form of prayer. He has taught us, for example, to have recourse continually to the Heavenly Father in all our needs and in all situations of life.

To-day we shall study the different forms of mental prayer practised by the Divine Master during the years of His mortal life, and we shall find in that study a powerful encouragement in our difficulties and precious lights for our personal conduct.

It is necessary however to bear in mind that our soul, enveloped by the senses and the flesh and a wayfarer on the earth, finds itself naturally influenced by a multitude of physical phenomena and by the various events which succeed one another.

It remains equally united to God in these various circumstances as long as sin does not destroy the bonds which bind it to its

---

[1] Conference to the Sisters : Advent. 1911.

Principle, but its interior relations necessarily undergo frequent variations and, consequently, prayer will vary in its form according to the different influences which the soul receives.

It is good to bear this in mind in order not to be surprised at the changes which are produced in our form of prayer and not to believe ourselves rejected by God or on a wrong road, when our interior attractions change, or when we suddenly find ourselves deprived of sensible helps which we had previously experienced.   These changes in our interior dispositions are only an ordinary consequence of our human life and we should endure them with peace and tranquillity, without being troubled or surprised.

Our Lord could have established His soul in one constant, unvarying disposition.   He has not willed to do so, and we see in the Gospels that He preferred to submit Himself to our human miseries and to pass, even He, through such interior vicissitudes.

The prayer of Jesus in the desert was an elevated contemplation by means of which His most holy soul, applying itself interiorly to adoration and absolute union with God, raised itself above the senses and freed itself from all the things of the earth.   He remained in that state for forty days, ignoring the necessities of nature and nourishing Himself at the table of His Father on His divine Will and on His ineffable beauty.

This happy state may be granted to us at times, and although we may not persevere in it for forty days, in those brief moments of intimate, heavenly union, we shall nourish our souls on the Divinity and forget during those moments the shadows and sorrows of this earth.

But, as we see in the Gospels, this supernatural contemplation of Jesus was followed by the temptation and, immediately afterwards, by the many labours and the fatigues without number of His apostolic life.   It was a preparation for labours and combats.

In like manner, these special graces, this intimate union in prayer, are often given to souls in order to prepare them for a new life, for great labours, for exceptional sufferings.

When Jesus commenced His public life, His prayer changed and we see Him vary its form according to events.   He had no longer any raptures and if he passed entire nights on the mountain, what did he do ?   He adored His heavenly Father and spoke to Him of souls ; He laid before Him the weakness of His Apostles ; He prayed for them, He prayed for the multitudes that had surrounded Him during the day, for the sick that they brought to Him from all parts, for His enemies who sought to bring about His death.

Alone, under the eyes of His Father, He found in His Heart new means of proving His love for men. He thought of the Blessed Eucharist before establishing It, He thought of the divine words that He was to utter in order to instruct us ; He made His prayer for us.

When the hour of His Passion drew near, He experienced its influence. He became sadder, His tears became more frequent and His prayer again assumed a different form. In the Garden of Olives, He was immersed in a sadness unto death ; His sorrows, the ingratitude of men during the Passion, which He saw in a vision, threw Him into a state of anguish and discouragement which cast Him down and reduced Him to a physical and moral agony of extraordinary intensity. In that state He was unable to say anything to His Father ; all He could do was to suffer in His presence, to struggle against the sorrows of His soul and the natural terrors of His senses.

He had to do violence to Himself to pronounce from time to time an act of acceptance, and it was not without repugnance and without violent combats that He succeeded in pronouncing " . . . . . Let not My will but Thine be done." (Luke XXII, 42).

On the Cross, exhausted by the sufferings of His Body and by the agony of His Heart, He gathered all His remaining strength to deliver up His Spirit, immersed in darkness, into the Hands of His Father.

Before this most admirable example of Jesus, how can we be surprised at the fluctuations of our interior state and at the instability of the form of our prayer.

Prayer is the intimate expansion of our soul in God, it is the very simple manifestation of our thoughts, of the sentiments by which we are influenced, made in the presence of the divine Goodness.

Let us leave to God Himself the care of guiding our prayers and let us remember well that every prayer is good when it produces in us the fruits of solid virtue.[1]

---

[1] Conference to the Sisters : 14-12-1907.

3. THE SPIRIT OF PRAYER

The true spirit of prayer does not consist in the number of formulas which we recite, but in that fundamental disposition of the soul, which we call the spirit of prayer. It is this spirit of prayer which we should develop in ourselves and which therefore we should understand well.

This spirit reposes on the two foundations of humility and confidence. In the first place, humility shows us how we can do nothing of ourselves, how we are powerless to direct events and things, how, in spite of the superiority of our nature, we are dependent on innumerable inferior creatures to whose influence we are subject. Ah! how often we are obliged to confess our powerlessness in presence of a malady which strikes down some dear friend of ours or which attacks ourselves, in presence of the thousand vexatious occurrences which harass us, which upset our plans and interfere with what we are doing, and which, with all the power of our will, we would like to drive away from us or reduce to naught.

This consciousness of our helplessness, which is truth and which, consequently, is true humility, is not difficult to acquire. Every day of our life and every hour of the day brings us proof of it and we should have to be very blind, or in bad faith, not to be willing to recognise it.

When we thus feel in ourselves this great void, this absolute impossibility to get the better of events and to direct them by our ability, we go instinctively to the Lord of all things, to the Omnipotent, Who alone holds in His hands the power of acting as Master. And if we know that this Omnipotent Being is also Infinitely Good, if we know that, because He is Creator and Father, He loves to come to our aid and to console us, then we shall implore Him with confidence and hope in Him and, in all our needs, we shall go towards our God as the little infant goes towards its mother. Thus our prayer will be continuous because our needs are continuous. There will, then, be one almost uninterrupted motion of our hearts towards Him, one constantly renewed recourse to Him.

It is no longer a prayer said at intervals, nor is it even a number of assiduous prayers; it is a spirit of prayer which the soul carries everywhere, by which it may be said to live; which becomes its breath and its respiration.[1]

---

[1] Conference to the Sisters : 31-8-1907.

4. WE SHOULD LOVE GOD AS GOD

Several people have very wrongly formed for themselves from the writings of our holy Founder (St. Francis de Sales) and of Venerable Mother Mary de Sales Chappuis a certain form of piety which appears to me to reside more in sentiment than in well-grounded Faith and in the true notion of Love. There is a certain familiarity with Our Lord which is not sufficiently dependent and respectful. When all goes well and when they are enjoying consolation, they love Our Lord somewhat in the same manner as they would love someone very amiable, and then if trials and troubles come to them, they have the audacity to lecture Almighty God and show open displeasure with Our Lord. They wish to break with Him, they get irritated, they want to give up prayer, and when they decide to return to the good Master, they think they are doing Him a favour. This, Father, is not confiding love for God. Oh ! Father, I would wish that people should love God, but as God, that they should approach Him with the simplicity of a very little child that is very conscious of its weakness, but also with profound respect.[1]

5. OUR LOVE FOR GOD SHOULD BE RESPECTFUL

The modern spirit wishes to bring everything to the same level ; what is below wishes to raise itself to the level of what is on high, and to arrive at it the sooner, it endeavours to bring down what is on high.

If these principles are dangerous in the social life, they are not less so in the world of piety, into which some people seek to introduce them.

These heavenly doctrines of confidence in God, of filial and loving intimacy with Him, wrongly interpreted by vulgar souls, are sometimes transformed into a too human familiarity and nonchalance which is too much the order of the day.

I do not know where this failing is to be found ; it does not seem to me to reign among our Sisters, but it exists, and Jesus condemns it.

We should never separate the Humanity from the Divinity in Jesus Christ, nor should we ever separate in our hearts the love which we

---

[1] Letter to Father Charrier : 5-11-1907.

have for Him from adoration ; true love cannot exist without respect.

Jesus is Mercy ; He stoops, He bends down, He gives Himself ; that is the humility of Jesus ; but if the creature can by love ascend to His Heart, he must, nevertheless, by the knowledge of his own nothingness, remain very low at His feet, waiting until He draws him to Himself. He must love this God, this Saviour, passionately, he must trust in Him for everything, accept everything from Him, go to Him, with the heart of a child that opens itself, that believes, that receives and that gives. However, in these outbursts of love, the creature must keep his distance ; it is for Jesus, if He so wishes, to approach the creature, and in an excess of mercy, to make a sort of equality.

It is not the holy familiarity of the Saints which Jesus condemns, nor even the words of loving reproach, nor the familiar way of addressing Him inspired by love, which I sometimes use. What displeases the Sacred Heart of Jesus, what grates on It is the nonchalance with which some people criticize His works, with which they importune Him for trifles. The people with whom He is displeased are those who, in a certain manner, separating His Humanity from His Divinity, would bring Him down to their own level, attribute to Him their own sentiments, make Him a prophet, perhaps, but not the God filled with tenderness and mercy, but with greatness and majesty.[1]

6. DEVOTION TO THE HOLY SACRIFICE OF THE MASS AND FAITH IN THE BLESSED EUCHARIST

(*a*) In the evening, when communicating Himself to my soul according to His ordinary manner, Jesus conveyed to me interiorly several things regarding the Holy Sacrifice ; He said to me that the greater number of Christians assist at this sacrifice of Him without hardly knowing what is taking place on the altar, or what they ought to do themselves.[2]

(*b*) O divine Sacrament, heavenly nourishment, Sun of the soul ; O Jesus, always living, always loving, in Thee is life, strength and light. I believe in Thy presence in the little, white Host which

---

[1] Intimate Notes : 8-1-1897.
[2] Intimate Notes : Sept. 1899.

the priest places in my mouth, I believe that Thy Flesh is living, palpitating ; I believe that Thy Blood is real, similar to that which runs in my veins ; I believe that Thy Heart, full of love, is beating within my breast ; I believe that Thy whole Soul, all pure and beautiful and good, is here present within me ; I believe that Thy unique and sovereign Divinity, Which Thou dost share with the Father and the Holy Ghost without lessening It, is here united to Thy adorable Body.

I believe all this and I adore ; I believe what my senses seem to deny, but what my faith discovers. O infinite Power, O Love without bounds, O Word made Flesh, O Sacred Flesh become my nourishment ; my understanding sinks down into the abyss of its nothingness, and my heart, penetrated with ardent love, would wish to melt and be entirely mingled with the Divinity. O Lord Jesus, come into my soul, nourish me with the bread that makes us valiant ; communicate Thyself to my soul, and render it unshakable. Lord Jesus, I am on unsteady ground, help me quickly, for fatigue makes me stumble ; a moment more and I shall fall, come to my assistance, O Jesus.

But what have I to fear. He who maintains the world on its poles is within me. I have eaten of the Bread which engenders virgins ; the Blood of a God circulates in my veins ; tremble no more, my soul. The Master of the world has taken you in His arms. He wishes you to repose on Him ![1]

7. ST. JOSEPH

Glory, honour, and benediction to blessed Joseph ! His power in heaven is boundless, his tender love for men is inexhaustible. Never has anyone asked anything in vain from the glorious spouse of the Virgin.

All seemed lost, but one cry to Mary and Joseph, and all is saved !

As Jesus was submissive to them when He was on earth, so is He also in heaven ; let us go to Joseph with confidence and let us publish everywhere the glory and power and love of the glorious and merciful spouse of the Virgin Mary.[2]

---

[1] Intimate Notes : 1899.
[2] Intimate Notes : 16-7-1890.

CHAPTER XI

MARY MOST HOLY, THE MODEL OF THOSE CONSECRATED TO INFINITE LOVE

The following pages present to us her who, after the sacred Humanity of Jesus, was the most beautiful creation of Infinite Love : the Blessed Virgin Mary.

And because her life was the most generous and the most perfect response to God, Infinite Love, Who had chosen her and conferred His choicest gifts on her, we find united in her all the characteristics which should distinguish those consecrated to Infinite Love.

We learn above all from Mary to give ourselves with the complete devotedness, profound humility and total abandonment which are contained in her : " *Behold the handmaid of the Lord.*"

And it will be Mary who will guide us to Love and who will be our benign star and our firm support on the way.

1. TO JESUS THROUGH MARY

Since Jesus, our sweet Saviour has been given to us by means of Mary, it is also by means of Mary that we must go to Jesus.[1]

On the eve of the feast of our holy Founder, (St. Francis de Sales) the most amiable Father of my soul in a communication with which He favoured me, has, it seems to me, spoken these words to me : " My daughters should always approach the Divinity through the sacred Humanity of Jesus ; they should approach Jesus through Mary, and Mary through the faithful imitation of her virtues."[2]

2. WE SHOULD IMITATE THE LIFE OF MARY

On the feast of the Purification, St. Francis de Sales said to me again : " The daughters of the Visitation who will imitate the simple, poor, and hidden life of the Virgin Mother and who will live in her spirit, will enter into her holy privileges ; they will bear the Saviour in themselves and give Him a form ; with the blood of their sacrifices

---

[1] Conference to the Sisters : 29-4-1910.
[2] Intimate Notes : 24-12-1894.

and the crucifixion of their hearts, they will, like the Virgin Mary, give birth mystically to a whole people of the elect."

The life of Jesus is divine ; but since He is to be the great Model of the whole body of Christians, on its human side, the life of Jesus is capable of being understood by all and is within the reach of all,— at least in the case of some of His actions.

Mary is the Mother of all, but her life, which is completely hidden, silent, and interior, offers hidden mysteries which only certain souls are able to penetrate.

The daughters of the Visitation are called in a special way to imitate Mary, to follow her and to enter into her various sacred roles.

We do not sufficiently study our heavenly Mother Mary ; her hidden life, her union with Jesus, her spiritual participation in the state of Victim of her divine Son, and her admirable and sacred relations with the Father and the Holy Ghost.

The action of the Holy Ghost on Mary, and the correspondence of the Virgin to this action,—these are thoughts to enrapture the soul and to provide it with delicious nourishment.[1]

3. THE IMMACULATE VIRGIN

When God the Father willed to select a pure creature to be His active co-operator in the work of the Incarnation ; when the Son wished to choose for Himself a mother from whom He could receive His humanity ; when the Spirit of Love had determined to exercise His fertilizing action on a virgin to make her give birth to Christ, the adorable Trinity did not make a new creation. It took a maiden sprung from the race of Adam, completely similar in nature to other women, her sisters ; the Blessed Trinity merely preserved her from the stain of sin. For her faithful co-operation with the loving designs of God, the Blessed Virgin, all pure and without stain, was inundated with grace. Jesus living in her, enriched her with His divine gifts ; as Immaculate Virgin, Mother of God, she surpasses all creatures in dignity, but she is, nevertheless, only one among them ; every man can call her mother and cherish her as a sister ; one same nature brings them together ; one same love unites them in Jesus.[2]

---

[1] Intimate Notes : 1896.
[2] Intimate Notes : Oct. 1906.

4. MARY WAS THE MOST LOVED CREATURE

Since God decided to create the world for Christ in order that it might be the kingdom of the Word, Who was to become incarnate, we can easily understand how, in the thoughts of God, our heavenly Mother, the Virgin Mary, had preceded the creation of the world. It is for that reason that the Church applies these words to Mary : " From the beginning and before the world, was I created." (Eccles. XXIV, 14). It is indeed true that, in the order of time, she was not the first of creatures, since she was born many centuries after the creation of the world, but she may be said to have been created before the beginning of time, if not in fact, at least in the intention of God.

Now, let us consider for a moment how sublime it is to have been, as was Mary, the object of the eternal thought of God. With what anticipatory, paternal love the heavenly Father surrounded this little creature who was to be the Mother of His Word ! With what special tenderness the Son already loved beforehand her whom He Himself had created with the intention of being one day born of her ! With what infinite love the Holy Spirit burned for her in whom He was to accomplish so many divine marvels ! And do you think that this immense love of the Trinity which had enveloped for so many centuries, while she existed only in the divine mind, remained inactive ?

Love is never inactive. Love is movement, it is movement *par excellence,* because life is movement, and love is the life of God ! This divine love, always and from such a long time, in internal movement for Mary, occupied itself in preparing all the gifts, all the adornments of which a creature is capable, for the predestined soul of the Virgin. There was, as it were, a rivalry among the three Persons to enrich her in the highest degree and, it appears that there has been in the Trinity a sublime accord to adorn the future Mother of the Word Incarnate and lavish every gift upon her.

How can we to-day be astonished at all the privileges which we see attributed to our heavenly Mother ? How can we doubt about her Immaculate Conception, or her glorious Assumption, or about any of the special graces which accompanied her from the first moment of her earthly existence to her last breath. No, nothing in Mary can astonish us ; it would suffice for us to know that the thoughts of God dwelt lovingly on her as being the future Mother of the Word Incarnate.

But the thoughts of God have dwelt on us also. If He has not seen in us the Mother of His Word, He has seen, from the moment of our birth, the humble spouse of His Christ. If He has not filled us with His gifts to the same extent as Mary, He has conferred many great and special favours on us.

If Mary has been raised up so high, it is not only because she has received much, but also because she has given much. She has given the co-operation of her obedience to the designs of God on her ; she has given her faithful co-operation to every one of the graces that were poured out on her with such profusion ; she has given her sufferings and the martyrdom of her heart as proofs of her love and gratitude.

We also have received much in proportion to our littleness ; have we learned how to give back much to God Who has given us so much ? Do we give filial obedience to all His wishes ? Do we respond by constant fidelity to the graces of our vocation ? Have we learned how to give the true proof of love which is shown by mortification of ourselves and by the humble acceptance of trials of the soul and sufferings of the body ?

Let us dwell a little on these thoughts at the feet of our Immaculate Mother. Let us ask her to teach us to be like her, generous with God Who has been so generous with us.[1]

5. MARY, MOST HOLY, THE MODEL OF THE HIDDEN LIFE

At this, the Vigil of the Nativity of Mary, this sweet feast, so full of promise and of holy joy, we cannot let any other subject occupy our thoughts than this blessed nativity. We shall find in it material for our souls, and our hearts will be excited to more filial and ardent love for our Immaculate Mother.

If we consider the Virgin at birth, so frail and so like all other infants, and consider to what graces and glory she is destined, we at first remain filled with wonder.

She was to be the Mother of the Word Incarnate, she was to co-operate in the redemption of the world, and to be the treasury of divine grace and mercy ; she was to be the blessed amongst women,

---

[1] Conference to the Sisters : 8-10-1909.

the unique, the favourite of God, the Queen of Angels and of men. And notwithstanding all that, there was no singular manifestation at her birth, and we can ask ourselves why at that dawn it had not pleased God to show forth His power and reveal His adorable designs on that privileged creature by working some miracle in her favour.

The Omnipotent God did indeed work a stupendous miracle in her Immaculate Conception and in the treasures of graces with which He enriched her soul and which Mary developed with the utmost fidelity during her whole life, but nothing of that appeared on the outside.

God accomplishes His works for Himself; it suffices for Him that they give joy to His divine eyes. God, Infinite Love, likes to have His secrets which, doubtless, He can reveal, and which He reveals when He wishes, but which He takes pleasure in hiding, and sometimes very long, under a mysterious veil which conceals them from profane eyes.

The birth of Jesus was enveloped in light. There were the canticles of the angels resounding in Heaven above, there was the star lighting up the East, there were the shepherds coming in haste to the Stable, the Magi bringing their gifts, the chief Priests troubled and all Jerusalem in commotion.

Jesus is the Son of God, the Saviour of the world, God Himself Incarnate Who descended on the earth ; it is natural that His coming should cause commotion in the world. The Blessed Virgin is only a simple creature, it is true, but how great and how holy ! And besides, has not God at times performed prodigies for His simple creatures ? For John the Baptist, for example, what heavenly signs did He not show at his nativity ?

At the birth of Mary there was nothing similar. Everything was simple and natural, nothing proclaimed beforehand the admirable designs of God. And why was this ? Mary was certainly destined for as great things as those to which God destined John the Baptist, and she was not less loved by God. Why then such secrecy, such silence, so great simplicity ?

Ah ! it was for a good reason ; it was because Mary was to be the model of Christian Virgins, and was from that first hour, to teach us that divine lesson which she will repeat for us in every page of her life. It was necessary that the Immaculate, our Mother and our Model, should teach us that great lesson of the interior life, which is veiled in silence and hidden in God.

Let us therefore love this life, so simple and so common in appearance, of which the Virgin, our Mother, gives us an example in her nativity and in the whole course of her life. Let us apply ourselves to adorn the interior sanctuary of our souls into which God alone penetrates, and let us prepare for His divine eyes those sights which He loves and in which He finds complacence. Let us meditate on the completely hidden life of Mary, the true model for ours; on her life of intimate union with Jesus, of loving conformity with His divine will and of simple obedience ; on her life of labour and poverty, in which serene joy and profound sorrow alternate, in which her soul remained always tranquil and docile, sweetly bending, without murmur or perturbation, beneath the divine breath which passed over her.[1]

6. MARY, THE MODEL OF DOCILITY TO THE DIVINE WILL

It is again of Mary, our heavenly Mother that we wish to speak to-day, because we wish that this month be entirely consecrated to her. We shall consider together one of the most perfect dispositions of the Virgin Mary, that one which, along with her admirable purity and her sincere humility, has made of her soul the place of delights of the Most Blessed Trinity. We wish to speak of the flexibility of her will under the breath of the Will of God.

Whether there were a question of sorrow or joy, of the highest elevation or the lowest humiliation, the will of our heavenly Mother has never placed an obstacle or even a delay to her humble obedience.

And we are not to think that Mary was devoid of will, of character, of personal initiative. Hers was not a weak spirit, without consistency, incapable of willing, submissive to the will of others, as if naturally, but incapable of willing herself. Certainly not. Mary in all the circumstances of her life has shown a generous spirit and a strong, virile will.

We see her as a child of four years making the resolution of consecrating herself to God, tearing herself away from her mother's arms and going resolutely to the Temple. As a young girl of scarcely fifteen, she knows how to defend her vow of virginity which was against all the traditions of her race and the laws of the time. As a mother, by the strength of her will, she triumphed over the

---

[1] Conference to the Sisters : 7-9-1907.

persecution which threatened to snatch her Son from her, and over the mortal anguish which she carried in her heart for thirty years. And again it is her will which keeps her standing at the foot of the cross on which her Son was dying in agony. Yes, Mary was endowed by God with a strong, active will, but she knew so well how to make it submissive to the divine inspirations that she never hesitated to bow to the divine will of God.

The will is always dominated by love ; love alone is able to subjugate it. The love of God so reigned in Mary, that she knew how to submit her will and bend it gently and without effort to every demand to renounce what was pleasing, to accept what was bitter and to sacrifice what was dear.

If Infinite Love reigns supreme in our hearts, our will under its influence will adhere almost naturally to the Divine Will. When then we feel such resistance within ourselves in presence of a sacrifice to be made, when we see our untamed will bending only by force under the hand of God, we can be sure that the love of God is too weak in us, that He does not reign over our wills and hearts as absolute Master Who is always obeyed.

Let us ask our heavenly Mother to teach us to love God as she has loved Him, and to give Him, as she has done, complete dominion over our hearts. Thus our will, subjugated by that ineffable and powerful love, will adhere without effort and without hesitation to the Divine Will. As soon as ever it is manifested to us, whether by events or the voice of legitimate authority, we shall say to the Lord, even though it may sometimes be in tears and in sorrow : " Behold the handmaid of the Lord " of the Virgin Mary—that acquiescence in the Divine Will, so humble and submissive, which has made her the Mother of God and the Queen of Heaven and earth.[1]

7. MARY MOST HOLY, THE MODEL OF FIDELITY

Mary at birth was filled to overflowing with the gifts of God. She appears to us at the first moment of her life more filled with grace than the great Saints have been after long years of merit. But all these gifts and graces would have availed her little, if she had not been faithful in corresponding with them. It was her fidelity at every moment which enriched her to such a degree as to make her

[1] Conference to the Sisters : 21-5-1909.

the Mother of God, Queen of Angels and of men, and made her the highest and most perfect creature after Jesus Christ.

We, in like manner, though in lesser proportion, have been filled with graces. Baptism has made us children of God ; Holy Communion has united us continually to Infinite Love living in Jesus Christ, the Source of all blessings ; our holy Religious Profession has united us indissolubly to Our Lord and elevated us to the dignity of Spouses of the Son of God. How many other graces besides these have been given to us successively, and what riches we could have acquired if our fidelity had been the response to the divine liberality !

From henceforth let us therefore be careful to put the gifts we have received from God to good account by the fervour and generosity of our love. Let us not reject any grace. Let us imitate our heavenly Mother in her fidelity at every moment, and let us ask of her to obtain for us the grace to correspond, as she has done, with the merciful designs which God has over our souls.[1]

8. MARY MOST HOLY, THE MODEL OF SOULS CONSECRATED TO GOD

How great the dignity of a true Visitandine ! She is a copy, a faithful reproduction of the Virgin Mary at the time of the Visitation.

Mary was intimately united to Jesus, she carried Him in her bosom ; He lived by her, according to the natural order ; but she lived by Him and her soul was nourished on His Divinity.

Not only did Mary live by Jesus, but she communicated Him to others. When she was with her neighbour, her own personality disappeared : she was but an outward covering enveloping the Word of Life. Jesus made use of her, as of a second Self, to do His work in souls. By means of her he sanctified the soul of John the Baptist, He filled the soul of Elizabeth with prophetic lights, He loosed the dumb tongue of Zachary.

In like manner, the Visitation Sister should have an intimate union with our Lord. She should live by Him, she should nourish her soul on His divine substance, she should attract Him and bear Him in herself. She herself should also be the nutriment of God : as a voluntary victim, she offers herself to placate Divine Justice ; she offers Him her heart, emptied of all human love, in order that He

---

[1] Conference to the Sisters : 4-9-1909.

may satiate His thirst for love ; she loses the possession of her soul in God, in order that nothing may be wanting to the divine fulness.

Bearing God in herself, she will communicate Him to her neighbour ; her words will be of God alone, her modes of action, impregnated with divine Charity, will reveal God hidden within her. From her whole being there will go forth a hidden life which will attract people to God.

At the time of the Visitation, Mary revealed the sentiments of her soul in these words : " My soul doth magnify the Lord. And my spirit doth rejoice in God my Saviour. Because He hath regarded the humility of His handmaid : for behold from henceforth all nations shall call me blessed. Because He that is mighty hath done great things in me : and holy is His name." (Luke I, 46-49).

This state of interior praise should be that of a true Visitation Sister. She glorifies the Lord by her self-abasement which recognises the divine Omnipotence, by her abandonment which recognises the rights of divine Justice, by her confiding love which recognises infinite Goodness. Elevated above herself in a divine transport, she finds her joy in God. This heavenly joy, which is not often tasted except in the most spiritual part of her soul, nevertheless reflects itself on her countenance, and the very sight of her opens hearts to God. The pure light which enlightens her soul makes her distinguish what is from herself and what is from God. She recognises her lowliness and her nothingness, and though favoured and sometimes caressed as a spouse, she recognises that she is only a humble servant.

She proclaims herself blessed, because God has done great things in her. She has allowed God to act in her : that is her whole part. God has raised the throne of His Mercy on the abyss of her miseries ; God has done His will in her and by her, because she had not done her own will, but had adhered at every moment to the divine pleasure. God, in fine, has been pleased to accept her sacrifices, and if He has made use of them for the salvation of souls, it is not on account of their intrinsic value, but because they were united to the sacrifice of Jesus Christ.

Oh ! what a beautiful and holy vocation ! It is a sublime state in which one's being is sanctified by means of union with God. It is a faithful image of Mary bearing Jesus ; it is the blessed way followed by the Mother of God ; it is indeed a humble, abject life in the eyes of creatures, but it is splendid and glorious in the life of

God and His Angels ; a life, common and vulgar in appearance, but superhuman, and, even in this life, celestial !

What a grace to have been called to this blessed vocation ! What a sign of divine predilection to have been invited to this life of intimate union with the Divinity ! But what a responsibility also for the soul if it does not correspond with such great love, if it does not understand what God wants from it and is remiss in carrying it out.[1]

PART III

THE MESSAGE OF LOVE

The selection from the writings of Mother Louise Margaret which we have given so far tell us of the great desire of God to be loved.
" God is Love and Love wishes to be loved."
The selection given in this third part tell us of the origin and nature of the Work of Infinite Love ; of the practical means that God has taken in our own times to remind the world through His priests of the immense love of God for men and of the love which He demands.

CHAPTER I.

THE DESIRES OF GOD

What are these desires ?   To communicate His love to men and to renew the world, not by a new deluge, but by fire, and the fire which He will employ is a spiritual fire, the fire of divine love.

1. THE NEW DELUGE

Yesterday, after Holy Communion, being intimately united to Jesus, I saw in His Sacred Heart His desires as God ; He wishes that Love be diffused, that it inflame the world and renew it.   It is no longer by the waters of a new deluge that God wishes to purify and regenerate the world, but by fire.   The minds and wills of men have been led astray ; the world that needs purification is above all the world of intellects and souls, therefore the fire which God

---

[1] Conference to the Sisters : 18-6-1910.

wishes to employ is an purely spiritual fire. Love and Mercy must be preached to every creature, for the Heart of God has an immense desire to pardon ; if He sees the least sign of love in a heart in response to His own, He pardons. My soul suffers strange sorrow at the sight of the indifference and coldness of the greater part of Christians and the lack of correspondence which the love of God finds in the hearts of creatures ; but how it suffers also on account of its little capacity to love what it sees to be so lovable and so desirous of love !

Who thinks of the love of God ? Who believes as he should in His mercy ? Nevertheless God is Charity ; His works are nothing but love, and His Mercy is eternal and infinite.

One day, prostrate at the feet of Jesus, I called Him the only good of my soul, the sovereign love of my heart, the infinite treasure of all riches, and in the end I said to Him : " My Jesus, how dost Thou wish that I call Thee ?" And He replied to me : " Call Me Mercy."

O my sweet Mercy, O Jesus, who died of love on the cross, grant us that being brought back to Thee by the attraction of Thy Mercy, we may live by Thy love and for Thy love.[1]

2. GOD IS LOVE, AND MUST REIGN BY MEANS OF LOVE

I finished my retreat in most sweet peace. Jesus, the divine Consoler of souls poured out into me the sweet unction of His presence. I felt Him to be good, infinitely good towards His little, miserable servant. Oh ! how the infinitely great God must have need to pour out His love, when He comes in this manner to a creature of nothingness without any other reason but that of His Love ! Yes, I have felt more than ever during the days of this retreat, that there is in God an incomprehensible plenitude of love. This superabundant plenitude has a need to pour itself out, and Jesus, God incarnate, Who contains in His Heart the superabundance of this Infinite Love, goes seeking for souls who may receive the overflow of this Love.

The Word became man in order to come in Person to conquer hearts for Love. He formed His Church in order to make a kingdom for His Love ; He gave the Blessed Eucharist in order to be the fuel of Love ; He founded His Priesthood in order to propagate the reign

---

[1] Intimate Notes : 13-4-1900.

of Love throughout the ages ; He showed His Heart to the world in order to rekindle Love ; He gives it to-day to His priests as a weapon of Love. God is Love, He must reign by love ![1]

3. A GREAT WORK OF GOD IS BEING ACCOMPLISHED IN THE WORLD

There are times when everything should keep silence in the soul ; no sound of words should be heard. These are times when God does His great works, and as everything which He does is the result of His speech, of His Word, eternally Creator, while this un-created Speech resounds, all created speech should be silent. It is thus in my soul these times.

I am conscious of a great work of God being accomplished in the world ; wordlings do not perceive it ; they affect to ignore God, and to do without Him. And He . . . . leaves them to themselves. He allows the world to follow its bent downwards . . . . everything descends.

But our great God disposes in Himself the materials for His work. In the higher regions, He speaks the ineffable word, the Word that makes operative the words of Love. At times, often, for some months past, I find myself thus in profound interior silence. Jesus does not speak to me as formerly ; I no longer hear His voice dis-tinctly striking the ear of my soul. I have asked myself why He has become silent ; I have asked myself ; I have looked whether my infidelities, my miseries have made Him turn away from me ; but no, misery only attracts His mercy and besides, I have known that God dwelt in this great silence which envelops me.

It is in the hearts and minds where recollection and silence reign that God prepares His work of love, and my soul, by the pure good-ness of God, united to this divine labour, should listen to the voice of Infinite Love alone to the exclusion of every other voice.[2]

---

[1] Intimate Notes : Oct. 1905.

[2] Intimate Notes : 24-2-1906.

CHAPTER II

THE WORK OF INFINITE LOVE IS ENTRUSTED TO PRIESTS

PREPARATION TO RECEIVE THE GREAT MESSAGE OF LOVE

(a) I do not know why for some days past I feel myself attracted by Infinite Love more than usual. At times it seems to me that my heart wishes to rush out of my breast and go and unite with this divine Love.

I suffer also as I have not suffered for a long time, in my feet and hands, and from pain in my right side ; it is sweet and painful however, but this state of suffering and of ardent desire which causes me to rush towards Infinite Love diffuses in my soul such sweetness and such entire peace that it is like a commencement of heaven.

Heaven will be life in Love ; the soul, heart and whole being of man will enjoy absolute satiety of love, while always being thirsty for love and full of desire for love.

I do not know what the good Master wishes me to do, but I feel an ardent desire to spend this month of June well.[1]

(b) In June, 1902, during the Novena of the Sacred Heart, my divine Master manifested Himself to me for several days, as I have noted down. I gave all the details of these graces to my Director ; afterwards I suffered extremely. I felt that what Our Lord had said to me must be communicated to someone. The weight of these divine communications was crushing me, and I waited for help and light from God alone.[2]

1. THE GREAT MESSAGE OF LOVE

Yesterday, I was alone before the Blessed Sacrament, I was in that weary and painful state in which I had been for some weeks, when Jesus made His presence felt to my soul.

---

[1] Intimate Notes : 30-5-1902.
[2] From her autobiography.

I adored Him, being sweetly consoled by His presence, and praying to Him for our little novitiate, I asked Him to give me some souls that I might form for Him. Then He replied to me : " I will give you souls of men." Profoundly astonished at these words, the sense of which I did not understand, I remained silent, endeavouring to find an explanation. And Jesus spoke again : " I will give you souls of priests." Being still more astonished I said to Him : " My Jesus, how wilt Thou do that ? " He replied : " It is for My Clergy that you will immolate yourself. I wish to instruct you during this Octave, write down all that I will tell you."

Yesterday evening He said to me : **" My priest is My other Self. I love Him, but he must be holy. Nineteen centuries ago, twelve men changed the world, they were not merely men, they were priests. Now once more twelve priests could change the world."**

This morning He said to me : " The priest is a being clothed with Christ to such a degree that He becomes almost a God ; but he is a man also, and it is necessary that he be so. It is necessary that he feel the weaknesses, the struggles, the sorrows, the temptations, the fears, the revolts of men ; it is necessary that he be miserable in order that he be merciful ; it is necessary also that he be strong, that he be pure, that he be holy, in order that he may sanctify others.

It is necessary that My priest have a large, tender, ardent heart capable of loving.

The priest has so much to love ! He must love Me, His Master, His Brother, His Friend, His Consoler, as I have loved him. I have loved him even to the mingling of My life with his, even to making Myself obedient to His Word. He must also love My Spouse and his, the Holy Church, and with what love ! with a passionate and jealous love, jealous for her glory, for her purity, for her unity, for her fruitfulness.

Finally, he must love souls as his children. And what father has so many children to love as the priest ! "

June 7th.—" The heart of My priest ought to be an ardent flame, warming and purifying souls. If the priest only knew the treasures of love which My Heart contains for him ! Let him come to My Heart, let him draw from It, let him fill himself with love until it overflows from his heart and spreads itself over the world !

Margaret Mary has shown My Heart to the world, do you show it to My priests and draw them all to My Heart."

On the evening of June 7th I went to Confession ; our Chaplain spoke to me of the Novena. I told him that I had great suffering during it ; he appeared to be astonished. I told him that I was always like that ; that I suffered always. He replied to me : " If that is the case, the reason is, doubtless, because you will receive some grace, He (Our Lord) will tell you something definite." I made no reply.

Yes, Jesus did tell me something definite ; I did not know ; I did not yet understand. I was afraid.

June 8th.—I withdrew from prayer as much as I could (on the advice of those who directed her) ; I did not make the meditation permitted at half-past one, and during Vespers, feeling myself attracted (to Our Lord), I resisted and took up a book. Oh ! how I have resisted Jesus to-day ! I do not wish to do so any more, I would perhaps cause pain to His Heart. That evening He showed me the greatness of the priest. Chosen from among men, the priest ascends even to God ; he is placed between man and God, a mediator like Jesus and with Jesus. He has been, so to speak, transubstant- iated into Jesus, and He enters thus into His divine roles and His divine prerogatives. He is with Jesus, offering, expiation, victim. From this state of special union with Jesus, all the acts of the priest acquire an incomprehensible excellence.

June 10th.—After Communion I said to Jesus : " My Saviour, when our Blessed Sister (Margaret Mary) showed Thy divine Heart to the world, did not priests see It ? Does not that suffice ?" Jesus replied : " I wish now to make a special manifestation of It to them." Then He showed me that He had a special work to do : to enkindle the fire of love in the world ; and that He wished to make use of His priests to do that. He said this to me with such a touching and tender expression that tears came to my eyes : " I have need of them to do My work." In order that they may be able to extend the reign of love, they must be full of it themselves and it is from the Heart of Jesus that they must draw it. " My Heart is the Chalice of My Blood," said He to me again ; " if anyone has the right and the duty to drink from It, it is not My priest, who each day brings the chalice of the altar to his lips ; let him come to My Heart and let him drink !"

June 12th'—All day yesterday, I had a view of a special grouping of priests around the Heart of Jesus, of a work exclusively for them ; I do not know if I am mistaken. Oh ! how greatly I need light and help ! I am suffering, nevertheless, my soul is in great peace ; all within me is calm, I have neither temptations, nor painful and fatiguing thoughts. The depths of my soul are sweetly rapt in Jesus.

When by myself I wish to think out any of the things which He has communicated to me, I cannot do so ; nothing clear or precise occurs in my mind ; on the contrary, as soon as He speaks or touches my soul with His divine impression, everything is clear, luminous and definite.

June 13th.—This morning when reflecting within myself, I thought that, perhaps, a special branch of the *Guard of Honour* might be formed for priests. Jesus said to me : " No." He gave me to understand that He did not wish His priests to be merely adorers of His Heart, but that He wished to form a body of knights who would fight for the triumph of His love.

Those who would form part of this body of knights of His divine Heart would engage among other things to preach Infinite Love and Mercy, and to be united themselves, having but one heart and one soul in their campaign for the triumph of what is good, and never to obstruct one another in their activities.

June 17th.—Since June 13th, Jesus has given me no further details about this matter. Perhaps He will tell me nothing more.

This morning at Holy Communion, I asked Him to tell the rest to someone else, to one of His priests ; as for me, what can I do except suffer for Him and offer myself as a victim for His glory and the triumph of His love ?

Oh ! I offer myself to Jesus for this intention with all the power of my heart, and for active work also if He wishes it, but it seems to me that I have more capacity for suffering than for action.

I feel my nothingness and my weakness in a manner that I cannot express ; everything in me appears to me to be broken and vanquished; however, I feel in myself great courage to suffer. Yes, the suffering which I foresee does not terrify me. Jesus wishes me to be docile, He wishes me to bend without effort and without agitation under all the storms of trial which I feel coming. Thus I wish to remain more and more in the divine hands without personal action or will.[1]

---

[1] Intimate Notes : Feast of the Sacred Heart, 1902.

2. MISSION OF LOVE FOR PRIESTS

I see in God a sublime movement which, at this time, He makes to draw His loved creature to Himself ; it is a movement of love and mercy.

He commences by inviting His priests to come closer to Him in order that He may press them to His Heart and then bathe them in love ; then, through His priests He will extend His influence over all souls.   Oh ! what a fine mission of love God is going to give to His priests !   When it is shown to me I am so enraptured by its grandeur and beauty and by the infinite goodness of the Heart of God, that I am sometimes on the point of fainting.   I know that I am the weakest and the most miserable of mortals, but it seems to me, nevertheless, that the knowledge which God gives me of His Infinite Love is above human strength, and that, besides this grace which He confers on me by giving me that knowledge, He must give me still another to render me capable of supporting it.[1]

3. "I WILL GO TO MY PRIESTS . . ."

God, Infinite Love, has placed in each soul at its creation a principle of eternal life, a little spark of love, and it is this spark of love which has gone out from Infinite Love that always attracts God towards souls.

There is, as it were, a need in God to go to souls in order to rejoin this spark of life gone out from Him, which is in them.

When a soul is pure, there is a mutual attraction ; God goes towards the soul and the soul also feels itself drawn towards God.   When the soul is not pure, it does not feel the impulse of attraction, it is insensible.

God, the infinitely Pure, feels always this divine impulse.   However, He cannot penetrate into souls that are not pure ; they have become in a certain way materialized ; successive sins, material cares, and especially the cooling of the heart have hardened them and petrified them ; Infinite Love cannot enter into them in order to unite with this little spark which is the principle of their eternal life.

[1] Intimate Notes : 30-11-1905.

Then the Word, our eternal and divine Mediator, presented Himself to His Father and said : " I have found a means to make Love penetrate into the world and thus purify it and warm it again. I will go to those whom I have instituted to participate in My eternal Priesthood, and who continue it on earth ; I will go to My priests. Their souls are purer and more disentangled from earthly solicitude ; I will draw them to My Heart, I will fill them with love, and through them Infinite Love will flow into souls." That is the whole plan of Jesus ; the priest filled with love will communicate the divine flames to souls under his direct influence ; (for each priest has a certain number of souls under his influence) ; in their turn, these will enflame the souls of those around them and thus, little by little, Infinite Love will regain possession of the world.[1]

4. OUR LORD'S GREAT DESIRE TO COMMUNICATE HIS GRACE TO PRIESTS

Our Lord has an incomparable desire to communicate His grace, His virtue and His Infinite Love to the world, but first of all to His priests. They are to be the channels which are to bring life to souls, the life of love without which Faith is dead. It seems to me that a small number of priests, completely penetrated with Infinite Love, would suffice to produce immense good.[2]

5. CURRENT OF LOVE ENVELOPING PRIESTS

On last Sunday, during Holy Mass, several ideas about the work of Infinite Love were communicated to me ; at evening prayer, my soul, withdrawn into the inmost depths of the Divine Heart, saw again this reign of Love desired by Our Lord in a manner so clear that it seemed to me that I would be able to explain it to other souls with facility and make it understood by them. Afterwards when, with pen in hand, I wish to describe what I have seen, I feel myself powerless.

However, I must say something about it, for it is not for myself alone that Jesus shows me this, but in order that I may transmit it to others.

---

[1] Intimate Notes : 1-5-1903.
[2] Letter to Monsignor Filipello : 29-10-1911.

I saw a current of love descend from the bosom of Infinite Love which is God, and which came and enveloped, not all, but a great number of priests throughout the whole world. I thought that I understood (but I do not know whether I am mistaken, I am so much afraid of mixing up my own ideas with the designs of Jesus) that in each nation, in each diocese, there are a certain number of elite among the priests and that these are the ones which Our Saviour wishes to unite together by a bond of love, in order that they may be made stronger by union.[1]

6. THE MIRROR TO REFLECT GOD'S LOVE IS THE HEART OF THE PRIEST

Infinite Love is a sun ; if It projected its rays directly on the world, souls would be dazzled and consumed by It, because they are neither sufficiently noble nor sufficiently pure. This divine Sun must be reflected in a mirror, and the reflection of its rays in this mirror will enlighten the world and rekindle love in it.

This mirror is the heart of the priest, but it must be pure, it must be transparent. The soul of the priest must become conformable to the soul of Christ. When the priest is truly another Jesus Christ, he will become a pure mirror which will reflect the divine rays of Infinite Love.[2]

7. I WISH MY PRIESTS TO BE SOWERS OF LOVE

Yesterday, on the feast of St. John the Baptist, having entered the choir, I placed myself simply at the feet of Jesus without saying anything. I soon felt my soul as if separated from all things, and in mind, I saw what appeared to be an autumn sky, sad, and cold ; a great wind drove thick grey clouds before it in the heavens ; below, the brown earth, on which no vegetation appeared, extended as far as the eye could reach, and then I saw men pass along ; they took seeds from their breasts and scattered them in handfuls over the earth, and the voice of Jesus said to me : " I wish My priests to be sowers of love."

---

[1] Intimate Notes : 20-12-1912.

[2] Intimate Notes : 27-8-1905.

Then I saw no more, the voice of Jesus had put me in a transport, an intense light filled my soul ; something burning penetrated my whole being.[1]

8. I WILL MAKE A LITTLE ARMY OF PRIESTS WHO WILL FIGHT FOR THE REIGN OF LOVE

(a) Jesus, my most sweet Master, attracts me always towards His priests. As I was praying for our dear France plunged in anarchy and giving the impulse of revolt and of evil to other nations, He said to me : " I will make from My dear priests a little army that will fight for good and make My Love reign." At the same time He gave me to understand that He wished to see all the priests of the world under that strict discipline which assures victory for armies. And that this discipline was the discipline of the spirit ensuring that all priests have but one same thought, one same end, one same teaching, one same movement to combat and to resist evil.[2]

(b) I went to the choir in these dispositions. Immediately after I had made an act of adoration, my soul was drawn above itself. I no longer felt my corporal sufferings, nor any mental obstacle.

As ineffable sweetness was diffused through my soul ; Our Lord was very near, He bent down towards me ; then I entered into that immense, luminous, most ardent and most sweet reality which is Infinite Love.

I remained in adoration with inexpressible repose and peace of mind, and general enjoyment of my whole being.

While I was there, I saw below me in an intellectual vision a very vast space where good and evil were in presence of one another about to engage in conflict. Then, at the call of God, priests in great numbers, presented themselves, a place was assigned to each of them and gradually they formed themselves into an army, drawn up to give battle.

There were battalions of every kind. Some were those who fought by the word, by the pen, by works of zeal ; others, the Religious Orders, were the reserves destined for assaults and bloody charges. But the great mass, the bulk of the army, those who fought the

---

[1] Intimate Notes : 25-6-1902.
[2] Intimate Notes : 6-5-1907.

regular combats and whose exact discipline, endurance and fidelity ensured victory,—those were the priests of the secular clergy, the Pastors, the Assistants, obscure professors who, in the towns and in the countrysides, had to have their weapons in their hands from sunrise to sunset to fight against evil.

I have to use many words to express what I saw ; but in God everything is so simple, so clear, that it requires only a movement of the soul to see it and comprehend it, and yet it was infinitely clearer and more distinct than I can express.

Then the vision vanished and I remained in adoration without understanding it.[1]

9. OPEN TO ME THE SOULS AND HEARTS OF PRIESTS

Just now, at prayer, Our Lord manifested Himself to me. He said to me : " I wish to fill souls with My Infinite Love." Then He added in an accent of prayer : " Open to Me the souls and hearts of priests in order that I may pour into them, and through them, on the world, the love which urges Me."

Our Lord then said that the object of this new work was to give, to reveal His Infinite Love to priests ;—that it was not to be an ordinary work—that it should be begun by choosing a small number of priests from each diocese, chosen souls to be nourished on the doctrine of Infinite Love.[2]

10. THE PURIFYING EFFECT OF INFINITE LOVE

In obedience to your wishes, I will tell you what I believe I saw at prayer yesterday. I saw that Infinite Love should be given to priests in the first place to purify them, and above all to those among them who have most stains ; and then to enlighten them and strengthen them. And when Infinite Love will have accomplished this function, when they have become pure, ardent, and strong, love will continue to fill them and impregnate them to such a degree that they will have a superabundance of it, and will be able to diffuse it in all directions over souls. Even stains and faults will not be able to prevent a priest from receiving this gift of Love which God wishes

---

[1] Intimate Notes : July, 1912.
[2] Intimate Notes : 1913.

to make, which He now makes to His priests. If the priest repents, if he is willing to surrender himself to Love, he will be able not only to become again what he was, but he can become an apostle of Love, and that all the better because he has been saved by merciful love.[1]

11. OUR LORD WISHES PRIESTS TO KNOW THAT HE HAS MADE TO THEM THE GIFT OF HIS HEART

Yesterday evening and this morning I have had several very clear and definite communications on the Work of Love. I do not know how to explain them. It seems to me that Our Lord wishes us to commence by revealing His Infinite Love and the gift which He has made of His Heart to His priests, to some at first. It would be necessary to imbue these with this love and make them all inflamed with it. They would be like a fire lighted in the diocese and when it would be well kindled it would spread outside.

Oh ! how willingly I would give my life in order that some one else might receive the overflowing torrents of Love and pour them out on priests. I am able to do nothing.[2]

(*b*) Just now at prayer, Our Lord again showed me this great army of priests, and He said to me : " I entrust you with the task of distributing weapons to them." At the same time He gave me to understand that these weapons are love ; that it was necessary to make to priests the revelation of Infinite Love which is God, which is in God, and which God has for them. This revelation will enkindle in the hearts of priests such a great desire to make a return of love that they will become filled with ardour to combat evil and powerful to gain souls for Christ.

Seeing my powerlessness to execute the will of Our Lord, I remained there before Him ; tears came to my eyes and I said : " What can I do ? I have got the little book which Thou hast dictated to me published ; I have poured all that Thou hast given me for Thy priests into the heart of my Bishop. What more can I do except pray and suffer ?" And I remained there for a long time sunk in the depths of my nothingness.[3]

---

[1] Letter to Father Charrier : 7-8-1908.
[2] Intimate Notes : 26-7-1912.
[3] Intimate Notes : 25-7-1912.

12. IT IS THE WISH OF JESUS THAT INFINITE LOVE SHOULD ENVELOP PRIESTS AND BE THEIR STRENGTH

For priests, Father, what shall I say to you? The more experience I have, the greater I feel the need of something which will protect them against evil, which will unite them with the Sovereign Pontiff and among themselves.

It is the wish of Jesus that Infinite Love envelop them and be their strength, their safeguard, their union, and their light.[1]

13. GOD HAS IMMENSE LOVE FOR PRIESTS

Yes, God has an immense, infinite love for priests. He wishes to make them understand this ; when they have understood it, they will sanctify themselves to a high degree and become capable of doing the works of salvation of Jesus Christ. But it is very necessary to make them understand well that God has this love for them. The Work demanded by Our Lord consists chiefly in this. The means to be employed, the exterior form of the Work, is all of lesser importance.

Certain priests marked out by God are to be chosen to be the first to receive the revelation of Love, they must become imbued with the Love, become completely inflamed with it and then they themselves will communicate the divine fire to their brethren. And thus Infinite Love will do Its work and make Its progress, like a fire which is lighted in the corner of a forest and gradually spreads to all the trees, causing a general conflagration.

Oh ! would that I had some priests who could understand what the Heart of God has for them and what He expects from them.[2]

14. THE SUN OF INFINITE LOVE NECESSARY TO RIPEN THE FRUIT OF VIRTUE

Yesterday evening I had retired into the chapel of our holy Founder ; while I was adoring the Blessed Sacrament, I had a singular interior vision ; it was of a great tree covered with a multitude of fruits. Some of these fruits were very fine, very ripe, and without spot ; others that were hidden under the foliage were sound, but less

---

[1] Letter to Father Charrier : 14-8-1907.
[2] Intimate Notes : 31-7-1912.

beautiful and not completely ripe ; others were of a blackish colour, small and blighted.

As I was gazing upon this, it was shown to me that this tree, with powerful roots and vigorous trunk, was the Catholic priesthood, and Jesus said to me : " Do not trouble yourself about those spoiled fruits, they will fall off themselves, but take off the leaves that are casting a shadow on the others, in order that the sun of Infinite Love may be able to ripen them, gild them, and make them like those which you see are so fine." My Jesus, what dost Thou wish me to do ? I know nothing about this ; I give myself to Thee to do Thy will, as I am Thine to serve Thee and to love Thee ; I abandon myself to Thee !¹

15. I WISH YOU TO TELL MY PRIESTS THAT I GIVE THEM MY HEART

(*a*) I was in adoration before the Blessed Sacrament exposed, yesterday during supper. A profound consciousness of the Divine Presence enveloped me ; Our Lord manifested Himself to me with His usual goodness and He said to me : **" I wish you to tell my priests that I give them My heart ; this gift is a testimony of the ardent love which I have for them. and a pledge of the graces which I will confer on those who will be faithful to Me."** I replied : "I do not see Thy priests, how shall I tell them this ? I can tell it to our Chaplain or to Father, but that is all that I am able to do." Jesus replied : " That is sufficient," and He added : " Tell Father that I have chosen him to be the bearer to My priests of the new gift which I make to them of My Heart. They must prepare the reign of My love over the world, and that is why I wish to pour out in them an abundant effusion of love !"

Then I saw, as it were, a representation of my misery, complete, absolute misery, and Our Lord said to me : " You see that I have left in you sufficient to prevent you from ever being elated by My graces."²

(*b*) It seems to me that Our Lord's desire is that we should commence by saying that He has given His Heart to His priests, that we

---

¹ Intimate Notes : 1903.
² Intimate Notes : 13-7-1907.

should then point out how much He loved them, with what love of preference, and with what tenderness. After that we should say how priests can respond to this love of Jesus by loving Him, by imitating Him, by making His love known in the world, by continuing His very Person in themselves, by doing His work. Then we should speak of the divine work of Infinite Love, of that Love which is, as it were, accumulated in the Heart of God, which wishes to be spread abroad in order to save the world, and which wishes to make of the Priesthood a pure and sacred channel by which it will pass to bathe, purify, and warm all souls.

We should then deduce from this explanation the proof of what has been said at the commencement about the special gift of the Sacred Heart to priests and conclude by giving an idea of an organization which would group the priests of the world around their bishops and around the Pope in order to form a chain of love with which to surround the world.[1]

16. THE HEART OF JESUS IS LIGHT, STRENGTH AND LIFE FOR THE PRIEST

I asked Our Lord several times if He would give me some light on these words : " If any man will come after Me . . . ." Each time He directed me towards His Heart.

It seems that it is less His Cross that He wishes to give to His priests than His Heart. He wishes to show It to them, to give It to them because He has said : " When they know My love better, when they love Me more, they will receive and carry My cross more easily."

If I could only show His Heart as I see It, so adorably sweet and tender towards souls, towards priests !

" The designs and desires of Jesus are so simple : to raise up the world, to save it from scepticism and coldness, from the spirit of paganism which is enveloping it ; He has need of helpers for this great work and He calls His priests ; and before employing them in this great task of uplifting the world, He opens to them the treasures of His never-failing love. He says to them : " Come and draw from My Heart light, strength, and life."

---

[1] Letter to Father Charrier : 17-2-1908.

He wishes to communicate an abundance of life, of divine, supernatural life of His priests, in order that they also may be able to communicate it to others and so give life to souls.[1]

17. THE TREASURES IN THE HEART OF JESUS FOR PRIESTS ARE IMMENSE

My adorable Saviour, Thou hast been silent for many days, and under obedience, I have kept away from my thoughts what Thou knowest well I cannot keep away from my heart.

Just now, after Holy Communion, Thou hast united me to Thee so closely, that in a certain manner I lost the consciousness of my own being and could neither see nor know anything but Thee.

And while Thou wast completely mine and I was completely Thine, while my thoughts were lost in Thy thoughts, and my will, in Thy divine will, it seemed to me that this organization for priests was indeed willed by Thy Heart.

It seemed to me that the love which overflows from Thy divine Heart wished to go to the multitude of souls by passing through the hearts of Thy priests.

It seemed to me that Thou didst wish to see them gathered around Thy Heart, drawing from this divine source a renewal of life and love.

Priests are mothers; they must give life, they must make the souls that Thou hast given to them grow and increase; in order that they may be able to give life to souls, they must have in themselves an abundance of life and warmth of love ever becoming more abundant and ardent, always being renewed.

The treasures of love of Thy Heart are immense, O most sweet Jesus, and now Thou wishest to reveal them to Thy priests, and by Thy priests, Thou wishest to distribute them through the world.[2]

18. I WILL CALL THEM THE BELOVED SONS OF MY HEART

Yesterday I had approached the Holy Table with sentiments of profound humilation.

I think that this was pleasing to Our Lord, for immediately after receiving the Sacred Host, I felt myself taken possession of by the

---

[1] Intimate Notes : 7-6-1903.
[2] Intimate Notes : 18-2-1903.

divine presence in a manner much more perceptible than usual.

I was so conscious that Jesus belonged to me ; He attracted me to Himself with such sweet goodness, that it caused an inexpressible rapture of love in my soul.

I asked Him, as my Director desired, whether He wished to tell me something more about the Work. My most sweet Master said to me, at least it seemed to me so, that He wished that those who will be members of this Work should be entirely devoted to His Heart and that they should embrace all the means of diffusing His love in souls, even if by doing so they will have to sacrifice themselves.

He said to me also : " I shall call them the beloved sons of My Heart," thus giving me to understand that He would give them a great abundance of light and special help to accomplish His work in the world.

But He wishes them to be entirely devoted to His Heart.[1]

19. I WISH TO CONQUER HATRED BY LOVE

Jesus said to me : " I suffer from hatred !" This short phrase, like all those of my divine Master, contained a world of thoughts which have impressed themselves in a single moment on my mind, but which I can express only by a great many words, and that very incompletely. I saw in these words that hatred is the absolute opposite to God, and that it is His one enemy, and the greatest evil of the creature. Hatred on the part of man has two forms : hatred of man for God ; hatred of man for other men. Each of these forms of hatred is a monstrous offence to the Being of God which is Love. Hatred is like the negation of God-Love ; it is a manner of annihilating God ; or rather, it is a desire, an attempt, an effort made to annihilate God, Infinite Love.

I have not been able to restrain my tears when considering this. Then Jesus said to me : " I wish to conquer hatred by Love ; I will send My priests to diffuse it throughout the whole world. I have given them My Heart in order that they may see the treasures of love which are in God, and that, after drawing from these treasures for themselves, they may draw from them for the world. Tell

---

[1] Intimate Notes : 3-10-1909.

them to go and spread abroad everywhere the treasures of Love !''

Jesus showed me that He wished to see His priests filled with love for souls ; to see them bend down towards them and warm them by contact with them.[1]

20. THE PRIEST SHOULD ENTER BY THE SACRED HEART INTO THE INTIMATE KNOWLEDGE OF JESUS CHRIST

I have just re-read what I had written yesterday, and my soul, ascending towards God, said to Him : " My God, what must I do to make Thee loved ?" The voice of Jesus resounded in the depths of my soul and He replied to me : " Show My Heart, good, merciful, full of compassion and sweetness." When this Divine Voice makes itself heard, it diffuses light at the same time. In this light I have seen, if I am not mistaken, that priests should acquire a profound and ever-increasing knowledge of Infinite Love.

The world is not able to receive this revelation of love directly, nor is it able to assimilate its fruits of grace and salvation. It is the priest, because he is nearer to God and already consecrated to Him who receives this manifestation of love and communicates it to the world, and it is through the Heart of Jesus, studied in the mystery of His divine virtues and imitated, that the priest will enter into the full possession of the mystery of Infinite Love. It seems to me that Our Lord wishes me to say the following : The priest should not be content with receiving the devotion to the Heart of Jesus, with professing it himself and communicating it to souls. That is without doubt good, but it was not the end which the Divine Master had in view when He made a special donation of His Heart to His priests. Jesus wishes something further. Priests should enter by this Sacred Heart into the intimate knowledge of Jesus Christ ; it is as a door through which the priest must pass in order to penetrate into the interior of Christ, and having become bathed in Him and completely impregnated with Him, he should become a shining mirror in which Infinite Love can be reflected.[2]

Jesus is in haste to open His Divine Heart to His priests, for He sees that for want of knowing His love, many are lost by turning away from true doctrine. Faith declines and becomes extinguished when it is not lighted up and warmed by Love ![3]

---

[1] Intimate Notes : 11-2-1905.
[2] Intimate Notes : 27-8-1905.
[3] Letter to Monsignor Filipello : 8-12-1911.

CHAPTER III.

NATURE, SCOPE AND CHARACTERISTICS OF THE WORK OF INFINITE LOVE

The passages quoted in this chapter were written by Mother Louise Margaret between 1902, the year during which she received the first communications about the Work of Infinite Love, and 1914, the year preceding her death.

In these passages she speaks of the Work demanded by Jesus, and transmits to us His wishes with regard to its nature, and essential characteristics.

The general outlines of the Work were given in the communications which she received from Our Lord during the Octave of the Sacred Heart, 1902. The details of the Work ; the establishment of the Priests' Universal Union of the Friends of the Sacred Heart and the foundation of the new monastery that was to be " the root hidden in the ground " of the work—which were the means designed by Our Lord to convey the message of love to the world— were communicated by Him to Mother Louise Margaret between 1908 and her death.

The present chapter deals with these details of the Work.

1. THE WORK OF INFINITE LOVE

Yesterday I had several communications on the Work of Love but I do not know how to express them in human language. It is something exceedingly simple that Jesus wants. Everything so simple in God and in Infinite Love ! It is human ideas, human activities, that complicate things.

The end of the Work is the knowledge of Infinite Love ; its spirit is Love ; its principle exercise is Love ; its means of action on souls is Love.

Everything is reduced to these divine words : " Infinite Love." For Infinite Love is God ; and God is the beginning and the end of all things and nothing exists without Him. Without Infinite Love there is no longer anything.[1]

2. LIGHTS ON THE WORK

Yesterday, Sunday, I went frequently and prostrated myself before the Blessed Sacrament exposed ; I asked Jesus several times

---

[1] Intimate Notes : 30-7-1912.

whether He wished to give me something for the Work; but He said nothing.

In the evening, during the Litanies, my soul was sweetly rapt in the Divine Presence and was filled by most sweet, pure lights.

There were three distinct lights: The first was a view of the Infinite Love of Jesus for souls; Jesus in His solicitude for them forming the priest, an other Self. The priest, an invention of the Heart of Jesus for souls. The priest being what He is only for souls, being the privileged one of Jesus, another Christ, only on account of them; from that, the tender and profound love which the priest should have for souls.

The second light was on the Work. The thoughts of God, always for souls. The end of the Work: souls saved by Love and Mercy. The means of action of the Work, the priest; but for that, the priest must be holy, zealous, filled with love himself, so as to diffuse it, as it were, naturally in souls.

Jesus living in the priest and afterwards operating through him. Accordingly, the priest first prepares himself, becomes filled with Jesus; that is the first part of the Work; then the priest-Jesus goes to souls and attracts them by love and mercy. These are the divine artifices of Jesus.

The third light was on the dangers the Work may encounter, the spirit of the Work, its end, remedies against these dangers. One danger is that it may become national rather than catholic; in order to avoid this, the Work from its beginning must be put in union with the Holy See, the Pope must be asked to bless it, recognize it, and encourage it. I explain myself badly, I do not wish to put any of my own ideas into this Work; if I could speak perhaps I could make myself better understood. My Jesus, I am but an ignorant person, do Thou Thyself tell my Director all that should be said. [1]

3. THE ORGANIZATION AND OBLIGATIONS OF THE PRIESTS' UNIVERSAL UNION

Our Chaplain has asked me to state definitely my ideas about this Work. In obedience to His request, I am going to give a summary of all that I have already said, written, or thought, on the subject,

---

[1] Intimate Notes : Nov. 1902.

and to make it as clear as it is possible for me.

The desires of Jesus.—The first desire of Jesus is the salvation of souls, the uplifting of the world through love, the reign of Infinite Love established over the whole world.   His second desire is to employ His priests for this great work ; to make them active helpers, to act through them on souls and in the world.   His third desire is, it seems to me, an organization which will group priests together, prepare them and sanctify them for this great mission.

The Work.—A Work, a confraternity or a society, if the term is preferred, exclusively composed of priests, to be established ; it is intended not only for the priests of France, but for those of the whole world ; it is intended to unite them, and put them under the influence of the Sacred Heart, of Infinite Love.

Its end.—Its end will be to sanctify priests, to unite them, to make them act in one same spirit ; to penetrate them with love ; to form them into a great army fighting everywhere for right, en-kindling everywhere the divine fire of love in souls ; to develop priestly activity by union.

Its means.—The means which the Work will use for the sanctification of priests are the following :

(1) Union with Jesus Christ by the study and practice of the sacerdotal virtues of His Sacred Heart ; the priests of this organization should model themselves on Jesus Christ, enter into His thoughts, adopt His sentiments, live His life.   They should endeavour to reproduce Jesus in themslves, in as perfect a manner as possible ; and they should often compare their moral being and their exterior personality with the divine Model, seeking by this means to perfect the divine resemblance more and more in themselves.

(2) Fraternal union in the love of God and of souls, good under-standing and co-operation in their activities, etc.

Its obligations.—If priests belonged already to some sacerdotal union like that of Montmartre, for example, they should be faithful in fulfilling its obligations, in following its directions, etc, ; always according to the spirit of this new Society.   This latter Society will impose no obligations beyond a meditation in the morning on the life of Our Lord, the duties of the priest, etc. ; a careful examination of the day in the evening (an examen according to the plan which we have recently drawn up). Besides, the priest of this new Society will attend some meetings, and, by their preaching, their writings, and their works, labour zealously to diffuse the knowledge of Infinite Love and Mercy.

The Organization.—This Society will have a general centre, and a general Director who will take his inspiration from the Founder.

The priests of each diocese will group themselves together under a diocesan Director who will be either nominated or recognised by the General Director and approved by and under the patronage of the Bishop.

The priests of each town or canton will group themselves together and meet on stated occasions, with a priest delegated or nominated by the diocesan Director presiding. The Society will have a general Director who will either nominate or recognise the diocesan Directors, and those latter will delegate priests to preside at the conferences in the towns or cantons of the diocese.

The Conferences.—These meetings of the priests could, it seems to me, be conducted in the following manner : The president would either give a conference himself, or nominate a priest (who might either be a member of the Society or a stranger) to give a conference on the duties of the priest, the sacerdotal virtues, conformity with Jesus Christ, etc.

This conference should be simple, apostolic, tending solely to the good of the souls of the listeners, rather than learned or literary.

There should be some exercise in honour of the Sacred Heart of Jesus living in the Blessed Eucharist. This first part of the reunion should be held in the chapel or church. Afterwards the priests should go to the house of the President, or to a special hall, for a familiar discussion in which they would excite each other to the love of Jesus and of souls ; they could have an exchange of views and state their difficulties, etc.

Young priests would find in these reunions direction for their zeal, for their studies, for their sermons, etc. Each one should seek to do good to his confreres. The President, especially, should show a special zeal in this regard ; he should direct the conference, maintain it in the spirit of the Society, visit the members at times, and if he should remark anything reprehensible, seek to remedy it.

The presidents of the conferences should be dependent on the diocesan Director, and they should keep in touch with the General

Director in order to bring about unity of views, of movement and of action.[1]

4. FURTHER LIGHTS ON THE NATURE AND OBLIGATIONS OF THE WORK

This association proposed would be one specially for priests, and would group them around the Heart of Jesus ; its object would be the sanctification of the members and the development of their apostolic zeal and through this, the salvation of souls in general.

The priest who would enter this association would undertake to make each day at least a half hour's meditation in the morning, and in the evening, before taking their repose, to make an examination, a sort of comparison between the sentiments of the Heart of Jesus, the divine Priest, and the sentiments of their own heart.—For souls : they would undertake to preach the love and mercy of God and to aid each other reciprocally in their works of zeal, without ever impeding or thwarting each other.

It should be a universal Work ; for not only France, but the entire world has need of being renewed and warmed again by God's love.

In each diocese there would be established a particular centre united to the general centre.

This Work might also include meetings in each town, in each canton, in which the priests of the organization would state their difficulties and rekindle their fervour.

Each diocese should have a Director dependent on the general Director, and each conference or reunion should have a President who would be chosen from among the most pious, serious and respected priests of the town or canton.[2]

5. THE SPIRIT OF THE WORK IS NOT A SPIRIT OF FAULT-FINDING

Jesus does not wish that anything in the Work should give the impression of reform, for He does not come in a spirit of reform, but in a spirit of love.

He wishes that there be nothing in what will be written or said,

---

[1] Intimate Notes : 1902.
[2] Intimate Notes : 1903.

capable of casting a shadow on His consecrated ones, on His beloved ones.

Our Divine Jesus wishes that in this Work of the sanctification of the priest infinite consideration be used.

Jesus is not pleased when, under pretext or redressing certain wrongs, of correcting certain faults, people speak about priests without respect or consideration, nor is He pleased when they tell the world about the failings of those who ought to be the salt of the earth and the light of men's intellects.[1]

6. BUT A SPIRIT OF LOVE AND MERCY

It seems to me that Our Lord wishes me to say that the spirit of the Work should be a spirit of love, of mercy ; a spirit which will raise souls above the earth, which will turn them away from the sight of its corruption, and elevate them on high in Infinite Love ; a spirit which will sanctify the priest, and by love make him another Jesus Christ.

This union with Christ by love will render the priest holy, strong, merciful, and powerful over souls.

This Work should show the priest the true end of his life, the real reason of his being, and by increasing his love, give him strength to be what he ought to be, in order that he may be able to accomplish the work of God in the salvation of the world.

7. A SPIRIT OF UNION

The thought came to my mind that perhaps this Work would not be approved, that it would be regarded as a novelty in the Church and as something superfluous. Although there are associations grouping a certain number of priests together, nevertheless it seems to me that there has never been a universal organization uniting all the priests of the world together by a special bond, over and above the bond by which they are united by the ordinary duties of the priesthood. And as I was speaking to Jesus of this, He showed me that the family spirit uniting priests together had existed since the dawn of the Church ; that He Himself, instead of making His priests labour apart in each of the provinces of the Holy Land,

[1] Intimate Notes : 7-6-1903.

always united them round Himself; that after His Ascension He
had commanded them to remain united in the Supper-room; that
after the descent of the Holy Ghost, they were, it is true, scattered
for the necessities of the apostolate, but according as new Christian
communities were formed, the priests who were appointed to minister
to them remained closely united.   In the early Church the priests
were grouped around their Bishop; they lived, if possible, in his
house and formed with him a single family of which he was the father;
and not only the priests but the other orders of the Priesthood were
also united together.

The spirit of the world, which incessantly seeks to break the bonds
of Charity and to divide in order the better to destroy, has gradually
brought about a great isolation; the family spirit has, in part, disappeared; it no longer exists in the sacerdotal body as in the early
ages of the Church.   And this is what Jesus wishes to bring back.
He wishes that this spirit of union should exist among all the faithful,
but first He wishes to see it reign in the Priesthood.   This Work is
for that purpose.   It will serve to make the same spirit permeate
the whole sacerdotal body, and to establish a more complete union
of view, a more uniform movement of action among them.

The priests who are members of this Work, which will depend
on the Pope and will receive movement and life from Him alone, will
form an immense chain surrounding the world of Christian souls,
guarding them from error, defending them from evil, and protecting them from the evil spirit that persecutes them.[1]

8. THE SPIRITUAL MEETING-PLACE OF MEMBERS WILL BE THE SACRED HEART OF JESUS, AND THE BOND OF UNION WILL BE THE ACT OF DONATION TO INFINITE LOVE

To be *one* is to have the same thought, the same aspiration, the
same impulse.   In order that all the priests of the world form but
one, they must be united in one same will, one same act; they must
have a spiritual place of meeting where they can find each other.
This place of meeting will be the Sacred Heart of Jesus; this act
which will unite them to each other and all together to God, Infinite
Love, will be an act of complete and entire consecration and donation
of themselves to the Sacred Heart of Jesus Christ, the Tabernacle
of Infinite Love.

---

[1] Intimate Notes : 21-9-1904.

9. THOSE CALLED TO CO-OPERATE ARE TWICE BROTHERS IN CHRIST

The Work on Infinite Love can be done only by the union of hearts and the fusion of souls in Jesus. All those who are called to co-operate in it are twice brothers in Jesus Christ and they must observe perfect charity in the bonds of the utmost meekness and peace.[1]

10. EVERYTHING IN CONNECTION WITH THE WORK SHOULD BE SIMPLE AND HUMBLE

It seems to me that Our Lord's wishes are that the little booklet that is to be made (about the new organization) be written in very simple language without loftiness of style or straining after effect ; that it be simple and humble like Jesus.

There is nothing more opposed to the spirit of God than vainglory and trust in human means alone ; it is only in simplicity, lowliness and humility that the works of Jesus are founded.

It seems to me also that the following means for propagating this Work would be very pleasing to Our Lord : To speak of it to a pious Bishop, a friend of the Sacred Heart, who, finding it good, would recommend it to his priests, either at the time of their retreat or at synodal reunions.

Preachers of priests' retreats might also, with the consent of the Bishop, speak of the Work and distribute the explanatory booklet. It seems to me also that at the present time the Work could be propagated outside France more easily than in France itself.

* * * * * * * * * * *

Universality is the dominant note of the new organization. The forces of evil have their international organizations ; it is the wish of Our Lord that not only individual priests, but clerical unions of the whole world be linked together by a strong but simple bond of charity.

From the following quotations it is clear that isolated clerical unions, excellent in themselves as they are, do not satisfy Our Lord's demands ; it is clear also that the new world-wide union demanded by Our Lord does not aim at supplementing existing unions, but at uniting them by a new bond and infusing new life and vigour into them.

---

[1] Intimate Notes : Oct., 1912.

11. UNIVERSALITY, THE DOMINANT CHARACTERISTIC OF THE WORK

On the day before yesterday several interior communications were given to me about Infinite Love and priests. This Work of Love, so long desired and demanded by the divine Master, is, it seems to me, a universal bond between priests, based on the love which Jesus has for them and which they should have for Jesus. This will necessarily have its beginning in a diocese, but it must not be a diocesan Work. Jesus wishes something on very broad lines, which can be accommodated to all places, all dispositions, and all customs. The words spoken to me in 1902 often recur to my mind these times, and seem to indicate to me how the Work will begin :

" Nineteen centuries ago twelve men enlightened the world ; now for the second time twelve men would be able to save the world."

Is it not a very humble commencement which Jesus wishes for His great Work? Is it not to a very small number of priests at the beginning that He wishes to entrust the treasures of His Infinite Love ? The Statutes which have been written might, perhaps, be suitable for one country, but I think, if I am not mistaken, that something on broader lines, something more adaptable is required. Each country, each diocese, can add the details that will make them suit the particular needs and customs of each place.[1]

It is true that some points in these Statutes are a little vague. But for an organization which is intended for the whole world, what is needed is to give the broad outlines and leave sufficient room for each nation, each diocese to adapt itself to it by adding particulars of practice which certainly cannot be the same for different countries, and sometimes even for different diocese of the same country.[2]

I believe, dear Father, that Our Lord wishes the revelation of His Infinite Love and the gift of His divine Heart for priests to be universal.[3]

It seems to me that Jesus wishes to form a bond of love and charity between His Sacred Heart and His priests. There are many very good, very fine sacerdotal organizations ; almost each diocese has its own ; new ones are continually being formed. None of them is universal and this is understandable, for each nation, each province

[1] Intimate Notes : 16-9-1912.
[2] Letter to Father Charrier : 23-9-1911.
[3] Letter to Father Charrier : 31-10-1909.

has its particular needs and the organizations that are founded cater for these needs.

Nevertheless, if I am not deceived, Jesus wishes something universal, something catholic. What is needed, therefore, is an organization on very broad lines ; an organization which will be suitable for all places, for all dispositions, and which will unite together, by a very simple and very strong bond, all other organizations already formed.[1]

The new union is not to be an additional association, in the strict sense, but an all-embracing bond between already-existing associations.

I showed the Priests' Universal Union as a bond of charity destined, not to be, strictly speaking, an additional Association for priests, added to others which are already numerous, but an all-embracing bond uniting together all other associations for priests and completely fusing all the priests of the world together.[2]

CHAPTER IV.

THE MISSION OF MOTHER LOUISE MARGARET

Mother Louise Margaret was the person chosen by God to be the instrument of His designs in the Work of Infinite Love.

God demanded from her, not so much exterior action, as the immolation of her whole being.

Our Divine Lord communicated to her His divine plan for rekindling His love in the world : the establishment of a world-wide organization for priests and the foundation of a monastery of Sisters who, by their prayers and sacrifices, would act as a spiritual foundation of the Work of Infinite Love. All this was submitted to the Holy See during the reign of Pius X and sanctioned. Since that time both the organization for priests and the monastery of Sisters have continued to grow and develop with the blessing of the three Popes who have reigned since.[3]

I HAVE CHOSEN YOU TO REVEAL MY LOVE TO MY PRIESTS

Being alone to-day before the Blessed Sacrament exposed, I felt my heart become very ardent and my breast inflamed with extraordinary fire. It seemed to me that my soul and my whole

---

[1] Intimate Notes : 29-12-1912.
[2] Letter to Mgr. Filipello : 16-12-1912.
[3] For further information see *The Life and Work of Mother Louise Margaret* just published.

being would melt like wax before a great fire, by contact with Infinite Love radiating from the Heart of Jesus. In the midst of the delights and sufferings which Love causes me I said to the divine Master : " Why lavish so many blessings on me?" He replied to me : " Because I have chosen you to reveal My love to My priests." I said : " Thou seest that I am not able to serve Thee in this ; of myself I am not able to do anything and this priest[1] whom Thou, it seemed, didst give me for this Work is not willing to do anything and now he is ill and perhaps Thou art going to take him to Thyself soon." Jesus said to me : " He has already done more than you think ; just allow Me to do My will in you." Jesus gave me to understand that all that I was required to do was to receive from Him and to allow His gift to pass to others without troubling about the rest. Since my retreat, which, however, I made very imperfectly, I feel myself still more taken possession of by Infinite Love ; at times I feel myself drawn outside myself by an attraction from on high.[2]

2. MY SAVIOUR, I BELONG TO THEE, DO WITH ME ACCORDING TO THY WILL

O my soul, fear not ; give yourself up entirely to the Infinite Love of your divine Master. See the ineffable tenderness with which His adorable Heart is filled ; go and plunge into this ocean of ardent love and most pure light, and in this day understand how this Christ Who died and rose again from the dead loves you. Understand what He Who fills you with His riches wishes to be for you ; understand what He, Whose adorably tender Heart seeks what is best to give you, demands from your heart.

O Jesus, my most sweet Master, I believe in Thy love. I wish therefore to love Thee passionately. Yes, in spite of my repeated infidelities and my falls, in spite of my resistance and my weakness, Thy love, stronger than Thyself, brings Thee to me. How inexplicable this love is which inclines Thee, great, immortal, omnipotent God, towards Thy feeble, ignorant, miserable creature ! How worthy of Thy adoration and passionate love, O Lord Jesus, is Thy Heart, so liberal and so sweet.

---

[1] Father Charrier.
[2] Intimate Note : First Friday, Oct., 1906.

" O Jesus, tell me why Thy Heart contains so much love and why Thou dost pour it out on Thy unworthy creature? " And Jesus replied : " My Heart is the living tabernacle of the Divinity ; It contains It in Its plenitude, and the Divinity is Love ; do you not understand that Love is always active ; like a stream with abundant water, It has need to flow and rush forward? "

" Yes, love should diffuse itself, but why pour it out on my misery? "

" Your misery attracts Me, because I am Mercy, your weakness captivates Me, because I am Omnipotent ; your faults call out for Me, because I am the most Pure and I have sanctified Myself for you."

" My Jesus, what, then, dost Thou wish of me? "

" Love Me, allow Me to love you. Allow Me to pour into your heart the superabundant love of Mine. Allow Me to make of you a creature so beloved by her God that no one, on seeing you, will be able to doubt of the immense desire of Infinite Love to pour Itself out on man.

" Jesus, why me, and not some other more worthy? "

" Why? Because the remembrance of your weakness and of the shadows of your past, while making your weakness known to you, will prevent you from attributing to your own virtue the predilections of My Heart."

" My Jesus, tell me what are the desires of Thy Heart? "

" The world is becoming frozen, egoism is contracting men's hearts ; they have turned away from the source of Charity, and they think that they are very far from their God ; nevertheless, I, Infinite Love, am quite near, and the bosom of divine Charity, all swollen with love, must needs open. Allow Me to love you, Margaret, and through you, to descend to the world."

" My Jesus, what can I do for the world since I am separated from it ; how shall I be able to bring Thee to it, since I have no communication with it? "

" Margaret, I wish to explain to you this mystery which is beyond your power to comprehend. I became incarnate in order to unite Myself to men ; I died to save men ; My sacrifice was powerful enough to redeem the entire human race and infinitely more, but man, endowed with free will, must co-operate in the work of his salvation. The superabundance of My merits obtains for him efficacious grace for that ; but how many there are who reject

my grace ! Then I take souls, I invest them with Myself, I continue
My passion in them. I separate them from others for My work ;
I unveil to them the mysteries of My Love and of My Mercy, and
making them like purified channels, by means of them, I pour out
on the world a new abundance of grace and pardons."

" My Saviour, I belong to Thee, do with me according to Thy
will."

" Yes, I take possession of you, I make of your soul the channel
of My Infinite Love, and although it is obscure and hidden, it will
do My work. All the love which I shall pour out into you will go
to the world, but retain none of it, nor ever seek your own interest
but Mine. Be faithful and cherish suffering."

Those are not altogether the words of Jesus, for this time no
word has come under the form of human language. I have translated as near as possible the divine impressions and expressed in
human language the thoughts of Jesus.[1]

3. WHAT I HAVE BLESSED, I WILL STILL BLESS ; WHAT
I HAVE COMMENCED I WILL FINISH

Yesterday (during retreat), I passed nearly the whole day before
the Blessed Sacrament. Oh ! how I have suffered ! I begged
Jesus with entreaty, with tears, to enlighten Father, to dispel his
doubts, to manifest His will clearly to him. I annihilated myself
at the feet of my divine Master. Prostrate with my face to the
ground,   I said to Him : " I am nothingness, misery, sin ; humiliate
me, break me if Thou wishest, I deserve only that, but enlighten
him, aid him."

I thought for a moment : Since Father says that I am always
deceived, perhaps I am always deceived, perhaps I thought that
something which really did not exist was from Thee ; if it be so,
do not permit me to deceive others ; rather let all creatures abandon
me ! but Thou, my God, Thou, my divine Master, Thou my Jesus,
do not abandon me !

What martyrdom ! and at the same time I felt in the depths of
my soul an ever-increasing assurance that Jesus wished this Work
and that He wished it through Father Charrier. This interior
assurance, this impression of a will which seemed to be of God

---

[1] Intimate Notes : March, 1902.

redoubled my suffering. I was crushed under the weight of this knowledge and this light, feeling myself alone to support it; yes, my martyrdom was to have such a strong impression that the will of Our Lord was for the Work and to see my absolute powerlessness to convince Father Charrier. However, I had no trouble in my soul; nothing but immense suffering, profound as the sea, an agony unto death.

There was always something firm and invariable about my impression with regard to the Work. Yesterday evening I went to sleep, broken by sorrow; this morning on awaking, even before I had completely opened my eyes, I felt the presence of Jesus. He was there and said to me : " **What I have blessed, I will still bless ; what I have commenced I will finish.**"[1]

Am I deceived O my Jesus, about the desires of Thy Heart? Is all this an illusion? I am sometimes afraid of being deceived, of deceiving Father Charrier, of dragging him into the way of error, nevertheless, at the time when I receive this impulse, when it seems to me that Thou showest me Thy will, I have no doubt; on the contrary, I feel a marvellous assurance that these are really Thy desires and Thy wishes.

My Jesus, I beseech Thee, tell all this to Father, have it told to him by his Superiors in order that he may believe it. I am so miserable, the fact that I say it is enough to make people doubt it, and they are right.

My Jesus, I am but sin, but it seems to me that it is Thou nevertheless.[2]

4. I WISH TO IMPRINT MY HEART ON THE HEARTS OF MY PRIESTS

Just now at the end of prayer, the voice of Jesus, my divine Master, made itself heard in my soul. He said to me : " **I wish to imprint My Heart on the hearts of My priests, and it is by means of you that I will do that.**" These words caused me to become profoundly recollected ; I felt myself completely retired within myself with Our Lord. As Prime was commencing, I had to make an effort to recite my prayers of obligation ; but thinking that I might not have time

---

[1] Intimate Notes : 8-10-1904.
[2] Intimate Notes : 18-2-1903.

later on I said them. I have just come up to our cell to write down
this before Mass.

. . . . At the commencement of Mass, I said to my Saviour :
" Jesus, what can I do to obey Thee ? I am so miserable ; and now
he whom Thou hast given to me resists Thy desires." Our Lord
replied to me : " Fear nothing for his resistance, I am the Master of
his heart and I incline it to My will. Hand over to him faithfully
all that I shall give to you. I am going to give you still more for
My priests." He added : " Be humble, faithful, and mortified, and
you will do My Work." For the rest of Holy Mass and even now,
I feel this profound recollection in the inward depths of my soul
and this disposition of expectation which I experienced at the time
of the first communications of Jesus about His priests, three or four
years ago. O sweet Jesus, teach me to do Thy holy will ![1]

5. IT IS YOU WHO ARE TO BRING THE SUPERABUNDANCE OF MY INFINITE LOVE TO ALL PRIESTS

It seemed to me that Our Lord really wished to have an organization for His priests ; an organization through which Infinite Love
would be communicated to them.

Just now I saw myself to be such utter nothingness, so powerless to
fulfil the Master's mission. I was there without strength ;
I was not even able to go to the end of the terrace, and at the same
time I heard in the depths of my soul a voice, a movement, a prolonged divine sound saying : " Nevertheless, it is you who are to
bring the overflowing abundance of my Infinite Love to all the
priests and through them to the extremities of the earth."

I said to Him : " How can that be done !" But immediately I
closed the eyes of my soul, bowed my head, and murmured in a
sentiment of blind, supernatural faith : " Nothing is impossible
to God !"

All that I ask of Thee, O my God, is not to be wanting to Thy
grace, not to give Thee this pain of seeing me refuse to co-
operate in the accomplishment of Thy designs.[2]

---

[1] Intimate Notes : 18-10-1904.

[2] Intimate Notes : 2-9-1910.

The Living Tabernacle of Infinite Love !

O Mary, conceived without sin, Mediatrix of all graces, pray for us who have recourse to Thee !

6. INFINITE LOVE WENT FROM GOD TO THE SOULS OF PRIESTS

To-day, the 10th, about half-past one, I wished to commence to write a conference for our Chapter, and as I was going to commence, something drew my soul out of itself and I felt myself urged to go to the Chapel.

On my knees before the altar, for some moments I lost consciousness of exterior things around me and it seemed to me that from the Heart of Jesus in the Tabernacle, Infinite Love poured forth on me like a torrent. It was so strong and at the same time so sweet ! But this Love which rushed upon me was not given for me. I was a channel and served to make the waves of love pass on. Infinite Love, life, true life in its strength, in its intensity, passed and went from God to souls ; to the souls of priests, for it is to them that Infinite Love goes first.

I asked Jesus what I should do. He said to me : " Nothing : just allow My will to be done in you."[1]

7. THE INSTRUMENTS OF INFINITE LOVE

Henceforward, we must forget ourselves completely, setting aside our own interests, our own judgment, our own desires, and become the ever-docile instruments of Infinite Love Which wishes to do everything by Itself and employs us only in order the better to show Its divine power and skill.

When God acts upon nothing, His divine power encounters no obstacles, it is free ; when it acts upon a creature, or when it employs a creature in some work, it often encounters resistance in the will or in the passions of this creature.

Divine Power and divine Goodness have, if I may so express myself, more difficulty in doing their work through creatures than if they did it directly themselves.

Well ! in this Work of His Infinite Love, God has deigned to make use of creatures as His instruments, and He has consented to see them resist and cause long delays to His adorable designs. He has not wished to do His work all alone, He has consented to be put to inconvenience by us ; He has consented to wait until we should

---

[1] Intimate Notes : 10-6-1910.

be disposed to enter into His views, to do His work. Should not this thought, Father, make our hearts melt with love towards this great God, good like a father who suffers to see his work delayed and spoiled by his little child, who is incapable of helping him !

But you have at last done what Jesus wanted ; now He is going to show you His will and you are going to follow it, for when a person has once given himself to Love, he can no longer resist its divine designs.[1]

8. BETHANY OF THE SACRED HEART

This afternoon when I was adoring the Blessed Sacrament, my sweet love Jesus favoured me with His presence and said to me : " I am seeking for a stone on which to rest My head." I replied to Him : " I have nothing to offer Thee, my sweet Jesus ; in the whole extent of the universe, I do not possess a single inch of ground, I am poor like Thyself ; come and repose on my heart ; doubtless, it is hard and cold like a stone, but contact with Thy divine Person will soften it."

And Jesus said to me—so it seems to me : **" I wish to build for Myself a dwelling in which the virtues dear to My Heart will reign ; humility, poverty, simplicity, and charity."** Then I said to Him : " My sweet Mercy, do as Thou wishest ; I do not see in what way I can be of help to Thee, but with all my heart I put my whole being, body and soul at Thy disposal ; I can give Thee nothing but myself, take all and do as Thou wishest."[2]

9. (A) THE WORK OF INFINITE LOVE WILL BE ACCOMPLISHED ONLY THROUGH SUFFERING

Jesus said to me : " The work of Love to be carried out by the Priesthood cannot be accomplished with money like other works ; it can only be accomplished through many sufferings, sacrifices and humiliations !" These words of Jesus excited in me an ardent desire to suffer and to be humiliated. Thus when I was told yesterday what a certain person said about me ; about my past and present, I experienced joy, a supernatural joy infinitely sweet to my soul, and if this person had been present and if I could have embraced her without causing astonishment, I would willingly have done so with my whole heart.[3]

---

[1] Letter to Father Charrier : 11-1-1912.
[2] Intimate Notes : First Friday of May, 1900.
[3] Intimate Notes : 6-7-1906.

(B) MIRACULOUS EFFECT OF PARTICIPATION IN THE SUFFERINGS OF CHRIST

Do you see, Father, Infinite Love must be the sole Master in our souls. It must rule them according to Its desires; It must fill them with Itself and make them carry out all Its designs without any consideration, however good, being able to induce us to resist. Yes, I can understand your dread. It is not pleasant for our human nature to be thus delivered up to Infinite Love; for we must to a great extent lose our own being in this divine fire, we must do what we would never have wished to do, and so go beyond and above the possible and the feasible.

I cannot tell you to what degree I feel, I see, I touch the divine action of Jesus in His work of love, especially for some time past. And I have not been the only one to remark it. Those of our Sisters who have been called to co-operate with me have often been astonished to see the action of Our Lord in such an evident manner in a thousand occurrences. As for me, I allow Jesus to do what He wishes from moment to moment, and I contemplate Him acting. It is so consoling to see Him doing His work Himself! He has no need of us to act; He wishes merely to make use of us by our suffering. He blesses these sufferings which He sends us, and He takes them and unites them to His own; and He works prodigies by this mingling of the human and Divine, just as He did when He cured the blind man by mixing a little earth with His saliva and applying this mixture to the sightless eyes. A little earth trodden under foot (hearts broken with sorrow, souls rent with anguish, bodies crushed with suffering), and a little of Jesus, God and man,—this is the sacred mixture which brings about miraculous results. All souls that will be called to co-operate in the Work of Infinite Love will suffer in the inmost recesses of their being. They must accept it and wish for it; but they must remain united in Love.[1]

10. THE WORK OF INFINITE LOVE MUST BE FOUNDED BY SUFFERING

The work of Infinite Love, of which this little Monastery is the first component part, must be founded and nourished by incon-

---

[1] Letter to Father Charrier: 27-4-1910.

ceivable sufferings.   Therefore, I am prepared for everything both
for you, for myself and for others ; but I feel also and I see as you
do, a will of God for this Work that is becoming even clearer and
although sometimes my inner sufferings are intense, I feel myself
carried along and sustained by this divine will and the depths of
my soul are almost continually in a state of adoration and admiring
immobility before Infinite Love which disposes all things with
power and sweetness.[1]

11. A FOUNDATION OF MYSTERIOUS DEPTHS

Our adorable Master wishes that both of us lay a foundation of
mysterious depths of suffering for His Work of Love ![2]

12. I FEEL AN INEXPRESSIBLE JOY THAT MY SUFFERINGS CAN BE OF SERVICE

I feel that I must suffer much and be very much humiliated in
order that the Work of Love be accomplished.   In the midst of
my sufferings of soul and heart, I feel an inexpressible joy at the
thought that all this can be of service to priests.   If I descended
to the depths of humiliation and suffering, it would be then doubtless
that the Work desired by the divine Heart would be done.[3]

13. MULTITUDES OF SOULS

Yesterday evening at prayers, I could scarcely think, as lately
I have been dejected and downcast ; for a moment, however, my soul, raised up by a superior force above the miseries
of my body, forgot everything else.   I found myself as if placed
on the shore of an immense ocean.   It was Infinite Love ! My
soul felt itself attracted and I would have wished to bathe myself
in it, to plunge into it and to lose myself in it.   Then I returned
to myself.

Just now, in the silence of our cell, a most sweet sentiment took
possession of my soul ; it seemed to me that a marvellously sweet

---

[1] Letter to Father Charrier : 17-12-1914.
[2] Letter to Father Charrier : 19-12-1909.
[3] Letter to Father Charrier : 27-8-1908.

voice said to me that I would soon plunge into this abyss of Love and that I would not be alone, that Father Charrier would plunge into this abyss, and after us a multitude of souls would come there also.

When a soul falls into this divine ocean, there is a commotion in its waves of Love, and this movement extends, is widened, communicates itself, and the Blessed Trinity,[1] the heavenly spirits and all creation receive the effects of it.[2]

14. A DAY WILL COME WHEN IT WILL GIVE AN ABUNDANT HARVEST

He then said to me words to this effect :

" I have deposited My love in the earth of your heart like a seed, it has sprung up in the midst of the miseries and corruption of your human nature, bathed with the dew of My grace and warmed by the rays from My Heart ! Its young shoot has appeared on the earth. A day will come when it will give an abundant harvest ; priests will come first and nourish themselves with its fruit and later, the souls of the faithful will be nourished by it."[3]

Jesus said these words in the depths of my soul slowly, gravely, but with a sweet and penetrating goodness. A little later He added : " The work is done, repose in My Love."

During these words of the Master and afterwards, an ineffable peace reigned in my soul and in my whole being. I experienced in my soul this most sweet repose which is sometimes enjoyed after a great sickness and long suffering when sleep returns again. I felt that Jesus was good, but so good ![4]

15. THE SUN OF INFINITE LOVE WILL SHINE OVER THE WORLD

It has pleased Thee, my divine Jesus, in the midst of my sufferings to light up my soul with a ray of joy. It seemed to me that I was present at the sunrise. An immense horizon stretched out before me, and became slowly purpled by the fires of Love, and this purple commenced to glow like a metal when melting. The Sun of Infinite Love was not yet shining in the heavens ; but some rays revealed

---

[1] Intimate Notes : 30-7-1905.
[2] Intimate Notes : 30-7-1905.
[3] By the external glory which the Blessed Trinity receives.
[4] Intimate Notes : 3-10-1905.

Its presence, and if the valleys still remained in shadow, the summits
of the mountains were already lighted up. The summits—pure souls,
holy priests, already presaged the rising of a more ardent sun. Oh !
to see Infinite Love shine over all souls, to see this divine Sun light
up the world ! My God, how glorious that would be !¹

16. THE DEVELOPMENT OF THE WORK

I saw in the depths of my soul, what? I do not know how to
tell it. I saw the Work commenced ; I saw a certain number of
priests already adherents of the Work (the Priests' Universal Union),
then soon I saw what appeared to be the entry of the Work into
a new phase, a phase of suffering and struggle, but also of development and of extension.

This vision has been for my soul like a divine radiation of joy,
and repose. Afterwards, I began to suffer again, for Father Charrier
demands some extraordinary vision before going forward, and
Jesus does not wish to give it.

Jesus ! Jesus ! I abandon everything to Thee, do Thou finish
what Thou hast commenced.²

PART IV

THE PRIEST, THE SOWER OF LOVE

CHAPTER I

THE GREATNESS OF THE PRIEST

The Sacred Heart and the Priesthood *should be read in connection with
this Section IV. The subject-matter of it is similar. Of* The Sacred
Heart and the Priesthood, *Cardinal Merry Del Val wrote on behalf of
Pius X as follows :* " *The subject-matter of this book is worthy of the deepest
consideration. It contains an exposition of the sublime relations of intimacy
and love between the Heart of Jesus and the heart of the priest of the touching
harmonies between the Heart of Jesus and the Priesthood ; it recounts all
that the divine Master has done for those whom He calls ' His Friends ' ;
it lays before the priest the necessity of forming his heart and inspiring his
life by the ineffable model of the Heart of Jesus.*"

¹ Intimate Notes : 24-4-1906.
² Intimate Notes : 8-10-1904.

1. THE GREATNESS OF THE PRIEST

(*a*) I had remarked the day before yesterday that Our Lord when speaking to me of my Director had called him His brother, and not His servant, or His son, or, as He usually calls him : " he whom I have given you ! " After Holy Communion, as I felt Jesus very near, I asked Him why He had used this name. He said to me : " I called him so because he is a priest. The priest is much greater than My servant. The share which he has in My Priesthood gives him a kind of equality with Me, he thus becomes the beloved son of My Father and the object of His divine complacence." Then Our Lord showed me the greatness of the priest in a manner which I cannot describe, after that He added : " I want you to revive in the world the respect due to My priests."[1]

(*b*) Jesus, having favoured me with His divine presence communicated several things to me about the Holy Sacrifice of the Mass. Then speaking of His priests He said it seems to me, these words : " If they saw their greatness and their dignity which surpasses that of the angels they would no longer dare to do any merely human action."[2]

2. THE PRIEST IS THE DISPENSER OF THE MYSTERIES OF GOD

The priest has been made the dispenser of the mysteries of God (1 Cor. IV, 1), and of the treasures of His love ; all has been placed in His hands in order that He may distribute them to souls. He has, then in himself, the deposit of the mysteries of uncreated Truth, and of the treasures of Infinite Love. Oh ! how great the priest is, and how worthy of respect and honour ! But if he is a dispenser he ought to dispense. Each soul should receive from him all that is necessary for his intellect and his heart. God gives some graces directly to souls, as the rich man gives some alms to the poor that he meets. But He wishes that the greater part of His graces go to souls by the hands of the priest, just as the rich man gets his larger alms distributed by the steward that he has chosen.

---

[1] Intimate Notes : 11-3-1904.
[2] Intimate Notes : 1899.

The priest, then, has in his possession, all the treasures of Truth and Love, not to keep but to distribute.   If he does not give these divine living gifts but holds them back, he hoards them unjustly, he deprives souls of them, and he renders himself blameworthy.   On the contrary, if he distributes them, he is a faithful and blessed dispenser; he is more than that, he is a living and vivifying channel by which Infinite Love makes its sacred streams pass.[1]

3. THE PRIEST, THE INTERMEDIARY BETWEEN GOD AND MAN

All human creatures may approach God personally with confidence, for God is the Creator of all, the Father of all, He loves them all.   The Word Incarnate, Christ-love, is the Divine Person Who introduces souls into the presence of His Father, and through Him they are certain to be lovingly welcomed.   Nevertheless, our great God wishes, our adorable Jesus wishes, that in a great number of circumstances His humble creature, in order to approach Him, make use of the intermediary Whom He Himself has designated to present to Him souls and the sacrifice and gifts which they wish to offer to Him.   The intermediary chosen by God is the priest.   God, in His wisdom and Love, has formed a sort of mystic ladder or, if one prefers, a sort of chain which goes from the creature of the Divinity; the material creature to man, man to the priest, the priest to Christ, Christ to God.   And from Infinite Love, from God Himself, all gifts and all graces descend by this same chain of love even to the humblest and last of creatures; God, Infinite Love, to Christ, Christ to the priest, the priest to the multitude of men, men to the material creation.   Infinite Love thus passes and repasses in a perpetual flow; from God to His creation and from creation to God.[2]

4. THE PRIESTHOOD IS A SORT OF NEW INCARNATION OF THE PERSON OF CHRIST

God has cherished humanity particularly because it was His last work of creation; He has loved His Priesthood in a singular manner

[1] Intimate Notes : Jan. 1909.
[2] Intimate Notes : 1904.

as being the last form given to His dreams of love. Jesus Christ, God and man, has been pleased to make of the priest a sort of new incarnation of His Person, and this out of love for humanity which He wished to favour with a visible representation, human and permanent, of Himself. Christ risen from the dead and ascended into Heaven wished to continue to live on earth in a certain manner in the priest, and through him to unite Himself again visibly and exteriorly to the successive generations that people the centuries. From the Heart of Christ, burning with the desire to remain always in the midst of men to instruct them, to console them, to purify them, the Priesthood has issued forth ! The union of the priest with Christ should resemble the close and complete union which exists between the divine nature and the human nature of the Word Incarnate ; Jesus and the priest should, in a certain manner and all due proportions being observed, form but one person in the respect and love of the faithful, as in the spiritual authority exercised over souls.

What love Christ has for His priests in whom He lives again ! But what love should the priests also have for Jesus from Whom he receives all his greatness !

Of himself, the priest is not indeed superior to other men. When Christ, fixing His eyes on a soul, marks it out to walk after Him and share in His eternal Priesthood, He does not give it a nature different from others. He draws it from the multitude, and without exempting it from miseries common to humanity, He takes possession of it, reserving for Himself, if it is faithful, to raise it up, to perfect it, to exalt it by the grace of His divine union. God has revealed Himself to man through Christ ; Christ continues to reveal Himself to man through the priest. The priest, after Christ, is then a visible and tangible revelation of God throughout the ages ; he is a merciful extension of the great mystery of the Incarnation.[1]

5. THE PRIESTHOOD IS THE MYSTICAL HEART OF THE CHURCH

The Heart of Jesus manifested Itself to me ; this time not His Heart of flesh humble and meek, palpitating in His human breast, not the sensible symbol of His ardent love, the sacred vessel in which

---

[1] Intimate Notes : 1906.

the redeeming blood was formed and which the iron of the lance opened on Calvary, but His mystical Heart. Has not Christ, the eternal Word of the Father, besides the body of flesh with which He clothed Himself in order to unite Himself better to our human nature, a mystical body which He formed lovingly and of which He is the Head? And has not this body, like every living body, members and a heart?

The Church is the mystical body of Christ, the faithful are its members, and the Priesthood is its heart! Yes, the Priesthood is the heart of this living body of which Christ is the Head. A body dies if its head or its heart is mortally wounded; for it is from the head and the heart that life radiates throughout the entire body; but it can see many of its members fall off without the source of life drying up in it. Thus the Church can sometimes see with sorrow some of its members perish without its life failing, for its Head, Christ-Love, is immortal, and its heart, its holy Priesthood, grafted on Jesus, the eternal Priest, cannot perish.

The Priesthood, the mystical heart of Christ and the true heart of the Church, is then for the latter an organ as necessary, as indispensable as the heart is for the human body.

Without its head, Christ, without its soul, the Holy Spirit, the Church would not exist; and without its heart, without its Priesthood which warms it and gives it life, it would be dead. It is by it that the divine movement which comes to it from its Head is communicated to all its members; that the life-giving blood of grace circulates even to its extremities; and that the vital heat of love warms its members.

But what is this holy Priesthood in itself? It is a single organ, no doubt, composed of a multitude of parts. The Pontiffs, the priests, all the orders of the sacred hierarchy are its parts, its molecules, if we may so express it, which, united together, form the body of the Priesthood. The Priesthood is therefore what the parts themselves which compose it are.

Now, the Priesthood is the heart of the Church and in order to perform in it its operation in life, it must be robust and healthy, it must be free and ardent, its movement must be full, always well-balanced, and always dependent.

It must be robust and healthy. It is its purity which makes it strong; the chaste priest is strong against himself, strong against the enemies that tempt him from within, and against those that attack him from without. By his purity, he is raised above other men ; he dominates them by the dignity and power given to him by this superhuman energy acquired by conquering himself. By his purity, he destroys the germs of sin which every man receives from his human descent, and if he cannot exterminate them completely, he renders them at least inactive.

The heart of the priest must be free and ardent : free, yes, from the obstructions which the impious place in his way, free from human and ambitious views, free from seeking after sensual gratifications and human comfort, free without and free within, with the true freedom which permits him to accomplish the work of Christ ; but certainly not with that false freedom demanded by certain independent, lawless spirits who trust only in themselves and who reject all legitimate authority.[1]

CHAPTER II.

THE LOVE OF GOD FOR PRIESTS

Jesus desires that His priests should know with what ineffable tenderness His Sacred Heart loves them.

1. LOVE OF THE BLESSED TRINITY FOR PRIESTS

I have not time to write ; nevertheless, I wish to note down what was given to me yesterday at Holy Communion. Our Lord showed me the extreme complacence which the Three Persons of the Most Holy Trinity take in the heart of the priest who is fervent, devoted, chaste, and humble.

God the Father sees in him the most perfect image of the Word Incarnate ; a second Jesus, so like the first that He might almost mistake him for Him. He sees in him a very bright mirror in which the virtues of His beloved Son are reflected. He hears the voice of Jesus in the voice of the priest.

The Word sees in the priest a brother, a friend, a creation of His Heart, His other Self by whom He continues all His works, and in whom His human life, His life as priest and victim, is, in a manner, prolonged throughout the centuries.

---

[1] Intimate Notes : May, 1906.

The Holy Spirit recognizes in him His special temple, the reservoir into which He can pour His gifts with the greatest abundance, the proper instrument for His action on souls and a material perfectly prepared for the flames of love.

Our Lord in showing me this, gave me a sort of participation in the excessive complacence, in the most sweet enjoyment of the Holy Trinity. Oh! how much the holy, pure priest is loved by God! If he knew it I think that he would be unable to endure its sweetness.[1]

2. THE LOVE OF JESUS FOR HIS PRIESTS

Jesus, my sweet Mercy, I would wish to be able to write what Thou dost unceasingly put before the eyes of my soul : Thy priests ! The object of Thy ineffable love, of Thy divine solicitude, Thy priests ! Oh ! how Thou dost love them ! And Thou dost call them to Thee with such sweet words, with such touching complaints ! I see Thee like a tender lamb wounded by the malice of men, moaning gently to call those who can comfort and heal it. Thou hast thirst for love, Thou hast thirst for souls, and Thou dost stretch Thy parched lips towards those who can quench Thy thirst,— Thy priests ! It is to them, divine Jesus, that Thou dost come to seek consolation for Thy Sacred Heart. It is in them that Thou dost wish to find all that the world refuses to Thee ; fidelity, devotedness, confidence, love. It is by them that Thou dost wish to operate all that Thy divine tenderness has resolved to accomplish for the salvation of humanity. It is by their voice that Thou dost wish to call the world to Thee ; it is by their arms that Thou dost wish to clasp men and press them to Thy breast ; it is by their labours and sweat that Thou dost wish to make the earth prolific ; it is by the ardour of their charity that Thou dost wish to warm the world again. It is on them that Thou dost count to conquer evil. It is from them that Thou dost wish to receive the glory of triumph.

O Jesus, merciful Goodness, how Thou dost love Thy priests ![2]

3. THE PRIESTHOOD IS A CREATION OF MY HEART

Jesus said to me yesterday : " Give yourself entirely to priests and I will give Myself entirely to you." I said to Him : " I have

---

[1] Intimate Notes : 10-2-1904.
[2] Intimate Notes : 1905.

given them my prayers, my sufferings, my thoughts, the little intelligence I have and my whole heart. Thou knowest that I would willingly give my life for them, what more then have I to give?" Jesus made no reply. Afterwards, I sought for something else that I could still consecrate to the priests of Jesus but could find nothing.

While I was writing these lines, the divine Master returned to me ; penetrated with the sentiment of His presence, I laid down my pen and joined my hands, I listened to what He said to my soul. He said to me that for two months past I had not given all my thoughts to His priests ; that under the pretext of making myself useful and of working, I had sometimes voluntarily turned away my thoughts and concentrated them on exterior objects, that He wished that I be still for some time completely consecrated interiorly to His priests. Then Jesus began to speak to me of His priests with inexpressible tenderness : " The Priesthood," he said to me, " is a creation of My Heart." And again : " I have always loved My priests, but the zeal which many of them have shown these last times to spread devotion to My Heart, has increased My love for them still more." And He added : " Tell them to come to the Source of Love ; when they shall have drunk deeply from that source, they will renew the world. I shall render those who come to My Heart pure and strong. I shall confirm them in truth, I shall give them a new power over souls. I make them suffer sometimes also, but it is by suffering that the Work of Love will be done.[1]

4. IN THE SACRED HEART THERE ARE DWELLINGS OF LOVE INTO WHICH PRIESTS ALONE WILL ENTER

Jesus said to me : " My priests have need of devotedness and love ; they should love much and give, give continuously ; let them then come to My Heart."

Jesus said also, if I remember aright, that there are in His Heart, parts still unexplored which He has kept for His priests, and that it was a domain reserved for them.

There are dwellings of love into which priests alone will enter, and

---

[1] Intimate Notes : 24-6-1904.

**in which they will find all that they have need of to be faithful represen-
tatives of Jesus Christ, and then, when they shall have entered them
they will go out clothed with a certain unction which will act on souls.**

Many have entered these divine dwellings without knowing it,
and those are they who truly continue the mission of Jesus. But
when the road is known, many more will enter there, and it will
be for the salvation of many souls. And this road is the Heart of
Jesus-Priest, known and meditated upon ; it is the priest yielding
place in himself to Jesus and always acting under His divine impulse. It is the heart of the priest transformed into that of Jesus
by knowledge and love.

It seems to me that Our Lord wishes to identify Himself with
His priests in such a way that they will be but one with Him. This
will be the realization of these words of Jesus to His Father : " That
they may be one as We also are one ; that they be made perfect in
one." (John XVII, 22-23).

It is the Heart of Jesus filled with ineffable love for His priests,
that is going to bring about this union.

I perceived in this Sacred Heart an opening already made by which
love has commenced to descend on His priests.[1]

CHAPTER III.

HOW JESUS WISHES HIS PRIESTS TO BE

*How great, how beautiful and attractive is the character of the priest
such as depicted by Our Lord to Mother Louise Margaret !*

*That is how Jesus wishes His priests to be. That is how Holy Church
demands that they should be.*

*That is what is expected of them by the faithful, who are prepared to
follow them on the road of love provided they lead the way.*

*Priests reading these pages will find themselves urged to make a great
effort in order to mould themselves such as Jesus wishes them to be.*

*The faithful who read will be stimulated to offer their prayers and
sacrifices with a view to obtain abundant graces for priests, in order that
they may become other Christs.*

---

[1] Intimate Notes : 6-6-1903.

1. THE LOVE OF THE BLESSED TRINITY FOR PRIESTS, AND THE LOVE WHICH PRIESTS SHOULD HAVE FOR EACH OF THE THREE DIVINE PERSONS

I had several lights on the love which Our Lord expects from His priests.

One day, being completely attracted (to Our Lord) and recollected within myself, I saw the loving complacence which the Three Persons of the most Blessed Trinity take in the priest, the most perfect image of the Word Incarnate : the ineffable complacence of the Father who contemplates the traits of His Son ; of the Son Who recognizes Himself, of the Holy Ghost Who considers one of the finest masterpieces. Then I saw the return of love and complacence which the most Blessed Trinity expects.

The priest should not love God merely as the faithful do, in a general manner ; he should have a special sentiment of love for each of the Three Persons ; for the Father, he should have a love of adoration and filial respect, like the love of Jesus for His Father ; for the Son, a love of union which will keep him in continuous relation with Him ; for the Holy Ghost, a love of dependence, of docility and of recourse.[1]

2. THE PRIESTHOOD IS THE BLOOD WHICH GIVES LIFE TO THE MYSTICAL BODY

Our Divine Lord said to me that the priest should increase his faith, strengthen it and make it secure by the exercise of love, and that it was want of love that brought on weakening of, and lapses from the faith.

Love is a vital sap ; if it be lacking or if it be not sufficiently abundant, everything grows weak, especially faith.

The Church is a great living body ; Jesus Christ is its Head ; it is He Who, in His divine wisdom, gives intelligence and direction to it. His Love, Infinite Love is its heart, and all life comes from the heart ; that is why there must be much love in the Church.

The Priesthood is like the blood which gives life to this great body ; it should go continually to the heart, to Infinite Love in order to have life and then to carry it to the extremities ; then, it should

---

[1] Intimate Notes : 1902.

go constantly to the Head, to Jesus Christ in order to communicate movement to the whole system.

The Priesthood, like sap vivified by love, should circulate through the whole body of the Church ; and in order that it may communicate health and life to it, it must be, like blood, pure, warm, and healthy. It is only by going up unceasingly to the Heart, to Infinite Love, that it will keep or recover these necessary qualities.[1]

3. NOW I WILL SHOW YOU THE LOVE WHICH MY PRIESTS OUGHT TO HAVE FOR ME

Yesterday, I made this sacrifice, it seems to me with all the sincerity of my heart. Jesus appeared to accept it, He made me feel that it was really the disposition in which He wished me to be.

I suffered during the whole day, I was exhausted, but at peace, happy to have done what Jesus wished. At evening prayer, being very tired, I placed myself at the feet of Our Lord to adore Him in silence ; almost from the beginning of my prayer, He manifested Himself interiorly to me, enrapturing my soul by His presence, and said to me : " I have shown you the love which I have for My priests, now I will show you the love which My priests ought to have for Me." Then He showed Himself to me as a divine artist modelling the priest to the divine image with His own hands ; giving him the most beautiful traits : goodness, mercy, wisdom, etc.

After prayer, considering this grace and these lights, I asked myself why, on the evening before, Our Lord had asked me for this sacrifice, seeing that He Himself comes to speak to me of His priests. My most sweet Master gave me to understand that He wished for this sacrifice in order to put my soul in a certain state in which He desired it to be. He wished that it might be without attachment to anything, that it be pliable and soft in His hands, that it be like a feather lifted up by the wind and changed from place to place ; without fear or desire except that of loving Him, without eagerness, without bonds ; He wished it to be entirely empty and free in order that Infinite Love may be able to fill it and employ it according to Its pleasure.[2]

---

[1] Intimate Notes : 1902.
[2] Intimate Notes : 1905.

4. THE PRIEST SHOULD HAVE IH HIMSELF ALL THAT IS GOOD IN OTHER CREATURES

Jesus gave me to understand that the priest is raised to a very perfect state, and that he ought to have in himself all the good that there is in other creatures.   Thus, he should have all the courage and all the energy of a man, all his vigour of action, his intellectual power, his strength of soul, and his moral virility, and that he should join to this all the gentleness, all the tenderness, all the delicacy of the woman, her uncalculating devotedness, her sensibility of heart, her attractive goodness, and her chaste reserve.   That is why, in the work of the sanctification of the priest, Jesus wished that the soul of a woman should contribute her humble part.[1]

5. IT IS HIMSELF THAT THE PRIEST MUST RENOUNCE

" If any man will come after Me, let him deny himself and take up his cross daily, and follow Me." (Luke IX, 23).

These words are the resumé of the divine programme which Jesus traces for His apostles, for His priests, and which is to serve as mould for their loves.   " If any man will come after Me."   That is the call of Jesus to His priests.

The life of this chosen one should be holy, pure and raised above earthly corruption ; therefore the Master does not force anyone to embrace it ; He invites : " If any man wishes."   It must be a free, enlightened, courageous will which replies : " I will."   And when the man has thus declared himself, when his free, strong will has cast him into the arms of the Priesthood, there must be no going back or weakening.   Leaning on Almighty God, sustained by the grace which flows from all the wounds of Christ for him, he must walk after Jesus without looking back.

When the priest has responded to this loving invitation of Jesus, what must he do ?   And Jesus replies : " Let him renounce himself."

It is not riches and worldly goods that the priest must renounce ; provided that he distributes his money to the poor, or uses it for the glory of God, he may legitimately possess it.   It is not from pure affections, from holy friendships, that he must detach himself ; the priest, living the life of Jesus, may cherish his own people and pour

---

[1] Intimate Notes : 28-9-1904.

out his heart into friendly hearts. It is not even honours and dignities that he must renounce, for although he should never desire them, or seek them, he may, however, if the will of God so ordains, bend his back humbly under their burden and carry them with courage in the name of the Master.

It is himself that the priest must renounce ; not this new being sanctified in Christ which Baptism should have formed in him, and the Blessed Eucharist, the gifts of the Holy Ghost, and the Sacerdotal anointing perfected ;   but this purely natural being, this human nature degraded by original sin, and sullied and debased by actual sin.

It is this inferior being, agitated by so much greed and ambition, and tossed about by so many passions, that the priest must renounce.

To renounce oneself is truly a great work ; it is not a task accomplished in an hour ; that is why Jesus adds : " Let him take up his cross daily." The cross of the priest is his devotedness to God, his conformity with Jesus, his fidelity to the Church, his solicitude for souls.

Every day he must take it on his shoulders again. Each morning the priest ascends the altar : there he takes up his cross again, the cross of holy duties, and he is to lay it down again only on the following morning when he ascends the steps of the sanctuary again.

During the too short moments of the Sacrifice, the priest does not carry his own cross ; he carries the cross of Jesus Whom He represents, into Whom he passes, so to speak ; beside the altar of God Who rejoices his youth, the priest lays down his own personal cross, for then he no longer lives himself, it is Christ Who lives in him.

Every day the priest, then, takes up his cross and Jesus calls him to follow Him with these words : " Let him follow Me."

To follow Jesus is to go to glory, but it is also to pass through suffering ; the priest knows it ; he knows that when walking in the footsteps of his Master, he will sometimes meet with humiliations, very often with sorrows, always with self-sacrifice and complete abnegation.

He knows that he will have to give his sweat, his tears, and perhaps his blood, but he is not afraid, Jesus carves out the way for him ; he has only to put his feet in the print of His steps, he has only to follow the divine Chief Who, at the head of His followers, sustains their efforts in the combat and Who, making a rampart of His own body for those who are following Him, protects them and assures them of victory.[1]

6. THE PRIEST SHOULD BELONG ENTIRELY TO JESUS

These words of St. Paul had come to my mind : " For all things are yours . . . . and you are Christ's and Christ is God's." (I Cor. III, 22, 23). These other words were immediately given to me : God is Christ's, Christ the priest's, and the priest belongs to souls. I found myself at the same time completely concentrated on the consideration of this, and, drawn beyond myself, I entered into the most sweet contemplation of the mysteries of love contained in these words. I am going to try to note down some of these things.

God is Christ's. Jesus Christ is God Himself. I saw the intimate possession which the humanity has of the Divinity, and which the Divinity has of the Humanity ; I saw the sacred union and the ineffable embrace which takes place in Jesus between His two natures, divine and human. From this mutual possession the marvellous charms of Christ take their origin ; His greatness allied to profound humility, His justice allied to the most tender goodness, His strength united to unwearying patience, His sovereign sanctity joined to most compassionate mercy. The brilliant rays of the Divinity of Christ which filtered through the transparent veil of His humanity appeared to me with such sweet radiance, and His humanity, transfigured by the divine light, seemed so beautiful, that my whole soul rushed towards Him and appeared to wish to abandon my body to go and join itself to this adorable marvel.

Christ is the priest's. He has given Himself voluntarily to him : by the Blessed Eucharist, in the Holy Sacrifice, He becomes the divine possession of the priest. The whole Jesus, His mind, His doctrine, His works, His most holy soul, His most loving Heart, His most pure body, His divinity belong to the priest, who can dispose of these things as of his own goods, of his private possessions. He takes Him in his hands, he slakes his thirst with His Blood, he nourishes himself with His flesh, and not only does he live by Jesus, but he makes others live by Him ; not only can he enjoy the possession of Jesus but he can give Him to other souls and make them also enjoy Him.

---

[1] Intimate Notes : 24-6-1903.

Christ is the priest's ! The priest also is Christ's, there must be reciprocity. And because Christ has given Himself entirely to the priest, in like manner, the priest should belong entirely to Jesus. Entirely ; his mind, his heart, his body, that is to say, his whole intellect and all his thoughts, all his affections and his wishes, all his works, all the activities of his life.

The priest is Christ's. Christ can dispose of all that belongs to him with the same power as the priest disposes of Christ. In order that there be equality, the priest, in the hands of Christ, must be such as the White Host is in the hands of the priest. And I saw how profound, how divine was this union of Christ with the priest and of the priest with Christ ; it is not like the union of the Word with the humanity of Jesus, but it is, nevertheless, something very close and very intimate.

The priest belongs to souls. He is their possession as he is the possession of Christ. He belongs to them, therefore he no longer belongs to himself, he can no longer live for himself ; he must be completely given to souls, completely consecrated to them. Does not the mother belong to her child? Does she not owe herself completely to him, and has he not the right to all the helps which she can give him in his weakness ? And does not the child belong also to his mother ? He is her possession ; she carries him wherever she wishes ; she caresses him or rebukes him, she disposes of him as she wishes and has the right to obedience from him. In that manner souls belong to the priest, and from this double possession, made in the spirit and the grace of Jesus, there should arise on the part of the priest, boundless devotedness, and on the part of souls, confidence without reserve. I considered all the exquisite delicacy that should exist in the heart of the priest for souls, which are his treasure, his goods, his splendid possession ; and all the respect and confidence that should exist in souls for the priest whom God has given to them in order to guide them. Oh ! what grand things God does ! How many marvels His Infinite Love has worked ! But the eyes of man are feeble and dim ! I feel myself powerless to express what I feel, and nevertheless I feel and understand only very imperfectly these divine mysteries. There is here reason to go into an ecstasy of love but the weight of my misery is too heavy ![1]

---

[1] Intimate Notes- : 17-4-1904.

7. FEED MY LAMBS, FEED MY SHEEP

These words of Our Lord to St. Peter had come to my mind :
" Feed My lambs . . . . Feed My sheep." (John XXI, 15, etc.).
According to the common interpretation the lambs are the faithful ;
the sheep are the priests.   And I considered that, in this one word,
" sheep," Jesus had included in abbreviated form, all the duties of
the priest ; his duties towards God, his duties towards the Roman
Pontiff, the Vicar of Christ, towards his brethren in the priesthood,
towards souls.

The sheep belongs entirely to her master ; she owes him her life,
her offspring ; he has a right to dispose of her as he wishes.

The priest owes himself entirely to God, his sovereign Master.
He belongs entirely to Jesus Christ ; he owes Him the work which
he accomplishes, and if need be, the sacrifice of his life.

The sheep should be docile to the shepherd who directs it in the
name of the master ; it should answer his voice ; it should follow
him to the pasture where he conducts it ; it should be obedient and
faithful.   In like manner, the priest should be obedient to the voice
of the supreme Pastor ; he should enter into his views ; nourish his soul
only on the doctrines of which he approves, and remain faithful and
unshakably united to the pastoral staff of Peter.

Each sheep of the flock has no other duties towards those around
her but of meekness, and union ; she must not go away from the
flock, she must not remain alone, for she would expose herself to
perish.   Jesus wishes His priests to have a close bond of union
among themselves ; He wishes that they guard the unity of faith in
the bonds of fraternal charity, and that, working in the same spirit,
they give peace to the world and glory to God.

Finally, the sheep is a mother, a mother of lambs ; she carries them
in her womb, she nourishes them with her milk, she warms them,
and she guards them.

The priest is not only a father of souls, he is their mother also ; he
should have for them the tender and delicate love of mothers, their
devotedness, even to sacrifice of himself.

He ought to give souls the best of his life, he ought to nourish
them, if I may express myself so, with his own substance, the substance of a soul that is spiritual and very pure ; he ought to warm
them with the flames of Infinite Love ; he ought to guard them
from evil.

As a result of these thoughts, which I abridge, I conceived a profound sentiment of adoration for Jesus ; I found in these considerations an adorable mark of the divinity of the Saviour.

We mortals require many words to express an idea. Jesus, by a single word, expresses a whole collection of thoughts. That is seen at each step in the Holy Gospels.

By this one word " sheep " thrown out in conversation, as if by chance, Jesus has said everything about the priest ; all that he ought to be, all that he ought to do, all that he should give of himself to God, to the Church, to souls. Ah ! it is because Jesus is the Word.

He is the divine Thought and the uncreated Word ; a single word fallen from His lips contains a thought of God.

How good it is to know Jesus, so grand in His divinity, so sweet in His humanity ! I catch but a mere glimpse of Him ; how I would wish, however, to be able to express the little that I know of Him, to make Him known, to make Him loved, to win for Him adorations, to surround Him with praises, with love, with glory, and to exalt Him to infinity.[1]

8. JESUS WISHES THE PRIEST TO BE TRULY A MOTHER OF SOULS

Jesus always insists on this idea of the maternity of the priest. I do not know how to express it. He wishes the priest to be truly a mother of souls, always ready to sacrifice himself for them, forgetful of himself. For a long time past Jesus has been showing me this. I believe that I am always saying the same thing. Since He always says it anew, I also must repeat it.[2]

9. JESUS DESIRES EAGERLY TO SEE PRIESTS DELIVERED FROM PURGATORY

I was praying for the souls in Purgatory, and I had a great desire to deliver the souls that are dearest to His Heart, those that He desires most to see soon in glory, by uniting my prayers to the infinite merits of Jesus.

It seems to me that an interior voice said to me : " Pray then for

[1] Intimate Notes : July, 1903.
[2] Intimate Notes : 4-4-1904.

the souls of priests." I had not yet thought of these souls of priests detained in Purgatory.

I saw that there were many of them in this place of expiation and purification, and I knew that the greatest number of them were there for being wanting in devotedness to the Church and in love for souls. It is less for the negligence of which they have been guilty in the direct service of God than for want of zeal and love for the Church and for souls that these privileged ones of Jesus remain in Purgatory. But Our Lord's desire to see them delivered from this place is immense. When I asked myself why God so often reproached His priests for want of zeal and love, this explanation was given to me : If a man abandons his chaste and faithful spouse, if he refuses his children the nourishment which is necessary for them, is he not very guilty? The priest is united to the Church as a husband to his spouse, a spouse who is most faithful and sovereignly pure ; if he is wanting in devotedness to her interests ; if he is indifferent to her sorrows and her joys ; if, without turning against her, he concerns himself neither about her glory, nor about her preservation, nor her development ; if he leaves souls whose father he has been constituted, without giving them the spiritual nourishment of truth and love which they need in order to live, in order to develop and grow up, does he not commit a great fault?

I shall offer all my prayers during this month for the souls of priests.

Oh ! how I would wish that at the end of this month, Jesus would receive into heaven and press to His Heart a great number of those priestly souls whom He loves so much !¹

10. JESUS WISHES TO SEE HIS PRIESTS CROWNED WITH A TRIPLE CROWN : ZEAL, PURITY AND LOVE

My most sweet Jesus has favoured me with communications several times these days ; I have not had the time to note down what they contained.

Five or six days ago they were on the purity of the priest ; I think that it was on the first Friday of the month that I received them. Jesus said to me, if I remember aright, that He wished to see His priest crowned with a triple crown formed by devotedness,

---

¹ Intimate Notes : 3-11-1904.

purity and love. He showed me how much He wished His priest
to be pure, and that He would arrive at this purity only by love. It
is love which purifies ; the more one loves, the purer he becomes.
It is only Infinite Love reigning over the heart of man that can
destroy those carnal instincts and raise him little by little from the
mud of his corrupt and sinful nature up to the serene and virginal
splendours of sacerdotal purity.

Infinite Love, when it is ardent in the heart of the priest, cauter-
izes the wound of impurity which man bears in his flesh. Jesus
showed me that the priest should find in the study and adoration
of His divine Heart, that is to say, in a more complete knowledge of
Infinite Love, the source of devotedness and purity. The divine
Master has deigned to urge me to reveal His Heart to His priests
and to make them enter by this Sacred Heart into a more entire
possession of Infinite Love.[1]

11. THE PRIEST SHOULD LIVE BY JESUS

Teach me, my Jesus, to live by Thee ! Thou art our life ; many
times hast Thou repeated in Thy Gospel : " I am the way, the
Truth, and the Life." (John XIV, 6). And again : " Not in bread
alone doth man live, but in every word that proceedeth from the
mouth of God," (Math. IV, 4).

This word which proceeds from the mouth of God is His Word ;
it is Thou, Divine Word become incarnate through love, Thou,
Jesus Christ, God and man. It is by Thee, Jesus, that we must live,
by Thee, the absolute life of our being ; by Thee, inexhaustible
source of life. In Thee our whole being finds its life ; by Thy
Truth, Thou art the life of our intellects ; by Thy Infinite Love,
Thou art the life of our hearts, the vital spring of our wills ; by Thy
immortality, Thou art the life of our souls ; by Thy Eucharist, Thou
art the germ of eternal life for our bodies, the prolongation and the
increase of their temporal life. Yes, our weak flesh finds in Thee,
during this transitory and temporal state the cure of its ills, and
its life. It seems to me, my adorable Jesus, that without communion with Thy adorable Body, I would long ago have breathed
my last breath. Christian life is drawn from Thee, from Thee,
my beautiful Christ-Love, Who, as Head of the Church and Re-

---

[1] Intimate Notes : 8-12-1904.

deemer of souls, must give movement and life to the multitude of Thy members still scattered over the earth. Thou wishest that everything should live of Thee and by Thee ; but how much more dost Thou wish this from Thy priests !

Oh ! how those who here below continue Thy divine Priesthood should live of Thee ! Each morning, after offering Thee, the ineffable victim of love, they receive Thee into their breasts and are vivified by Thee. Their souls, their intellects live also of Thee by the study of Thy Truth ; but their hearts—their hearts do not always live sufficiently of Thy love ; that is why zeal has become cold in many, and apostolic devotedness dead in some. Jesus ! Jesus ! enliven the hearts of Thy priests by Thy Heart ; warm their love by Thine. Let them live entirely in Thee ; let their flesh live by Thy most pure flesh ; their intellects, by Thy divine intellect ; their hearts, by Thy most ardent and gentle Heart. Jesus ! the world has need of love ! It has such need of light. Pour out on it Thy light, pour out on it love through Thy priests, and live ever more in them ; live in Thy Priesthood ; speak, act, think, love in Thy priests and by them.[1]

12. JESUS AND MARY, MODELS OF HUMILITY FOR THE PRIEST

What are the sentiments which dominate the humanity of Christ? What is, if one may so express it, the attitude of the human nature of Christ with regard to the divine nature? Without the smallest doubt, it is one of humility. That is why we see Jesus incessantly humbling Himself before the heavenly Father. That is why we see Him, the Son, the only Son, the Beloved Son, in His thirst and desire for humiliations, offer Himself for insults, for reproaches, for blows, for ignomony, and seem never to have enough of these things. The most beautiful and most sweet humanity of Jesus knew so well all that it has received from God by the Incarnation ; it knows so well that it is only a creature, elevated solely by the choice of Love up to the hypostatic union.

Mary replied by the " Behold the handmaid of the Lord," to the words of the angel saluting her " Mother of God " ; later on Jesus was to say : " The words which I speak to you, it is not of Myself

---

[1] Intimate Notes : Nov. 1903.

that I speak them to you, and My works, it is the Father dwelling in Me Who accomplishes them." (See St. John XII, 49, 50 and X, 25, 32, 38, etc.). The Virgin abased herself at the moment when she is called to the most incomprehensible greatness. Jesus Christ, the Word Incarnate, humbles Himself and annihilates Himself before His Father, referring to Him all the wisdom of His words and all the greatness of His works. And what will the priest do? By the grace of his Priesthood, he has been, like the Blessed Virgin, elevated to an incomparable dignity ; he should, like Christ, make the divine Word resound in souls and accomplish superhuman works. Like Christ and the Blessed Virgin, he will refer to God all the praise and all the glory, he will humble himself before the Word incarnate, before the eternal Priest-Jesus, from Whom he holds all these things.

At the feet of the adorable Master Whose Priesthood he continues visibly, of this noble Benefactor Who has drawn him from the multitude of other men and has enriched him with such marvellous gifts, the priest will prostrate himself in annihilation, saying with St. Paul : " Gladly therefore will I glory in my infirmities, that the power of Christ may dwell in me." (11 Cov. 9).

The more a creature has received from God, the more it should annihilate itself before Him ; for the more it has received the more it should give back, and what could this human creature whose patrimony is poverty, give back that is more personal to itself and at the same time more glorious to God, than this voluntary abasement and this profound humiliation !¹

13. EXAMINATION OF CONSCIENCE FOR PRIESTS

The Heart of Jesus, the divine Priest was dominated all the days of His life by three sentiments : an ardent thirst for the glory of His Father, a passionate desire for the salvation of the souls of His brethren, and an irresistable and constant need of sacrifice and immolation.

Have these three sentiments dominated my heart to-day? What have I done to glorify my heavenly Father? What have I undertaken for the good of my brethren? What sacrifices have I made in union with Jesus immolated?

I. Jesus, the divine Priest, accepted opprobrium and humilia-

---

¹ Intimate Notes : Oct., 1906.

tions willingly in order to repair the glory of God. Have I to-day, humbled myself before God, recognizing my nothingness and my miseries, and referring to Him the glory of the good which I have by His grace accomplished? Have I received contempt and outrages from men with joy?

II.   Jesus, the divine Priest, never thought of Himself ; He left all, stripping Himself of everything and becoming poor, in order to give Himself completely to the salvation of His brethren. What have I done to-day for my brethren with my time, with my heart, with my goods ; if I have not given of my material goods, have I at least used my intellectual and spiritual gifts for them?

III.   Jesus, the divine Priest, having lived in a spirit of continual sacrifice, at the end, offered Himself on the cross, immolating His own life by love. Have I manifested the spirit of sacrifice in my actions of this day? What sacrifice have I made to-day of my satisfactions of heart, of my contentment of mind, of my strength, of my repose, of my life for the love of Jesus and for souls?

Profound and sorrowful regrets for the shortcomings of this day. Offering to the Sacred Heart of the good accomplished.[1]

CHAPTER IV.

MARY MOST HOLY AND THE PRIEST

The priest will find in Our Blessed Lady the masterpiece of Infinite Love. Following in her footsteps, and with her maternal assistance, it will be easier for him to give Jesus to the world as she has done.

1. OUR BLESSED LADY, THE MODEL FOR THE PRIEST OF THE LOVE HE SHOULD HAVE FOR JESUS

My Divine Master told me that the love of the priest for Him should be different and singularly more ardent than the love of other men.

He showed me then, as in a mirror, all the special gifts and graces with which He has enriched the souls and hearts of His priests, and afterwards He said these words to me : " He who has received more

---

[1] Intimate Notes : 1902.

loves more !" I cannot give in detail all that I saw, by a single glance, of the divine gifts in the priest ; he who has received them has not even an idea of them, and even when he believes that he has received much, he cannot know all the lavishness of graces that Infinite Love has bestowed on him.   It will be one of the enjoyments of the priest in heaven to see and know all that Love has done for him and how privileged he has been among other men.   Perhaps the term which I am about to employ is not the accurate one, but it seems to me that the priest, in a certain manner, passes to the state of being divinized by the union which he has with Christ, and by the power which he has, through Christ, over souls for their good and for their salvation.

After showing me all the motives for which the priest is obliged to have for God, Our Lord, a love quite particularly strong, tender and ardent, Jesus again said to me : " There is only one creature who has loved Me, and who loves Me as the priest should love Me ; there is only one heart that can serve as a model for this love : it is the Heart of My most Holy Mother."   Then He showed me in an adorable manner how the love of the priest ought to be in everything like the love of Mary for her divine Son.   Like Mary, the priest, elevated very high by a grace of preference, remains nevertheless an inferior creature in submission under the divine Master ; like her, he touches on nothingness by his nature, and on intimacy with the Divinity by a privilege of love ; like her he should be more enlightened on the truth of his own misery and lowliness, and more illuminated by the divine radiations of Infinite Love. Like her he receives from the Holy Ghost the power to produce the Word Incarnate in the world ; the Mother produces Him in the truth of His visible flesh ; the priest, in the truth of His Eucharistic Flesh.

The love of Mary for Jesus is the love of a privileged creature, it is a love of ardent gratitude and profound humility, a love which abases itself and devotes itself, which gives itself entirely by the necessity of returning all possible to Him from Whom so much has been received.   The love of Mary is also the love of a mother, a tender, delicate, eager love, a love which defends and protects, which devotes itself again but in a different manner, which gives itself not in order to give back, but in order to give again to Him to Whom she has already been given.

The love of the priest for Jesus, his adorable Master, should be altogether similar. He should have a love of humble gratitude ; a love of a beloved creature which adores, which thanks, which gives itself without counting, a love full of exquisite delicacy, a jealous love which guards with vigilance, which protects, which surrounds with loving attentions, which sacrifices itself even to the forgetfulness of self.

Mary had for Jesus not only the love of a privileged creature and a loving mother, she had in addition, she had always for her beloved Son the love of a virgin. It is a humble love too, love ought to be always humble ; but a confiding love, faithful, single, full of chaste familiarities, exquisite tenderness and respectful ardour. Such should also be the love of the priest for Jesus : a pure love, a love free from entanglement, faithful and confiding. The priest has not, it is true, the ideal whiteness of the Immaculate ; his heart has not the sublime purity of the heart of the Virgin Mother ; but he has only to draw from the graces of his priesthood ; he will find there fountains of virginal tenderness and heroic devotedness.

Jesus wishes to be loved by His priests as He has been loved by the Virgin Mary, and He has included in the privilege of the priesthood graces similar to those contained in the privilege of the divine maternity ; graces of intimate and altogether singular union with His adorable Person ; divine and human ; graces of ineffable purity, graces of unreserved devotedness.[1]

2. THE MYSTERY OF THE VISITATION AND THE PRIEST

The mystery of the Visitation was not of a day. Like all the mysteries of Christ, it was to be prolonged to the end of the ages ; it was to be reproduced for the profit of all generations ; to be continued always vivified by Christ eternally living. As the Virgin on the day of the Incarnation had received in her womb the Word of God, so the priest, on the day of his ordination receives in his soul the same sacred deposit. And immediately that he has received it, he feels himself, like the Virgin, urged to communicate it, he cannot enjoy it egotistically ; a new activity takes possession of him, makes him go out of himself and carries him towards the souls with whom he wishes to share his treasure. On the morrow of his sacerdotal consecration, Peter said to the blind man at the door of the Temple :

---

[1] Intimate Notes : 25-6-1905.

" Silver and gold I have none, but what I have I give thee ; in the name of Jesus Christ of Nazareth, arise and walk." (Acts, III, 6).

Peter, the priest, felt the divine Word living in himself, and he must needs give Him, distribute Him to men. When beaten, threatened, imprisoned, the first Apostles kept this Word of love in themselves ; they were urged on and sustained by Him, they announced untiringly the words of Truth and purified the hearts of men at the same time as they enlightened their intellects.

The Word lives in the priest and the Word cannot be inactive. Thus the priest, the true priest of Christ, feels an insatiable need for acting on souls, for converting them, for sanctifying them, for communicating to them always more and more this supernatural life which fills him and moves him to action. It is by his words, into which the divine Word, passes that the priest, like the Virgin on the blessed day of the Visitation, enlightens and purifies.

The accents of the Magnificat should, verse by verse, pass into the voice of the priest.[1]

On the Feast of St. John and yesterday, Jesus kept my soul in profound recollection in Himself. This mystery of the Visitation has always been a source of grace and light for my soul. Mary represented vividly the action of the Priesthood. The priest has Jesus in himself, he carries Him in his soul which is marked with the sacerdotal character, he carries Him in his heart by love, and he goes to souls, and he speaks and acts, and Jesus hidden invisibly in him does His work of mercy. But for that, Jesus must be truly living in the priest, as He was in Mary, and the priest, like the Virgin, must be docile to the inspiration of the Spirit, he must allow the divine Word, which he carries, to act in liberty in him and through him.[2]

---

[1] Intimate Notes : Oct. 1906.
[2] Intimate Notes : 3-7-1906.

THE ESTABLISHMENT OF THE WORK OF INFINITE LOVE

The main theme of the selections from the writings of Mother Louise Margaret given in the present volume is the Work of Infinite Love, the propagation of which was entrusted to her by Our Divine Lord. Let us see briefly how far that Work has been realised.

Mother Louise Margaret spent twenty-four of her forty-seven years of life as a Sister in a Visitation Monastery; during fifteen of these years (1890-1906) she lived in the Visitation Monastery at Romans in the South of France, the remaining nine years were spent as an exile in different Visitation Monasteries in Italy. She began to receive communications from Our Divine Lord soon after her entry into religious life and these continued down practically until her death. In 1900, Our Lord showed her in a vision the little house in which she should found a monastery of the Visitation where the virtues dear to Her Heart, humility, poverty, simplicity and charity would reign. On the Feast of the Sacred Heart and during the following seven days (now the Octave), He dictated to her His message for the clergy of the world and entrusted her with the mission of conveying it to them.

To her anxious enquiry as to how she, a Contemplative Sister shut up in a monastery, was to accomplish this task, Our Lord replied : " Fear not, I am faithful."

In 1906 the Sisters of the Community to which she belonged were expelled from France and found a temporary home at Revigliasco in Northern Italy. They were soon compelled to move again and found a home in the neighbouring diocese of Ivrea of which Monsignor Filipello was bishop. Monsignor Filipello, a man of great learning and profound piety, was the bishop chosen by Our Lord to aid Mother Louise Margaret in carrying out her mission.

The Community in exile, beset with difficulties from all sides, chose Mother Louise Margaret as Rev. Mother though she was one of the youngest of the Community. This unexpected appointment was, she said, the work of the Lord and was interpreted by her as an indication from Him that she should use the opportunities which that position gave her to carry out His behest. Monsignor Filipello had already been interested in a work for the clergy similar to that entrusted to her and asked prayers for its success. In that manner he learned of the communications which she had received from Our

Lord and found that they not only corresponded with his ideas but went far beyond them. The reigning Pontiff, Pius X, had similar ideas which He embodied in His Encyclical to the Clergy.

Monsignor Filipello studied these communications carefully and after a year's considerations decided, subject to the approval of the Holy See, to give the Work of Infinite Love his whole-hearted support.

In the meantime, after vainly endeavouring to have a book composed by her Director which would give Our Divine Lord's message to priests, as He had commanded, Mother Louise Margaret was told by her Director and by other priests who had examined her writings, that the composition of the book could not be the work of anyone except the person who had received these communications, and that therefore she should compose it herself.

She did so. In the book, *The Sacred Heart and the Priesthood,* she delivered the first part of Our Lord's message—His love for His priests, the gift of His Sacred Heart to them, the virtues which He expected them to cultivate and the zeal which He expected them to exercise in winning souls for Him. His Holiness Pius X, who had been informed about the circumstances in which the book was composed, sent a beautiful letter through His Cardinal Secretary, Merry del Val, commending the book.

The second and more difficult part of her mission remained to be accomplished,—the establishment of the Priests' Universal Union and the foundation of the new monastery. Divine Providence aided her in carrying out this also.

When her second term in office came to an end in 1912, at a time when it appeared that she was still indispensable to the Community it happened in a mysterious way that she had to leave the Monastery and was sent by the new Superioress to a convent of the Visitation in Rome. Monsignor Filipello took advantage of the opportunity to have herself and all her writings and projects examined by the Holy See. The great work which she was commissioned to establish to which all her other projects were subsidiary, the Priests' Universal Union of the Friends of the Sacred Heart, was sanctioned by the Congregation of the Council and blessed by Pius X. The foundation of the Little House in which the virtues dear to the Heart of Jesus should reign and which was to serve as the root hidden in the ground for the Work of Infinite Love was entrusted to her by the Congregation for Religious. Monsignor Filipello invited her to make the foundation in his diocese and she left Rome with a blessing from Pope Pius X written by His own hand.

A house was offered to Monsignor Filipello and accepted by Sister Margaret, her companion. When she went to inspect it she found that it was the very house which Our Lord had shown to her in a vision fourteen years previously.

When the foundation was made, God gave her another year to complete her work on earth—the training of the first postulants for the Little House of the Work of Infinite Love—and then called her to her reward.

Humanly speaking, the community in the little rented house with its two professed Sisters (one of whom returned to the Mother-house) and four postulants, was doomed to be dissolved. The Visitation Order, unaware of the fact that it was the work of Our Lord, petitioned the Holy See to dissolve it. But Divine Providence watched over it and the reigning Pontiff, Benedict XV, protected it and even contributed to its upkeep. Pius XI sent the princely gift of 25,000 lire towards the building of a new wing to house the numerous postulants who sought admittance. His present Holiness, Pius XII, has sent repeated messages of encouragement to the Sisters and to the Priests' Universal Union.

The little Community which at the death of Mother Louise Margaret was composed of two professed Sisters and four postulants has grown to be a mother-house with fifty-three professed Sisters and a large number of postulants and novices representing nearly every country in Europe. It has a branch at Orleans in France and has received applications from many countries to found other branches.

Monsignor Filipello lived to see the Priests' Universal Union of the Friends of the Sacred Heart firmly established in Italy and France and spread into Germany, Belgium, Holland, Poland and even Roumania.

Since then it has spread to the Middle East and in spite of the troubles in the Far East the books of the Priests' Universal Union have been translated into Chinese with a view to establishing the Union there ; they have found their way also to India, Burma, the Philippines and Japan.

Everywhere that the Priests' Universal Union has been established, branches for the Associates of the Union and Faithful Friends of Bethany have been organised and are making satisfactory progress.

PRAYER FOR THE GLORIFICATION OF THE SERVANT
OF GOD, MOTHER LOUISE MARGARET

O Infinite Love, living in the Heart of Jesus, make Thyself known to men, in order that they may love Thee as Thou wishes to be loved.

And since it has pleased Thy divine goodness to make use of Mother Louise Margaret Claret de la Touche to make better known to priests the abysses of Thy Love and of Thy Mercy, and to draw men toward the Christian Priesthood, deign, we beseech Thee, to crown Thy works by glorifying Thy humble Servant and, through her intercession, realise in the world, under the guidance of the Supreme Pastor and the Bishops of Thy Church, unity of mind and heart in the light of truth and in the peace of Charity.   Amen.

Those who receive favours through the intercession of Mother Louise Margaret are asked to communicate them to :

The Monastery of Bethany of the Sacred Heart,
Vische Canavese,
Torino,
Italy.

THE WORKS BY AND ABOUT
MOTHER LOUISE MARGARET CLARET DE LA TOUCHE

The Sacred Heart and the Priesthood
The Book of Infinite Love
The Little Book of the Work of Infinite Love
The Love and Service of God, Infinite Love (Containing a Message from Our Divine Lord for the Clergy of the World)
The Life and Work of Mother Louise Margaret Claret de la Touche (Containing a Message from Our Divine Lord for the Clergy of the World)

With the publication of this volume in 1987, all five books have been returned to print by TAN Books and Publishers, Inc.

Today the "Work of Infinite Love" envisioned by Mother Louise Margaret Claret de la Touche has four branches:

1) The Priests' Alliance
   Via Lamarmora, 31
   10030 VISCHE (TO), ITALY

2) Sisters of Bethany of the Sacred Heart
   Betania del Sacro Cuore
   10030 VISCHE (TO), ITALY

3) Missionaries of Infinite Love (a secular institute for women)
   Soggiorno Caritas
   10010 CANDIA (TO), ITALY

4) Friends of Bethany (for lay people)
   Betania del Sacro Cuore
   10030 VISCHE (TO), ITALY

The Sisters also have houses in France and Argentina.

The director of the Work of Infinite Love for the United States is:

Father Vergil Heier, C.M.M.
Mariannhill Missionaries
23715 Ann Arbor Trail
Dearborn Heights, Michigan 48127

If you have enjoyed this book, consider making your next selection from among the following...

Prices guaranteed through December 31, 1987.

How Christ Said the First Mass. Fr. Meagher................... 12.00
Too Busy for God? Think Again! D'Angelo........................ 2.50
St. Bernadette Soubirous. Trochu............................ 12.00
Passion and Death of Jesus Christ. Liguori.................... 5.00
Treatise on the Love of God. 2 Vols. St. Francis de Sales...... 10.00
Confession Quizzes. Radio Replies Press......................... .60
St. Philip Neri. Fr. V. J. Matthews............................ 3.00
St. Louise de Marillac. Sr. Vincent Regnault.................. 3.50
The Old World and America. Rev. Philip Furlong............... 12.00
Prophecy for Today. Edward Connor............................ 3.00
The Active Catholic. Fr. Gabriel Palau........................ 4.00
What Will Hell Be Like? St. Alphonsus Liguori................. .40
The Book of Infinite Love. Mother de la Touche............... 3.00
Chats With Converts. Fr. M. D. Forest......................... 5.50
The Church Teaches. Church Documents........................ 10.00
Conversation with Christ. Peter T. Rohrbach.................. 5.00
Purgatory and Heaven. J. P. Arendzen......................... 2.00
What Is Liberalism? Fr. Sarda y Salvany....................... 3.00
Spiritual Legacy/Sr. Mary of the Trinity. van den Broek...... 6.00
The Creator and the Creature. Fr. Frederick Faber............ 9.50
Radio Replies. 3 Vols. Frs. Rumble and Carty................ 27.00
Incarnation, Birth, Infancy of Jesus Christ. St. Alphonsus... 5.00
Light and Peace. Fr. R. P. Quadrupani........................ 3.50
Dogmatic Canons & Decrees of Trent, Vat. I. Documents....... 5.00
The Evolution Hoax Exposed. A. N. Field...................... 3.00
The Primitive Church. Fr. D. I. Lanslots...................... 5.50
The Priesthood. Bishop Stockums.............................. 7.00
The Priest, the Man of God. St. Joseph Cafasso............... 7.00
Blessed Sacrament. Fr. Frederick Faber...................... 11.00
Christ Denied. Fr. Paul Wickens.............................. 1.25
New Regulations on Indulgences. Fr. Winfrid Herbst.......... 1.50
A Tour of the Summa. Msgr. Paul Glenn....................... 12.50
Spiritual Conferences. Fr. Frederick Faber................... 9.00
Latin Grammar. Scanlon and Scanlon.......................... 9.00
A Brief Life of Christ. Fr. Rumble........................... 1.50
Birth Prevention Quizzes. Radio Replies Press.................. .60
Marriage Quizzes. Radio Replies Press.......................... .60
True Church Quizzes. Radio Replies Press....................... .60
St. Lydwine of Schiedam. J. K. Huysmans..................... 5.00
Mary, Mother of the Church. Church Documents............... 2.00
The Sacred Heart and the Priesthood. de la Touche.......... 5.00
The Passion and Death of Jesus Christ. Liguori.............. 5.00
Revelations of St. Bridget. St. Bridget of Sweden........... 2.00
Magnificent Prayers. St. Bridget of Sweden.................. 1.00
The Happiness of Heaven. Fr. J. Boudreau.................... 6.00
St. Catherine Labouré of the Mirac. Medal. Dirvin.......... 7.50
The Glories of Mary. (pocket ed.). St. Alphonsus Liguori.... 5.00
The Love of Mary. D. Roberto................................. 5.00
Begone Satan. Fr. Vogl....................................... 1.50
The Prophets and Our Times. Fr. R. G. Culleton.............. 6.00
St. Therese, The Little Flower. John Beevers................ 3.50

Prices guaranteed through December 31, 1987.

At your bookdealer or direct from the publisher.

Prices guaranteed through December 31, 1987.